MW00529618

FROM INCARCERATION TO REPATRIATION

A VOLUME IN THE SERIES

Battlegrounds: Cornell Studies in Military History
Edited by David J. Silbey
Editorial Board: Adela Cedillo, M. Girard Dorsey, Michael W. Hankins,
Ellen D. Tillman, and Edward B. Westermann

A list of titles in this series is available at cornellpress.cornell.edu.

FROM INCARCERATION TO REPATRIATION

GERMAN PRISONERS OF WAR IN THE SOVIET UNION

SUSAN C. I. GRUNEWALD

CORNELL UNIVERSITY PRESS

Ithaca and London

First published 2024 by Cornell University Press

Library of Congress Cataloging-in-Publication Data

Names: Grunewald, Susan C. I., 1989– author.
Title: From incarceration to repatriation : German
    prisoners of war in the Soviet Union / Susan C. I.
    Grunewald.
Other titles: German prisoners of war in the Soviet
    Union
Description: Ithaca : Cornell University Press, 2024. |
    Series: Battlegrounds: Cornell studies in military
    history | Includes bibliographical references and index.
Identifiers: LCCN 2023040583 (print) | LCCN 2023040584
    (ebook) | ISBN 9781501776021 (hardcover) |
    ISBN 9781501776038 (epub) | ISBN 9781501776045
    (pdf)
Subjects: LCSH: Prisoners of war—Soviet Union. |
    Prisoners of war—Germany. | World War,
    1939–1945—Prisoners and prisons, Soviet. | World
    War, 1939–1945—Prisoners and prisons, German. |
    Reconstruction (1939–1951)—Soviet Union.
Classification: LCC D805.S65 G784 2024 (print) |
    LCC D805.S65 (ebook) | DDC 940.547247—dc23 /
    eng/20230914
LC record available at https://lccn.loc.gov/2023040583
LC ebook record available at https://lccn.loc.gov
    /2023040584

In loving memory of my mother, Barbara S. Frees

Contents

ACKNOWLEDGMENTS

The roots of this project started in fall 2003, when my mother signed me up for Russian 101 as an elective my freshman year at Wilton High. That eventually spiraled into choosing Lafayette College for its Russian and East European Studies program. My mom's collection of Soviet history books proved to be quite useful during my career, and I am particularly indebted to her marginalia. I must also thank my father and brother for their unwavering love and support during this whole process, especially for the many trips to and from JFK and LaGuardia at odd hours.

This book would not have been possible without several key people and institutions. At Carnegie Mellon, Wendy Goldman, Donna Harsch, Paul Eiss, and Steven Barnes were instrumental to this work. Kate Lynch and Scott Sandage provided key feedback on research seminar papers that later became the backbones of three chapters. Naum Kats provided insight for the commemoration chapter and donated hours of his time to help me translate an early version of it into Russian for presentation before the Russian Academy of Sciences and for publication. Scott Weingart, Daniel Evans, Jessica Otis, Jessica Benner, Matthew Lincoln, Emma Slayton, Ann Marie Mesco, Wilpen Gorr, Rikk Mulligan, and Casidhe Hutchison all helped with the digital mapping process. I appreciate the support and friendship of the students in the history program at Carnegie Mellon, especially my cohort of David Busch, Christine Grant, Mark Hauser, and Clayton Vaughn-Roberson. Jesse, Sue, Amy, Natalie, Andrew, and Lisa in the department office never failed to provide me assistance and always improved my mood. To the members of the CMU Sport Taekwondo Club, thank you for letting me reduce my stress on targets and your bodies, especially Jordan Tick, who had the unlucky role of being my sparring partner for five of my six years at Carnegie Mellon. Thank you to Brad Johnson, Franceska Xhakaj, Matteus Tanha, Milda Zizyte, Jennifer Golda, Susan Tanner, Maria Pia Gomez-Laich, and Natalie Suzelis for help and friendship outside my department. To Danielle, thank you for the fish fries.

My three years as the Digital History Postdoctoral Fellow at the University of Pittsburgh World History Center gave me additional time and resources to work on this manuscript. Thank you very much to Ruth Mostern, Molly Warsh, and Ali Straub during this time for support and feedback on materials. Jonathan Harris provided wonderful comments on earlier drafts that vastly improved the manuscript. My colleagues Aaron Sheehan-Dean and Sue Marchand at Louisiana State University also provided key feedback on this book. Vielen Dank to Günter Bischof for advice on this project as well.

I am grateful for the research support that I received from the Association of Slavic, East European, and Eurasian Studies and its Cohen-Tucker Dissertation Research Fellowship; the A. W. Mellon Foundation and its Digital Humanities Fellowship at Carnegie Mellon; the Central European History Society; the Department of History at Carnegie Mellon University; and the University of Pittsburgh World History Center; Center for Russian, East European, and Eurasian Studies; and European Studies Center for research and writing support for this project.

The staff of the Russian State University of the Humanities, especially Irina in the international department and history professor Aleksei Alekseevich Kilichenkov, helped immensely with my research process in Moscow. I wish to especially thank Tat'iana, Dar'ia, and Evgeniia at the Russian State Military Archive, who made sure that I always received my documents and intervened when necessary with the troublesome coat-check attendant. The staff at the State Archive of Contemporary History of the Ulyanovsk Region (GANI UO) also went above and beyond to help me with my research. The staff of Ulyanovsk State Technical University, or the "Politech," also continued to assist me in whatever ways possible. Without the continued friendship of history professor Vladimir Gurkin, I would not have a chapter examining the commemoration of German POWs. Marina Sergeevna patiently improved my Russian while I served as a Fulbright ETA at the Politech and introduced me to Ol'ga Tyurina, who facilitated my approval to work at GANI UO. Fate also intervened and helped me make the acquaintance of Gennadii Demochkin in the reading room of GANI UO; his personal archival collection gave me the missing information for the commemoration chapter that would otherwise have been akin to finding a needle in a haystack. Irina, Lena, George, Masha, Sasha, Kirill, Nikita, Katya G., Katya M., and Natasha in Ulyanovsk gave me places to stay, drove me around, fed me, and provided me with friendship over the years. Anne-Marie (Russia twin), Jean Louis, Alla, Terry, Gustave, Linda, and Jacob made sure that life in Moscow was never dull. Linda also helped me with some research in Berlin and Frankfurt an Oder.

I must thank my cohort of Soviet historians, all of whom studied at institutions other than Carnegie Mellon. Jonathon Dreeze, Erin Hutchinson, Kelsey Norris, Jack Seitz, Dakota Irvin, John Romero, Rebecca Hastings, Sean McDaniel, and Tyler Kirk all contributed in one way or another to survival abroad and the finished product. I will never be able to thank them enough for their research tips, drafting advice, and friendship. Erin and Tyler graciously agreed to read full drafts of the later-stage manuscript. I owe you both at the next ASEEES.

Finally, I must thank the staff at Cornell University Press for their help with this process. Emily Andrew, David Silbey, and Bethany Wasik have been wonderful and encouraging editors. My two anonymous readers also provided a wealth of supportive and constructive feedback to make this the best possible project.

Abbreviations

CPSU	Communist Party of the Soviet Union
FRG	Federal Republic of Germany
GDR	German Democratic Republic
GKO	State Defense Committee (Gosudarstvennyi komitet oborony)
GlavPU RKKA	Main Political Administration of the Red Army (Glavnoe politicheskoe upravlenie Raboche-krest'ianskoi Krasnoi armii)
GULAG	Main Administration of Camps (Glavnoe upravlenie lagserei)
GUPVI	Main Administration for Affairs of Prisoners of War and Internees (Glavnoe upravlenie po delam voennoplennykh i interovannykh)
MID	Ministry of Foreign Affairs (Ministerstvo vnutrennikh del)
MVD	Ministry of Internal Affairs (Ministerstvo inostrannykh del)
NKFD	National Committee for a Free Germany (Nationalkomitee Freies Deutschland)
NKVD	The People's Commissariat for Internal Affairs (Narodnyi komissariat vnutrennikh del)
OGPU	Joint State Political Directorate (Ob''edinënnoe gosudarstvennoe politicheskoe upravlenie)
SED	Socialist Unity Party of Germany (Sozialistische Einheitspartei Deutschlands)
SVAG	Soviet Military Administration in Germany (Sovetskaia voennaia administratsiia v Germanii)
UPVI	Administration for Affairs of Prisoners of War and Internees (Upravlenie po delam voennoplennykh i interovannykh)
VdH	Association of Returnees (Verband der Heimkehrer)
VKP(b)	All Union Community Party (Bolsheviks) (Vsesoiuznaia kommunisticheskaia partiia [bol'shevikov])

FROM INCARCERATION TO REPATRIATION

Introduction

In November 2017, Russian high school student Nikolai Desyatnichenko gave a speech in front of the German Bundestag in which he discussed his discovery of information about a previously missing German soldier who had been taken prisoner by Soviet forces and had died in 1943. Desyatnichenko noted that the remains of the soldier might lie in a mass grave in the Chelyabinsk region, deep in the Urals and far from the frontlines. He said, "I saw the graves of innocently lost people, many of whom wanted to live peacefully and did not want to fight. They experienced incredible difficulties during the war." The Russian Federation's prosecutor general accused Desyatnichenko of being a Nazi apologist for stating that not every member of the Wehrmacht had been a murderer or a Nazi. The prosecutor general's office investigated the student and his teachers under Russia's Criminal Code statute on "Rehabilitation of Nazism."[1] It is unclear what happened to Desyatnichenko after these initial charges.[2] He did, however, turn into a viral Russian meme,

Note on transliteration: this book uses the Library of Congress Russian Romanization Table standards.

1. "Rossiiskii shkol'nik pokayalsya za nevinno pogibshikh soldat vermakhta," *Lenta.ru*, November 20, 2017, accessed January 29, 2018, https://lenta.ru/news/2017/11/20/nazi_shkolnik/ and "Genprokuratura proverit uchitelei rasskazavshego o nemetskikh soldatakh shkol'nika," *Lenta.ru*, November 21, 2017, accessed January 29, 2018, https://lenta.ru/news/2017/11/21/zaverte/?utm_medium=more&utm_source=rnews.

2. "A byli li Kolya iz Urengoya. Skandal-to druzhno zatushili," *Dzen.ru*, January 24, 2021, https://dzen.ru/a/YArQTLfJOU0wijA7; "Kuda podevalsya chelovekolyubivyi mal'chik Kolya iz Novogo Urengoya?"

that of "Boy Kolya" (*Mal'chik Kolya*). A search of "Boy Kolya" in Yandex, Russia's equivalent of Google, results in hundreds of images of Desyatnichenko either wearing Nazi or SS outfits, looking like Hitler, or with the phrase "Forgive us, fascists!" The legacy of the World War II German POWs in the Soviet Union resonates to this day in contemporary Russian politics.

Two reasons for the continued importance of the German prisoners of war to present-day Russia are the sheer number of them and the length of their captivity. The Allied Powers combined captured over 11 million Germans during the war: the Western Allies captured a staggering 7.745 million compared to the 3.349 million of the Soviet Union.[3] However, Soviet officials continued to detain more than 1.5 million German POWs in the months and years after the war. The prisoners were released in phases, but the last group was held until 1956, seven years longer than any other Allied victor nation. At first glance, this long-lasting incarceration might seem to be a story of Soviet retribution, a desire to punish at least some group of Germans for the war. For many Germans and others, the continued incarceration of POWs served as yet another example of Soviet vengeance, such as the mass atrocities and rapes committed by Soviet soldiers across Germany and Austria toward the end of the war, or as a result of the proliferation of war crimes trials across Soviet territories. The German prisoners were seen as another group caught up in Stalinist repression, consigned to either the Gulag or to Gulag-like camps to labor as punishment for their wartime transgressions.

Many arguments about the vindictive nature of the camps also stem from the difficulties in ascertaining how many German POWs died in Soviet captivity. Not every prisoner returned home: many died in Soviet captivity, although scholarly estimates for the figures vary greatly between Russian and German authors. Russian sources claim about 381,000 German POW deaths; German calculations range from a similar figure to perhaps as many as one million.[4] As of 2017, many of the files relating to POW deaths remained classified in the Russian archives. Unfortunately, obtaining an accurate accounting of the

Dzen.ru, March 24, 2021, https://dzen.ru/media/motivators_demotivators/kuda-podevalsia-chelove-koliubivyi-malchik-kolia-iz-novogo-urengoia-605b017f37297b3abd6b17a8.

3. Ann-Kristin Kolwes, *Die Frauen und Kinder Deutscher Kriegsgefangener: Integriert, ignoriert, und instrumentalisiert, 1941–1956* (Bielefeld: transcript Verlag, 2021), 18.

4. For Russian estimates, see G. F. Krivosheev et al., *Soviet Casualties and Combat Losses in the Twentieth Century* (London: Greenhill, 1997), 276–278. Rüdiger Overmans believes that it is possible to confirm 363,000 German deaths in Soviet captivity from Wehrmacht records, which also list almost 700,000 soldiers missing in action on the Eastern Front. It is possible that these missing men were captured and died in Soviet camps. Rüdiger Overmans and Ulrike Goeken-Haidl, *Soldaten hinter Stacheldraht: Deutsche Kriegsgefangene des Zweiten Weltkriege* (Munich: Ullstein, 2000), 246. See also chapter 5 for a full discussion of factors complicating German POW death statistics.

mortality rates is probably impossible, especially considering the renewed importance of the cult of the Great Patriotic War in contemporary Russia.

Unquestionably, the captivity of the German POWs did serve as a form of punishment for the war. Long understudied due to the politics of the Cold War and a lack of access to sources, the viciousness of the German–Soviet war is poorly understood. The Eastern Front's war of ideological annihilation resulted in 80 percent of Germany's military casualties.[5] The opening of a second major front in Europe did not dramatically change the stationing of German troops. After D-Day, two-thirds of Germany's army remained on the Eastern Front.[6] The war did tremendous damage in the Soviet Union: the country lost 26.6 million soldiers and civilians, one-third of the 6 million Jews murdered by the Nazis were killed on Soviet soil, and the industrial and agricultural infrastructure in the occupied territories was nearly destroyed.[7]

Yet, even amidst the violence in the "bloodlands" of Eastern and Central Europe caught between the Nazi and Soviet dictatorships, the brutality of the war did not greatly influence the Soviet treatment of captured German soldiers.[8] Despite vast evidence of Nazi mass murder and atrocities against Red Army POWs, Soviet authorities did not respond by perpetrating the same actions against their prisoners. In many ways, Soviet officials followed the international standards and practices of the Geneva Convention, even though they were not compelled to do so because they were not signatories. Critics often represent this lack of obligation as evidence of Soviet brutality, but as chapter 1 illustrates, this argument is not supported by the newly available sources. Soviet authorities, in compliance with the Geneva Convention, segregated officers from enlisted men, exempted officers from labor, and attempted to give captives rations on par with those of similar rank and status within the Red Army. Soviet officials recognized that intentionally retributive treatment of German POWs would be an international relations disaster, especially while trying to portray the Soviet Union as a peaceful nation rather than an aggressor during the early years of the Cold War.

This study, based on Russian and German archival sources as well as geographic information system (GIS) mapping, argues that the economic realities of the wartime and postwar Soviet Union, not retribution, motivated

---

5. Richard Overy, *Russia's War: A History of the Soviet War Effort: 1941–1941* (New York: Penguin, 1998), 327.

6. Wendy Z. Goldman and Donald Filtzer, *Fortress Dark and Stern: Life, Labor, and Loyalty on the Soviet Home Front during World War II* (New York: Oxford University Press, 2021), 8.

7. E. IU. Zubkova, *Russia after the War: Hopes, Illusions, and Disappointments, 1945–1957* (Armonk, NY: M. E. Sharpe, 1998), 20.

8. Timothy Snyder, *Bloodlands: Europe between Hitler and Stalin* (New York: Basic Books, 2010).

policies and practices toward German POWs. The Soviet government initially detained the POWs as a labor source to aid in postwar reconstruction. After the country emerged from the war with a dire shortage of manpower and a ruined economy, the Soviet government chose to harness the labor of able-bodied German POWs for as long as possible to aid in reconstruction. The postwar agenda of rebuilding the Soviet Union and establishing a socialist Germany superseded a wartime campaign of hate. The Soviet Union's initial policies on POWs were influenced both by the existing Gulag system and the 1929 Geneva convention. After 1949, however, Cold War considerations began to dominate Soviet decision making, especially about whether to detain or repatriate POWs.

The Main Administration for Affairs of Prisoners of War and Internees (GUPVI) system, like the Gulag on which it was modeled, was an inhumane and brutal one. The memoir-based literature has conditioned much of what has been written about the GUPVI system without contextualization. This book downplays the role of memoir literature, not to silence the voices of the men who suffered through the system but to prioritize the unused and understudied Soviet sources. Presenting the rationale behind Soviet bureaucratic decisions in creating and maintaining this system is not meant to serve as support or apology for either the Gulag or POW camp apparatus. The goal of this study is to understand the logic that drove Soviet leaders to administer the system in the circumstances of the war and early Cold War. This work strives to provide that context, which I argue is crucial for understanding the system. Certainly, the GUPVI system, much like the Gulag, was an extremely harsh form of incarceration; forced-labor conditions were dangerous, and the prisoners often suffered from a lack of supplies. However, this brutal system was generally a byproduct of contemporary conditions, rather than intentional deprivation. Soviet officials expended resources to try to ensure the well-being of foreign prisoners in ways that they rarely did for Soviet inmates in an effort to avoid providing international critics with additional ammunition with which to condemn the Soviet Union.

Drawing on numerous archives, newspapers, memoirs, and author-generated maps, this book is the first composite picture of German POWs in the Soviet Union in any language. German POWs are mentioned only briefly in sources concerning World War II, the Gulag, the postwar reconstruction of the Soviet Union, and postwar German politics and memory.[9] Currently,

---

9. This is by no means an exhaustive list, but for cursory information on POWs during World War II or their uses in reconstruction, see Alexander Werth, *Russia at War: 1941–1945* (New York: E. P. Dutton, 1964); Antony Beevor, *Stalingrad: The Fateful Siege, 1942–1943* (New York: Penguin, 1999); Steven M. Maddox, *Saving Stalin's Imperial City: Historic Preservation in Leningrad, 1930–1950* (Bloomington: Indiana

there is not a single monograph about the experiences of German POWs in the Soviet Union in English. There are, however, two monographs in English on the captivity of Italian and Japanese POWs in the USSR at the same time.[10] The only authors to write substantially about German POWs in English are concerned primarily with their reintegration, lives, and memoirs after repatriation to East and West Germany.[11] Their books examine the role of POWs in Cold War politics but do not deeply explore their lives in captivity or their contributions to Soviet reconstruction. Russian literature on the topic largely comprises published collections of primary documents. Until the fall of the Soviet Union, it was forbidden to discuss or write about the POWs, and the archival documents related to this topic were classified and restricted.[12]

Not surprisingly, there is a fair amount of secondary German-language literature on the POWs. West German scholarly writing about the POWs began to be produced almost immediately after the return of the final prisoners. In 1957, the West German government created the "Scientific Commission for the History of German Prisoners of War" to officially study German POWs in all Allied hands. Dr. Eric Maschke headed the commission, and so it came to be known as the "Maschke Commission." After almost sixteen years, the study produced twenty-two volumes on all possible aspects of POW life in various countries of captivity.[13] Though still influential, the Maschke Commission findings

University Press, 2014); Karl D. Qualls, *From Ruins to Reconstruction: Urban Identity in Soviet Sevastopol after World War II* (Ithaca: Cornell University Press, 2009); and Jeffrey W. Jones, *Everyday Life and the Reconstruction of Soviet Russia during and after the Great Patriotic War, 1943–1948* (Bloomington, IN: Slavica Publishers, 2008). Again but by no means an exhaustive list, some major recent works on German postwar politics or memory that discuss the POWs include Robert G. Moeller, *War Stories: The Search for a Usable Past in the Federal Republic of Germany* (Berkeley: University of California Press, 2003); Jeffrey Herf, *Divided Memory: The Nazi Past in Two Germanys* (Cambridge, MA: Harvard University Press, 1997); Donna Harsch, *Revenge of the Domestic: Women, the Family, and Communism in the German Democratic Republic* (Princeton, NJ: Princeton University Press, 2007); and Elizabeth D. Heineman, *What Difference Does a Husband Make? Women and Marital Status in Nazi and Postwar Germany* (Berkeley: University of California Press, 2003).

10. Sherzod Muminov, *Eleven Winters of Discontent: The Siberian Internment and the Making of a New Japan* (Cambridge, MA: Harvard University Press, 2022); Maria Teresa Giusti, *Stalin's Italian Prisoners of War*, trans. Riccardo James Vargiu (Budapest: Central European University Press, 2021).

11. See, for example, Frank Biess, *Homecomings: Returning POWs and the Legacies of Defeat in Postwar Germany* (Princeton, NJ: Princeton University Press, 2006); Christiane Wienand, *Returning Memories: Former Prisoners of War in Divided and Reunited Germany* (Rochester, NY: Camden House, 2015).

12. V. B. Konasov and A. L. Kuz'minykh, *Nemetskie Voennoplennye v SSSR: Istoriografiia, Bibliografiia, Spravochno-poniatiinyi Apparat* (Vologda: Vologodskii in-t razvitiia obrazovaniia, 2002), 18; S. G. Sidorov, *Trud Voennoplennykh v SSSR: 1939–1956gg.* (Volgograd: Volgograd University Press, 2001); A. L. Kuz'minykh, *Inostrannye voennoplennye Vtoroi mirovoi voiny na Evropeiskom Severe SSSR (1939–1949 gg.)* (Vologda [Russia]: Knizhnoe nasledie, 2005); A. L. Kuz'minykh, *Voennyi plen i internirovanie v SSSR (1939–1956 gody): monografiia* (Vologda: Drevnosti Severa, 2016).

13. For a brief history of the commission and its major components see Rolf Steininger, "Some Reflections on the Maschke Commission," in *Eisenhower and the German POWs: Facts against Falsehood,*

were very one-sided due to the lack of archival access. Even though German and Austrian scholars have received access to archival sources in the former Soviet Union since its collapse in 1991, more recent studies continue to focus on the treatment of the POWs during captivity and repatriation but do not evaluate the contributions of the POWs to the Soviet economy.[14] They largely emphasize German suffering in Soviet captivity and frame it as punishment for the war, evoking at times the legacy of the Gulag without analyzing the similarities and difference between the Gulag and POW labor camp systems.[15]

It is impossible to understand the German POW experience in the USSR without understanding and comparing different aspects of forced labor and the Soviet economy. Treatment of the POWs fit into an already well-established framework of forced labor within the Soviet Union. The People's Commissariat of Internal Affairs (NKVD), which administered the Gulag, also administered the GUPVI POW forced labor camps. The Gulag (*Glavnoe Upravleniye LAGerey* or Chief Administration of Camps) was created by the Politburo, the central governing and policy-making body of the Soviet Union, in 1929 to conserve state resources: the network of self-supporting camps was to replace the nation's existing network of prisons. In addition to helping the penal institutions become self-reliant, administrators intended these camps to colonize remote regions of the Soviet Union and "develop mineral deposits using convict labor."[16]

Using their previous experiences from the Gulag in housing, feeding, clothing, reeducating, and mobilizing prisoners, GUPVI officials primarily concerned themselves with how to most effectively assign their charges to the state's industrial and reconstruction needs. Archival evidence shows that the state was eager to release prisoners who were ill or injured and could not work, a policy that suggests an approach less retributive than economic in motivation. Treatment of the POWs was not especially punitive, and they were not singled out

ed. Günter Bischof and Stephen E. Ambrose (Baton Rouge: Louisiana State University Press, 1992), 171–173. Appendix B of *Eisenhower and the German POWs* includes a bibliography of each of the twenty-two volumes of the Maschke Commission, 241–243.

14. See, for example, Stefan Karner, *Im Archipel GUPVI: Kriegsgefangenschaft und Internierung in der Sowjetunion 1941–1956* (Vienna: R. Oldenbourg, 1995), Michael Borchard, *Die deutschen Kriegsgefangenen: in der Sowjetunion: Zur politischen Bedeutung der Kriegsgefangenenfrage 1949–1955* (Düsseldorf: Droste Verlag, 2000), Andreas Hilger, *Deutsche Kriegsgefangene in der Sowjetunion, 1941–1956: Kriegsgefangenenpolitik, Lageralltag und Erinnerung* (Essen: Klartext Verlag, 2000); and Overmans and Goeken-Haidl, *Soldaten hinter Stacheldraht*.

15. For a detailed discussion of German memory, Soviet captivity, and suffering, see Susan Grunewald, "'Victory or Siberia': Imaginings of Siberia and the Memory of German POWs in the USSR," *German History*, 40, no. 1 (March 2022): 88–106, https://doi.org/10.1093/gerhis/ghab088.

16. For information on the founding of the Gulag and its governing bodies, see O. V. Khlevniuk, *The History of the Gulag: From Collectivization to the Great Terror* (New Haven: Yale University Press, 2004), esp. xvi, 2, 9, and 84.

among other prisoners. Indeed, certain subsets of the POW population received better treatment not only than did Soviet prisoners in the Gulag but also free Soviet citizens, an example of the tempering effects of international relations and international standards established by the Geneva Convention. As for all other convicts in the USSR, the conditions for POWs improved or worsened depending on those in the nation overall. When provisioning and consumption gradually improved after the war, so did conditions in the camps.

Thus far, there has been little effort to examine the forced labor of the German POWs in conjunction with the prevalent scholarship on the Gulag forced-labor camp system. Over the years, scholars have debated the motivations of Soviet leaders—political, economic, or ideological—in creating and maintaining the Gulag forced-labor camp system. Some scholars emphasize the role of political dictatorship and terror.[17] A more recent, archivally based scholarship argues that economics, politics, and ideology all played a role in the Gulag's creation but carried different weights as the system developed over time.[18] Some historians assert that although prison labor was widely deployed, the camp system never made a significant contribution to the economy. Others believe that the Gulag was, in fact, central to the development of the Soviet economy, primarily by developing inhospitable areas rich in natural resources and accomplishing large-scale construction tasks in short periods of time.[19]

Situating the mobilization of POWs in the context of the widespread use of forced labor in the Soviet Union sheds new light on these debates over economics and politics. Earlier Gulag forced-labor construction projects of the 1930s served as the model for how to mobilize POW labor, and German POW labor within the camp system did contribute significantly to the Soviet economy after the war. This finding, revealed by new archival documents concerning POW deployment and output, encourages a reexamination of the role of prison labor in the economy over time, suggesting that the labor contribution of prisoners must be evaluated within the context of different historical periods.

The study of German POWs also contributes to the debate about the role of ideology in the camp system. Recent scholarship on the Gulag has examined

---

17. See, for example, Aleksandr Isaevich Solzhenitsyn, *The Gulag Archipelago, 1918–1956: An Experiment in Literary Investigation* (New York: Harper & Row, 1974); Robert Conquest, *Kolyma: The Arctic Death Camps* (New York: Viking Press, 1978); Anne Applebaum, *Gulag: A History* (New York: Doubleday, 2003).

18. See, for example, Lynne Viola, *The Unknown Gulag: The Lost World of Stalin's Special Settlements* (Oxford: Oxford University Press, 2007), and Khlevniuk, *History of the Gulag*.

19. Paul R. Gregory and V. V. Lazarev, *The Economics of Forced Labor: The Soviet Gulag* (Stanford, CA: Hoover Institution Press, 2003); Mikhail Morukov, "The White Sea-Baltic Canal," in *The Economics of Forced Labor: The Soviet Gulag*, ed. Paul R. Gregory and V. V. Lazarev (Stanford, CA: Hoover Institution Press, 2003), 151–162; Khlevniuk, *History of the Gulag*, 84.

the role of ideology and refashioning of nonpolitical criminals in the system.[20] If inmates were to be rehabilitated, it would be via refashioning through their productive work and contributions to the construction of a new society. This study on the treatment of POWs shows that ideology and refashioning remained a consistent part of camp life. Despite the emphasis on the labor contributions of the POWs, antifascist reeducation was an important part of their experience. Archival findings show that the state devoted considerable resources to instructors, curricula, lectures, books, and pamphlets.[21] Thousands of POWs went through antifascist schools while in the labor camps. The goal was to repatriate the former Nazi soldiers as reeducated antifascist activists who would be sympathetic to the Soviet Union and its values. Indeed, some received special training to work as propaganda agitators on their release to a divided Germany.[22]

One final aspect of the scholarly debates over Soviet forced labor concerns the permeability of the camp system. The Gulag is often represented as sharply isolated from Soviet society, a world apart. However, more recently, scholars have shown that the Gulag was neither remote nor cut off.[23] Instead, the "archipelago" was intertwined with Soviet society. The same holds true for the GUPVI system. The POW camps were located near major industries in and around towns and near sites that used both compulsory and free labor. Camp officials loaned POWs out on contract to the major economic commissariats. The prisoners worked alongside Soviet prisoners and free workers. Memoir literature and anecdotal material from Russians and Germans alike suggest a significant amount of interaction.

Although the GUPVI system prioritized the economic contribution of the POWs to postwar reconstruction, the POWs also played a significant role in

---

20. See, for example, Steven Anthony Barnes, *Death and Redemption: The Gulag and the Shaping of Soviet Society* (Princeton, NJ: Princeton University Press, 2011); Julie Draskoczy, *Belomor: Criminality and Creativity in Stalin's Gulag* (Brighton, MA: Academic Studies Press, 2014); Alan Barenberg, *Gulag Town, Company Town: Forced Labor and Its Legacy in Vorkuta* (New Haven: Yale University Press, 2014); Wilson T. Bell, *Stalin's Gulag at War: Forced Labour, Mass Death, and Soviet Victory in the Second World War* (Toronto: University of Toronto Press, 2018); and Steven Maddox, "Gulag Football: Competitive and Recreational Sport in Stalin's System of Forced Labor," *Kritika: Explorations in Russian and Eurasian History* 19, no. 3 (2018): 509–536.

21. See, for example, RGVA, f. 4p, which is an entire collection of documents related solely to the Antifascist Department of the Administration of POWs and Internees. Individual camps also had their own antifascist departments and record keeping. For example, RGVA, f. 39p, op. 7, which include Antifascist files for the Moscow region camps.

22. RGALI, f. 3715, op. 1, d. 35; ll. 18–19, RGVA f. 4p, op. 33, d. 3, ll. 6–7; and RGVA f. 105p, op. 16, d. 3, ll. 18–19ob.

23. Barenberg, *Gulag Town, Company Town*; Wilson Bell, "The Gulag and Soviet Society in Western Siberia, 1929–1953," (PhD diss., University of Toronto, 2011); Wilson Bell, "Was the Gulag an Archipelago? De-Convoyed Prisoners and Porous Borders in the Camps of Western Siberia," *Russian Review* 72, no. 1 (2013): 116–141; and Golfo Alexopoulos, "Amnesty 1945: The Revolving Door of Stalin's Gulag," *Slavic Review* 64, no. 2 (Summer 2005): 274–306.

the development of relations between the Soviet Union and an eventually divided Germany. This topic, which is critical to our understanding of the Cold War, has been largely neglected. The incarceration of German POWs proved a major diplomatic stumbling block to Soviet relations with both German states after the war and continued to inform diplomatic relations for many years. Thus, the POWs played a central role in shaping German–Soviet relations during the early Cold War. Additionally, the relevance of the POWs to Cold War politics was not limited to the two Germanys and the Soviet Union. The long-lasting imprisonment of German POWs motivated the attempted intervention of the United States, Great Britain, the UN, and the Red Cross motivated by both human rights concerns and more nakedly political motivations. As such, the fate of German POWs contributes to transnational studies of the Cold War.

The impact of these men on domestic Soviet politics and international relations did not end with the final returnees in 1956. The memory of these men and their incarceration continued to inform aspects of commemoration and diplomatic affairs in the Soviet Union, Russia, East and West Germany, and the German Federal Republic. Drawing on works that focus on commemoration, war, and mourning, this book shows the changing role of POW memory, which continues to play a role in contemporary Russian politics and society.[24] Soviet and Russian war memorials clearly illustrate that collective memory of the war shapes their content, despite political powers heavily controlling their form. Although different interpretations of the past exist in different periods, newer iterations of Russian war memorials also harken back to original themes. The past is never fully rewritten; rather, it is modified to suit the changing needs of politics and communities. Although memory studies of the Holocaust and the First World War have exploded in number, the field of Soviet war memory is still relatively young and underdeveloped.[25] Existing studies of Soviet war memory show that the state controlled the narrative of the war at every point and in every period and that political changes

---

24. For studies on the First World War or the Holocaust, see Jay Winter, *Sites of Memory, Sites of Mourning: The Great War in European Cultural History* (Cambridge: Cambridge University Press, 2014); J. M. Winter, *Remembering War: The Great War between Memory and History in the Twentieth Century* (New Haven: Yale University Press, 2006); James Young, *The Texture of Memory: Holocaust Memorials and Meaning* (New Haven: Yale University Press, 1993); Peter Novick, *The Holocaust and Collective Memory: The American Experience* (London: Bloomsbury, 2001); Shoshana Felman and Dori Laub, *Testimony: Crises of Witnessing in Literature, Psychoanalysis, and History* (New York: Routledge, 2013); Thomas Trezise, *Witnessing Witnessing: On the Reception of Holocaust Survivor Testimony* (New York: Fordham University Press, 2014); and Lawrence Langer, *Holocaust Testimonies: The Ruins of Memory* (New Haven: Yale University Press, 1991).

25. See Nina Tumarkin, *The Living & the Dead: The Rise and Fall of the Cult of World War II in Russia* (New York: Basic Books, 1994), for the first major and still influential work on this topic.

occasionally caused variations in state-sponsored narratives and monuments.[26] No scholar has yet to examine the portrayal of German POWs in Soviet and Russian monument production. Yet, as this research reveals, German POWs serve as an excellent case through which to study the evolution of Soviet war memory since World War II.

To make its claims and engage with such a diverse range of entangled but disconnected topics of research, this book uses a wide range of sources. It relies on archival sources together with published and unpublished accounts of POWs to support its central claims about the relationship of economics and politics in shaping the long-lasting incarceration of German POWs in the USSR. Most of the evidence comes from former Soviet archives, including the State Archive of the Russian Federation (GARF), the Russian State Economic Archive (RGAE), the Russian State Military Archive (RGVA), the Archive of Foreign Policy of the Russian Federation (AVP RF), the Russian State Archive of Socio-Political History (RGASPI), the Russian State Archive of Literature and Art (RGALI), the State Archive of Contemporary History of the Ulyanovsk Region (GANI UO), and the Research Institute of History and Culture of the Ulyanovsk Region in the name of N. M. Karamzin. Local camp administrators, central camp officials, and Soviet leaders such as Joseph Stalin, Lavrentii Beria, and Vyacheslav Molotov all directed and evaluated the conditions and use of POWs in the USSR and left ample documentation. These sources have been declassified since the collapse of the Soviet Union—some in the early 1990s and others as late as 2012. Although deeply informative, these documents also present a series of problems. First, despite ongoing declassification efforts, many documents concerning POWs are fractured or remain classified, especially those regarding repatriation and mortality statistics. Second, these sources are largely top-down, bureaucratic documents. They reveal much about state motives but little about the actual conditions faced by the POWs. Third, as the labor chapter of this book discusses, documents of this type, especially concerning forced labor, are often highly problematic. As scholars of the Gulag note, plans did not always translate into reality, and camp commanders frequently falsified output figures. Local archival sources and memoirs show that padding statistics and failures to realize state directives were commonplace. Thus, this book uses a variety of other archives, sources, and methodologies to present a fuller analysis of POWs in the USSR.

Government documents and unpublished POW accounts from German and American archives have proved useful in assessing information contained

---

26. James V. Wertsch, *Voices of Collective Remembering* (Cambridge: Cambridge University Press, 2002); Lisa A. Kirschenbaum, *The Legacy of the Siege of Leningrad, 1941–1995: Myth, Memories, and Monuments* (Cambridge: Cambridge University Press, 2006); Steven M. Maddox, *Saving Stalin's Imperial City: Historic Preservation in Leningrad, 1930–1950* (Bloomington: Indiana University Press, 2014).

in Russian archival sources. Nazi, West German, and East German official government documents from the Federal Military Archive (BA-M), the Federal Archive–Foundation Parties and Mass Organizations of the GDR (BA-SAPMO), and the Political Archive of the Federal Foreign Office (PA AA) all contributed to my investigation of labor, reeducation, and repatriation. Unpublished POW accounts from the Archive of the German Caritas Association (ADCV), the Evangelical Central Archives in Berlin (EZA), the German Red Cross Archive (DRK), and the Hoover Institution Library and Archives in California, as well as published memoirs, address the same questions. The memoir and personal accounts supplement the official documents, showing to what degree lived experience measured up to policy.

This work also makes extensive use of German newspapers and magazines, including *Neues Deutschland, Der Spiegel, Bild (Zeitung),* and *Frankfurter Allgemeine Zeitung,* to explore the role of POWs in German–Soviet relations in the early years of the Cold War. Their reporting reveals how citizens and family members reacted to the situation and pushed their governments to secure the release of the POWs. Finally, GIS mapping provides a highly valuable means to circumnavigate the lack of centralized accountings of POW labor contributions, providing support for wider arguments about the role of POWs in the wartime and postwar Soviet economy.

This book is organized in thematic chapters about camp life, labor, reeducation, politics, and memory that tell a distinct chronological story. The Soviet government created the organization that would become the GUPVI in 1939. With the end of the Battle of Stalingrad in 1943, the Soviets began to house large numbers of prisoners and concentrate on their labor deployment. By the end of the war, Soviet officials worked to release POWs incapable of labor and to assign the remaining men to the most pressing reconstruction tasks. Taken together, the first four chapters show that both economic needs and national conditions influenced POW detention and treatment. Yet, forced labor did not solely shape the POW experience. Ideological reeducation played an important role in POW camp life and, before 1953, served as a major reason, other than illness and injury, for repatriation. Indeed, in 1949 when West and East Germany officially became separate states, ideology surpassed economics as the main motive behind repatriation. As the Soviet economy moved closer toward complete recovery, the dwindling number of POWs in Soviet captivity were increasingly used as pawns by both East and West in the expanding Cold War. Those who returned did so to undertake political work on behalf of the Soviet Union, and those who remained served as bargaining chips.

The fifth and final chapter examines the memory and commemoration of the German POWs in the Soviet Union and Russia. It explores the recollections of these men after their repatriation and shows how they have become a key part of World War II commemoration and Soviet and Russian politics. Although the war ended in 1945, the legacy of its German captives still remains a topic of importance to both the Russian state and its people to this day. The study of Russian war memory is vital to the understanding of contemporary Russia, where legacies of the war have been used to develop nationalism and justify wars on neighboring nations.

CHAPTER 1

The Soviet POW Camp System

International Law and Daily Life

During the industrialization campaign of the 1930s and the Great Patriotic War, the needs of the Soviet economy deeply affected policies toward prisoners and free workers. While in Soviet captivity, German prisoners of war were the responsibility of the Main Administration for Affairs of Prisoners of War and Internees (GUPVI) under the People's Commissariat for Internal Affairs (NKVD). Later known as the Ministry of Internal Affairs (MVD), the NKVD ran both the forced-labor POW camps and the infamous Gulag camps. Its experience in creating and running the Gulag system formed the basis for how to feed and house POWs, mobilize their labor, and, to a certain degree, reeducate them. At the same time, experience with POWs from World War I, as well as international conventions regarding their care, meant that the two parallel NKVD forced-labor systems differed in various ways.

The Politburo, the highest policy-making organ of the All-Union Communist Party (Bolsheviks) (VKP(b)), created the Gulag in 1929 to conserve state resources and colonize remote areas of the nation. The system aimed to be self-sustaining—punishing all internees for their crimes against the state, isolating dangerous individuals from society, and refashioning redeemable prisoners into proper socialist citizens through labor. In essence, the GUPVI would do the same for its POWs. Soviet leaders used their experience running the Gulag to mobilize German POWs into the national economy. Although the GUPVI system was based on that of the Gulag, state officials differentiated between the two types of prisoners. Despite not ratifying international conventions for the treatment of POWs, Soviet leaders enacted policies that mostly conformed to international standards. Their failures to comply with international standards often resulted from national shortages of food and medicine, rather than intentionally retributive policies toward captives. Labor needs in the USSR, especially for postwar reconstruction, shaped most aspects of camp life. Conditions in camps improved as national conditions did overall.

Soviet leaders used the structure of the preexisting Gulag forced-labor camp system to shape the treatment of German POWs. Although labor needs in the USSR motivated many aspects of camp life, international standards and previous war experiences may have tempered the treatment of the POWs. The ability to repatriate ill or injured POWs, especially during periods of extreme postwar hardship, ensured that the state could better distribute its scarce resources to maintain the health of its working prisoner population. If the state had been primarily motivated by retribution, it could have easily worked its captives to death through starvation rations as the Nazis had done with their Soviet captives. The labor needs of a damaged economy and a drastically reduced labor force, however, outweighed desires to punish their former foes. Indeed, over time, Soviet leaders bettered the conditions for German captives whenever possible to increase their potential to contribute to the national economy.

International Law and World War I Experience

Policies for keeping prisoners of war during World War II were based on practices that emerged during and after the First World War, when combatant nations captured mass numbers of prisoners and assigned many to labor tasks. During this conflict, the 1907 Hague Convention governed how to treat the captives through its stipulations about feeding, clothing, housing, and employing the men. After World War I, representatives of many nations again convened to draft the 1929 Geneva Convention, which would guide the treatment of captives during World War II. Even though the Soviet government did not ratify either the 1929 or the 1949 Geneva Conventions, Soviet officials used some of the 1929 provisions as guidelines for their own series of regulations regarding prisoners of war.

Each of the major combatant nations of World War I kept mass numbers of prisoners, and most also used these men for forced labor. Indeed, the large number of prisoners taken on all sides during the conflict suggested that labor use was a normal practice, rather than an exception.[1] Over the course of the war, around ten million Europeans were taken captive and spent an average of three or four years in captivity.[2] For all combatant nations, the 1907 Hague Convention set guidelines for how to treat POWs. The Hague Convention of 1907 was the result of two meetings of international powers, one in 1899 and the other in 1907. Tsar Nicholas II suggested in 1898 that a Hague Conference be held, and it was convened by Queen Wilhelmina of the Netherlands. The conference met from May 18 to July 29, 1899. More than one hundred representatives from multiple nations attended. Although committees for armaments, rules and customs of war, and arbitration were established, nothing came of the 1899 conference beyond reports from those committees. A second conference was then called for by U.S. president Theodore Roosevelt and convened by Nicholas II. Representatives from every independent nation, with the exceptions of Costa Rica, Honduras, Abyssinia, and Liberia, met at the Hague from June 15 to October 18, 1907.

Ultimately, the nations adopted fourteen conventions, including "Convention (IV) respecting the Laws and Customs of War on Land and Its Annex: Regulations concerning the Laws and Customs of War on Land. The Hague, 18 October 1907." One of its sections, "Chapter II: Prisoners of War," comprised seventeen articles.[3] According to the articles, POWs were to be "humanely treated" and had the right to receive shelter, food, and to write and receive correspondence on par with the treatment that men of their rank received in the capturing nation's armed forces. The most important article was Article 6, which read, "The State may utilize the labour of prisoners of war according to their rank and aptitude, officers excepted. The tasks shall have no connection with the operations of war."[4] Thus, Convention (IV) outlined what would be considered the acceptable and baseline levels of treatment for prisoners and permitted their use for labor off the battlefield and outside the military.

Most of the combatant nations of World War I took advantage of this access to a labor force. By August 1916, 90 percent of Germany's 1.6 million prisoners of war were mobilized in agriculture or industry. In France, prisoner

---

1. Heather Jones, "A Missing Paradigm? Military Captivity and the Prisoner of War, 1914–18," *Immigrants and Minorities* 26, nos. 1–2 (July 2008): 21.

2. Alon Rachamimov, *POWs and the Great War: Captivity on the Eastern Front* (New York: Bloomsbury, 2014), 1, 4.

3. Benjamin Franklin Trueblood, *The Two Hague Conferences and Their Results* (Washington, DC: American Peace Society, 1914), 3–4, 9, 11; International Peace Conference, The Hague, Official Record, International Committee of the Red Cross, https://ihl-databases.icrc.org/ihl/INTRO/195.

4. Hague Convention, "Chapter II." International Peace Conference, The Hague, Official Record, International Committee of the Red Cross, https://ihl-databases.icrc.org/ihl/INTRO/195.

labor was essential to the home front where "the captive rapidly came to be identified in terms of his value as a worker."[5] On the Eastern Front, the Germans and Russians used their prisoners for labor. The Russians developed practices that shaped how they treated their enemies some twenty years later. In Russia, German POWs were deployed on labor assignments across the nation from Minsk and Kishinev to Vladivostok and Murmansk. Beginning in fall 1915, the POWs worked in agriculture, construction, and mining. Initially, Russian government officials issued regulations that limited the use of German POWs, especially among the free population. They feared that interactions between Russian citizens and the Germans could be problematic, but as the war continued and more men were drafted to the front, the Russians turned to large-scale mobilization of their prisoners.

By 1916, German POWs were heavily involved in the Russian economy. They worked in a 2:1 ratio in agriculture to industry. The two sectors competed strongly for POW labor and wrangled constantly over the allocation of prisoners. As would be the case in World War II, prisoners employed in agriculture had better conditions than those in industry, mainly because of their proximity to food and the nature of their work. Men drafted to the front generally were the most able-bodied members of the population. After soldiers were captured, the state assigned these healthy, strong men to the most physically demanding jobs such as mining or foundry work. Factory managers preferred to employ these men rather than members of the free population because they could pay the soldiers less, and they were often in better physical shape than the elderly, women, children, and teenagers who remained on the home front. POWs constituted 27 percent of the industrial force of the Moscow-Tula, Donets, Ural, and Western Siberian districts, a statistic that would be replicated during World War II.[6] The use of German POW labor even continued after the Russian Revolution and into the Civil War.[7] In this period, the Bolsheviks mandated weekly inspections of their German captives and the completion of special forms in the event of the death of a prisoner.

Unlike in other nations, many of the POWs in Russia were not confined to camps enclosed with barbed wire and barracks. Indeed, many POWs lived in small to medium-sized groups on estates or peasant farms. German officers received excellent treatment while in Russian captivity, per the terms of the Hague Convention. They did not have to work, and they received salaries, which enabled them to buy additional food, clothing, and other sundries that

5. Jones, "Missing Paradigm," 28–29.
6. Rachamimov, *POWs and the Great War*, 89, 92, 108, 111.
7. GARF, f. 393, op. 89, d. 1, ll. 131 (ob) and 132, Hoover Institution Archives Reel 3.3983.

would improve their quality of life. At times, German officers behind Russian lines enjoyed a higher quality of life than the free residents of their homeland, who suffered severe shortages of food and other goods during World War I.[8]

Although there were guidelines for the treatment of POWs, the German POW experience related directly to the course of the war. Living conditions did not remain static. Both military successes and failures had negative impacts on camp life. When the Russian Army launched successful offensives and captured more men, the camps became overcrowded and were ill equipped to meet prisoners' needs for housing, sanitation, medicine, and food. Eventually, supplies would be imported to the camps, and they would be expanded to handle the higher population, but this took some time. In these interim conditions, typhus outbreaks ravaged the camps, yielding mortality rates ranging from 50 to 70 percent. Later, as the war progressed and the Russian home front began to experience difficulties, so too did the German POWs. Military failures, supply issues, and revolutions all led to an unintentional decrease in the quality of life of POWs.[9] As was the case during World War II, overall national conditions dictated the living conditions of the POWs. When the free population experienced hardships, so too did the prisoners. Poor conditions in the camps were not the result of an attempt to punish the enemy.

Just as the Russians gained experience in caring for and mobilizing German POWs during World War I, so too did the Germans. Like the other combatant nations, the Germans put their Russian prisoners to work. They began using Russian prisoners for labor in 1915 and their Western Front captives one year later.[10] According to one Russian scholar, much is still unknown about the treatment of Russians in German hands because the central German archives burned in 1945. Some evidence suggests, however, that Russian prisoners of war suffered from a shortage of medical care and from epidemics. Tuberculosis was the main killer of Russian POWs during World War I. Moreover, the Germans used 90 percent of their Russian prisoners for forced labor, and the rough conditions that the Russians faced were seen as a justification for the treatment that the Germans received in Russian captivity, suggesting the emergence of a retributive dynamic.[11]

As mentioned, the practical experience gained during World War I was not the only factor shaping how POWs would be treated in the next world war. The Hague Convention of 1907 was deeply influential, and it led to the 1929

8. Rachamimov, POWs and the Great War, 92–93, 98–99.

9. Rachamimov, POWs and the Great War, 103–104.

10. Jones, "Missing Paradigm," 30.

11. O. S. Nagornaia, "Drugoi Voennyi Opyt": Rossiiskie Voennoplennye Pervoi Mirovoi Voiny v Germanii, 1914–1922 (Moscow: Novyi Khronograf: 2010), 12, 105, 116, 119, 129.

Geneva Convention. Its protocols, which were signed and ratified by the United States, the United Kingdom, France, and Germany, included the stipulations of the 1907 Hague Convention. A few years later, in 1934, the government of the German Reich, various branches of the armed forces, and the Wehrmacht High Command agreed to uphold the regulations of the Hague and Geneva Conventions, signed by the nation's previous governing bodies.[12]

The officials of the Soviet Union, as noted, did not sign the 1929 Geneva Convention, breaking with international law and with the stipulations of the 1907 Hague Convention, which Russia had played such a prominent role in creating. According to international law, the Russian Empire's obligations to the Hague Convention would transfer to the new government of the Soviet Union. The Soviet government, however, broke all treaties signed by the tsarist regime except for a select few. Before World War II started, the Soviet government had already refused to subscribe to the stipulations of both the Hague and the 1929 Geneva Conventions.[13] The motivation for Soviet officials' refusal to sign the 1929 Geneva Convention remains unclear. One scholar suggested that it was due to the Swiss government's refusal to acknowledge the Soviet government. He also stated that Soviet officials announced they did not sign due to Article 9 because it mandated that captured soldiers needed to be racially segregated, which the Soviet government rejected on the grounds of its constitution. Another author suggested that Soviet leaders refused to sign because it viewed the mandated Red Cross camp inspections to be avenues for spying.[14]

In refusing to uphold or sign the conventions, Soviet officials did not have to comply with rules such as publishing lists of POWs or providing them the right to send and receive letters. Most importantly, by not upholding or signing the conventions, the Soviet government ignored Hague Convention IV,

---

12. Alfred Streim, "International Law and Soviet Prisoners of War," in *From Peace to War: Germany, Soviet Russia, and the World, 1939–1941,* ed. Bernd Wegner (Providence, RI: Berghahn Books, 1997), 294–295; List of Signers, "Convention relative to the Treatment of Prisoners of War. Geneva, 27 July 1929," International Committee of the Red Cross, https://ihl-databases.icrc.org/applic/ihl/ihl.nsf/States.xsp?xp_viewStates=XPages_NORMStatesParties&xp_treatySelected=305.

13. Streim, "International Law and Soviet Prisoners of War," 294. Aleksandr Kuz'minykh disagrees with Streim and states that, although the Soviet government initially refused to continue to abide by the 1907 Hague Convention, in April 1942 it confirmed its intentions to maintain the standards of that convention. Kuz'minykh, *Voennyi Plen i Internirovaniye v SSSR (1939–1956): Monografiya* (Vologda: Dvernosti Severa, 2016), 96. List of Signers, "Convention relative to the Treatment of Prisoners of War. Geneva, 27 July 1929."

14. For arguments against rejection of the international conventions based on the failure of the Swiss government to recognize the Soviet state, racial issues, and the Soviet constitution, see Chris Bellamy, *Absolute War: Soviet Russia in the Second World War* (New York: Knopf Doubleday, 2008), 20–21. On the notion of this rejection based on the danger of spying, see James D. Morrow, *Order within Anarchy: The Laws of War as an International Institution* (Cambridge: Cambridge University Press, 2014), 217.

Chapter II, Article 20, and the 1929 Geneva Convention on the Treatment of Prisoners of War Part IV, Section II, Article 75, which stated that POWs would be repatriated as quickly as possible after the conclusion of peace.[15]

Although they did not sign or uphold the conventions, Soviet officials did base their standards for care of POWs on them. On July 1, 1941, the Soviet government issued Decree No. 1798–800s, "Provision on Prisoners of War," a truncated version of the 1929 Geneva Convention. Instead of the ninety-seven articles of the Geneva Convention, the Soviet "Provision" had only thirty-one, and it differed from the convention in several key points. It made no mention of a minimum food ration, allowed POWs to be used in industries connected to the war effort, and did not require noncommissioned officers to be separated from enlisted men in work details.[16] Essentially, the Soviet "Provision" enabled use of the maximum number of POWs in the nation's economy, including economic sectors supporting the defense industry, such as construction, timber, and mining.

Whether a nation signed the Geneva Convention of 1929 should not be given too much weight when discussing POW treatment. Although scholars have pointed out the failure of Soviet representatives to sign and abide by it, the Soviet government never aimed to intentionally mistreat the captives of enemy nations. At the same time, Nazi Germany, which upheld Weimar Germany's signing, flouted every stipulation for care regarding prisoners on the Eastern Front.[17] Of the 5.7 million Soviet POWs who fell into German hands during World War II, about 3.3 million died, with roughly 2 million POW deaths occurring between June 1941 and February 1942. The Nazis routinely used starvation to kill substantial numbers of Soviet POWs. Either they supplied insufficient quantities of food or no food at all to their Soviet captives. The soldiers who clung to life turned to cannibalism to survive. Other Soviet POWs died of disease or exposure caused by "camp" conditions: many camps were open fields without shelter that had been cordoned off with barbed wire. Although the prisoners attempted to make their own shelters in the form of dugouts or sod houses, they had little protection from the elements. Typhus and dysentery ravaged the camps, and the captives had no access to medical treatment. Others died from overexertion while marching or working.

15. Hague Convention, "Chapter II, Article 20," International Peace Conference, The Hague, Official Record, International Committee of the Red Cross, https://ihl-databases.icrc.org/ihl/INTRO/195; "Convention relative to the Treatment of Prisoners of War. Geneva, 27 July 1929."

16. Kuz'minykh, *Voennyi Plen*, 96–97; Maksim Matveevich Zagorul'ko, *Voennoplennye v SSSR 1939–1956: Dokumenty i materialy* (Moscow: Logos, 2000), 27–28.

17. Alfred Streim, "International Law and Soviet Prisoners of War," 294; Frank Biess, *Homecomings: Returning POWs and the Legacies of Defeat in Postwar Germany* (Princeton, NJ: Princeton University Press, 2006), 45.

The vast majority of Soviet POWs were simply shot outright.[18] One German soldier, Leonard Ferk, told his Soviet captors, "In Toropetz, on the Velikoluzhskoi road, I saw dead Russian POWs. The SS group shot them only because they did not want to give themselves the difficulty of taking them back with them."[19] Another German soldier in Soviet hands, Rolf Wezel, told of the capture of Mogilev, Belarus, at the end of July 1941. The Germans rounded up at gunpoint all the Red Army soldiers, many of whom were wounded. They led them out of the city and had them all bend down to drink from a ditch. While they drank, Senior Lieutenant Fall told his men, "Kill them; we have enough without them."[20] The Nazis also used their Soviet captives to clear minefields and as test subjects for what would become the mechanized mass killings of the Holocaust. Captured Red Army soldiers served as the first victims for Zyklon B gas at Auschwitz in September 1941.[21]

Other Allied nations also failed to follow the stipulations of the Geneva Convention both during and after the war. After the war, U.S. administrators and Red Cross officials cited the French for not treating their German POWs according to the stipulations of the 1929 Geneva Convention. These officials noted instances of starvation of German POWs in French hands.[22] The United States also intentionally neglected to comply with the rules governing the rights of captured soldiers because of strategic concerns. In one instance, the U.S. Navy captured the German submarine U-505 and its crew on June 4, 1944. Although the German crew attempted to scuttle the vessel, the U.S. sailors succeeded in acquiring an Enigma code machine complete with up-to-date ciphers. To prevent the German military from learning that the Americans possessed the ability to decode their encrypted communications, U.S. officials segregated the crew from other German POWs, hid their identities from the local population, and did not report their existence to the Red Cross. Camp officials in Louisiana even went so far as to remove them from camp during a Red Cross inspection.[23]

---

18. David Stahel, *The Battle for Moscow* (Cambridge: Cambridge University Press, 2017), 41–42; Karsten Linne, "Hunger und Kannibalismus bei sowjetischen Kriegsgefangenen im Zweiten Weltkrieg," *Zeitschrift für Geschichtswissenschaft* 58, no. 3 (March 2010): 248; Rebecca Manley, "Nutritional Dystrophy: The Science and Semantics of Starvation in World War II," in *Hunger and War: Food Provisioning in the Soviet Union during World War II*, ed. Wendy Goldman and Donald Filtzer (Bloomington: Indiana University Press, 2015), 5–6; Christian Streit, *Keine Kameraden: Die Wehrmacht und die sowjetischen Kriegsgefangenen 1941–1945* (Bonn: J.H.W. Dietz, 1997).

19. RGVA, f. 1p, op. 21a, d. 61, l. 21.

20. RGVA, f. 105p, op. 4, d. 14, l. 213.

21. Stahel, *Battle for Moscow*, 44.

22. Ruth Beaumont Cook, *Guests behind Barbed Wire: German POWs in America: A True Story of Hope and Friendship* (Birmingham, AL: Crane Hill, 2007), 465.

23. "Navy Department Immediate Release Press and Radio," pages 1–3, May 16, 1945, folder 7, 5750/351—CNSG—U-505 (Code Name Nemo) Navy Department Documents, box 198, Records of the Office of the Chief of Naval Operations, RG 38, NARA; R. S. Edwards "Secret Memorandum," Janu-

THE SOVIET POW CAMP SYSTEM

After World War II, various nations again met in 1949 to refine the Geneva Conventions and shape international law based on their wartime experiences. This time, the Soviet Union sent a delegation and took part. The Soviet Ministry of Internal Affairs (MVD, the successor organization to the NKVD) closely tracked the discussions and suggested changes to be included in the 1949 Geneva Convention. As part of this process, the Soviet delegation consulted the Main Administration for Affairs of Prisoners of War and Internees (GUPVI) for its input and practical experience. In the end, the Soviet representatives did not agree with all the convention's terms and again refused to sign and ratify it, although they did so within five years on May 10, 1954.[24] Once again, it was likely that the provision requiring immediate repatriation of prisoners at war's end and the Soviet unwillingness to open their camps to Western monitors proved sticking points. Thus, the Soviet Union was not bound by international law to give their German POWs certain rights that they would have received if held captive by the other Allied victor nations. The lack of international monitoring served as the basis throughout the Cold War for Allied nations to attack their communist rivals.

POW Capture, Distribution, and Labor Classification

When the Soviet Union entered World War II on June 22, 1941, the nation already had a well-established government entity for prisoners of war, the Administration for Affairs of Prisoners of War and Internees (UPVI) of the NKVD. The Gulag, another suborganization of the NKVD, informed UPVI policies and practices. Although previous experience and legal conventions

---

ary 25, 1944, and Clayton Bissel "Letter to the Provost Marshall General," January 25, 1945, folder 2, 5750/351—CNSG—U-505 (Code Name Nemo) Navy Department Documents, box 198, Records of the Office of the Chief of Naval Operations, RG 38, NARA; TG serial 0021, June 4, 1994, box 108, Records of the Office of the Chief of Naval Operations, RG 38, NARA; Wesley Harris, *Fish out of Water: Nazi Submariners as Prisoners in North Louisiana during World War II* (Ruston, LA: RoughEdge, 2004), 12, 20–21; Gary W. Moore, *Playing with the Enemy: A Baseball Prodigy, a World at War, and a Field of Broken Dreams* (Philadelphia: Casemate, 2006), 92, 95, 97, 99, 101; James E. Wise, *U-505: The Final Journey* (Annapolis, MD: Naval Institute Press, 2005), 89, 95; Arnold Krammer, *Nazi Prisoners of War in America* (New York: Stein and Day, 1979), vii, 27, 36.

   24. Full drafts of the 1949 Convention with suggested changes can be found in RGVA, f. 1p, op. 21a, d. 38 and 39. These include typewritten drafts in Russian with changes penciled in. The folders do not give a reason for the ultimate refusal of the Soviet delegation to sign. They do, however, include a letter dated February 23, 1949, to the Minister of Internal Affairs, S. N. Kruglov, asking for GUPVI's input and expertise in shaping the discourse of the 1949 Convention. For this letter, see RGVA f. 1p, op. 21a, d. 38, l. 1; "Russian Federation," International Committee of the Red Cross, https://ihl-databases.icrc.org /applic/ihl/ihl.nsf/vwTreatiesByCountrySelected.xsp?xp_countrySelected=RU.

both played a part in shaping how Soviet leaders thought about the organization and administration of their POWs, the Gulag forced-labor system served as the primary model. The NKVD used the norms it had developed for Soviet prisoners and applied them to the POWs in the UPVI system. The need for POW labor motivated the Soviet state to continue to detain its German POWs for many years after the end of the war and influenced most aspects of camp life. As was the case in the Gulag, labor needs greatly dictated UPVI rations, work hours, medical inspections, and cultural work.

The NKVD created the UPVI in September 1939, coinciding with the Soviet Union's movement into Poland after the Molotov-Ribbentrop Pact. The UPVI soon proved important in the Winter War with Finland in November. When the UPVI became operational, it consisted of a system of 267 camps that oversaw 392 work battalions and 178 special hospitals.[25] Within the first month of operation, it handled almost nine thousand POWs of various ethnicities and nationalities.[26] After the Germans invaded the Soviet Union on June 22, 1941, the Red Army sent their Axis captives to NKVD-run collection points (*priemnye punkty*) along the front. From there, the NKVD sent the soldiers toward the rear to distribution camps (*lageri-raspredelitel'nye*). Modeled on the Gulag camps, the distribution camps temporarily cared for and housed captured soldiers before they could be interrogated and sent either to larger camps away from the frontlines, to hospitals, or for trial. As of June 5, 1942, the NKVD operated six distribution camps, which served every major battlefront. Each distribution camp worked in tandem with the collection points, which multiplied as the war progressed. Over the course of 1942, the number of collection points increased from nineteen to forty-five, or roughly 2.5-fold.[27] During this year, the Soviet military also disseminated propaganda to encourage Germans to turn themselves in to the Red Army. After Stalin's Order No. 55 was promulgated on February 23, 1942, the Red Army began issuing paper passes to German soldiers printed in German and Russian to encourage them to surrender. The passes stated that every German officer and soldier had the right to cross the front and be taken captive, that every Soviet citizen had the obligation to turn over Germans to the nearest Red Army post, and that prisoners would be guaranteed life, good care, and a return to their homeland after the end of the war.[28]

---

25. I. P. Kuz'micheva, *Skvoz' Plen: Nemetskiye Voennoplennye v Sovetskom Soyuze* (Moscow: Sabash-nikovykh, 2007), 10, 26.

26. RGVA, f. 1p, op. 2a, d. 1, l. 76.

27. Kuz'minykh, *Voennyi Plen*, 135,

28. Passierschein, undated, Klaus Kirchner Collection, box 4, folder 2401–2405, Hoover Institution Archives; RGVA, f. 4p, op. 3, d. 3, ll. 41–42.

Thus, each prisoner went from collection point to distribution camp to a more permanent home front camp or hospital camp. Home front camps generally looked like the model of a typical camp. They frequently, but not always, featured some sort of barbed-wire enclosure with gates and security posts. The camps had barracks, a mess hall, latrines, and bathing facilities, plus infrastructure for the camp administration.[29] Not all prisoners lived in traditional camps, however. As chapter 2 notes, prisoners could be loaned out to local industries under labor contracts. In some cases, local enterprises had to house the prisoners in factory barracks. Moreover, there is a popular contemporary Russian anecdote that German POWs lived on various floors of the flagship building of Moscow State University as they worked to construct it.[30]

Regardless of whether the prisoner lived in the home front camp or in local factories, his assigned labor camp determined his work detail. According to the Council of People's Commissars' Decree No. 1798–800s, "Provision on Prisoners of War" of July 1, 1941, POWs were to be mobilized for labor tasks through the UPVI system.[31] By 1942, labor assignments became standardized when the NKVD ordered the POWs to work in nickel and coal mines and for the timber industry. It also assigned POWs captured before 1942 to work in peat extraction to fuel power stations in the Sverdlovsk Province. Yet the numbers of captured soldiers and POW laborers remained low. The first year and a half of the war saw mostly retreats and defensive fighting for the Red Army, and consequently, it captured only a small number of soldiers. Before the Battle of Stalingrad (August 23, 1942–February 2, 1943), only 10,528 Germans had been captured by the Red Army. At Stalingrad, however, the Red Army captured 91,000 German soldiers, including 22 generals.[32] The Battle of Stalingrad was thus a major turning point not only in the war but also in the capture and deployment of POWs.

Unfortunately, many of the Germans captured at Stalingrad perished because of a lack of supplies and leadership decisions made by both the German and Soviet sides. In November 1942, Soviet forces began to encircle a large

---

29. For diagrams of camps, see GARF, f. 9526, op. 6, d. 384, l. 64; RGVA, f. 105p, op. 6, d. 23, l. 1; RGVA, f. 105p, op. 6, d. 23, l. 17.

30. Katherine Zubovich does not mention the POWs in connection to Moscow State University, although she notes that they did participate in the construction of the Kotel'nicheskaia Building, another of Stalin's Seven Sisters skyscrapers. Katherine Zubovich, *Moscow Monumental: Soviet Skyscrapers and Urban Life in Stalin's Capital* (Princeton, NJ: Princeton University Press, 2021), 242n92.

31. Kuz'minykh, *Voennyi Plen*, 96–97; Zagorul'ko, *Voennoplennye v SSSR*, 27–28.

32. Kuz'micheva, *Skvoz' Plen*, 12; Antony Beevor, *Stalingrad* (New York: Penguin, 1999), 396; Ian Garner, *Stalingrad Lives: Stories of Combat and Survival* (Montreal: McGill-Queen's University Press, 2022), 189; Iain MacGregor, *The Lighthouse of Stalingrad: The Hidden Truth at the Heart of the Greatest Battle of World War II* (New York: Scribner, 2022), 280.

number of German soldiers. A Sovinformbureau report from January 1, 1943, indicated that the Red Army had encircled twenty-two enemy divisions in the city. Surrounded, the Germans faced diminishing rations and temperatures that dropped to as low as minus 40 degrees—the point at which the Fahrenheit and Celsius scales converge. Field Marshal Friedrich Paulus's troops had been surrounded since November 23, 1942, and promised airdrops had diminished in both frequency and quantity. The Soviet commanders offered the Germans the chance to surrender on January 8, which Paulus rejected. On January 10, the Soviet forces launched another offensive against the encircled Germans. After days of fierce fighting, Soviet commanders offered Paulus the chance to surrender on January 17, which he again rejected. The Red Army again launched an offensive on the last of the firmly entrenched Germans in the city, advancing slowly, building by building. As the Red Army approached German headquarters, more and more German and Romanian soldiers began to surrender to the Soviet military. Eventually, Soviet forces captured Field Marshal Paulus in the basement of the city's central department store on January 31. The remaining pockets of German soldiers relented and finally surrendered on February 2. Because of Hitler's refusal to permit their surrender, more than 200,000 German soldiers died from hunger, exposure, disease, or Soviet advances between the initial encirclement in November 1942 and their surrender on February 2, 1943.[33]

As was the case with tsarist camps for Germans following major Russian military advances in World War I, the rapid influx of German POWs after Stalingrad overtaxed the UPVI system, and Soviet officials failed to properly care for the massive number of prisoners. Negligence and lack of coordination resulted in the deaths of many. Even though the Red Army and NKVD had realized by the end of 1942 that surrender was imminent at Stalingrad, few preparations had been made to guard, feed, supply, or house the increasing number of prisoners, most of whom were in poor physical condition from months of encirclement. The German soldiers were also woefully underdressed for the harsh Russian winter. The freezing German prisoners marched to camps near Stalingrad. Along the way they were rarely given shelter and had to spend evenings sleeping outside in insufficient clothing. Compounding these hardships was the lack of food or water.[34]

Many of the 91,000 German prisoners marched to their deaths on their way to the camps or died on arrival. These men, and their Italian and Romanian allies, were very weak at capture. In this poor condition, they were more sus-

---

33. Alexander Werth, *Russia at War, 1941–1945* (New York: Dutton, 1964), 533–540, 542.

34. Werth, *Russia at War*, 500.

ceptible to disease, and many died due to epidemics, gangrene, or scurvy.[35] When rations finally did arrive at the Stalingrad camps, they were pitiful. There was rarely more than a loaf of bread for ten men.[36] By April 15, 1943, the NKVD reported that 55,228 of the 91,000 Stalingrad prisoners had died, or almost 61 percent in three months.[37] Although some of these deaths could be attributed to a combination of negligence and indifference motivated by a desire for retribution, many were the result of the painful wartime conditions within the Soviet Union. The winter of 1942–1943 was the height of the food crisis sparked by the Nazi invasion of 1941. There was a deep reluctance to provision German POWs when the nation was desperately short of food. Mortality rates rose in the Gulag system and in the country as a whole. During the early war years, the Wehrmacht had occupied the Soviet Union's largest farmlands in Ukraine and Western and Southwestern Russia. The state turned to a complex rationing system to try to feed both the Red Army and the home front but struggled to do so. Civilians tried to supplement their allocations with garden plots and collective farm markets to stay alive.[38]

It was also difficult to give POWs medicine for typhus and diphtheria, as well as delousing equipment when the same problems plagued most Red Army soldiers and civilians. Throughout the country, civilians went for months without washing due to a lack of soap, and subsequently they suffered from lice or rashes and skin infections.[39] In the Gulag, prisoners also heavily suffered from the lack of rations. The Gulag faced the same rapid influx of prisoners as the POW camp system in this period: the tide of the war brought a rapidly increasing number of both German captives and Soviet citizens into Soviet penal institutions. After the liberation of territories, Soviet authorities interrogated the remaining population and harshly convicted tens of thousands of citizens of treason, regardless of whether they had committed anti-Soviet activities during the war. In some cases, their survival alone merited punishment. A similar fate befell those convicted in postwar filtrations, who found themselves sentenced to the severely undersupplied camp system.[40]

35. Maria Teresa Giusti, *Stalin's Italian Prisoners of War*, trans. Riccardo James Vargiu (Budapest: Central European University Press, 2021), 100.

36. Beevor, *Stalingrad*, 410.

37. Beevor, *Stalingrad*, 413.

38. Donald Filtzer, "Starvation Mortality in Soviet Home-Front Industrial Regions during World War II," in *Hunger and War*, ed. Goldman and Filtzer, 267–268, 270, 329; Wendy Goldman, "Not by Bread Alone: Food, Workers, and the State," in *Hunger and War*, ed. Goldman and Filtzer, 45–46.

39. Beevor, *Stalingrad*, 409–410; Goldman, "Not by Bread Alone," 83.

40. Alan Barenberg, *Gulag Town, Company Town: Forced Labor and Its Legacy in Vorkuta* (New Haven: Yale University Press, 2014), 60–63; Wilson T. Bell, *Stalin's Gulag at War: Forced Labour, Mass Death, and Soviet Victory in the Second World War* (Toronto: University of Toronto Press, 2018), 57–60.

The preferential treatment of soldiers and civilians versus prisoners was not a new development in the Soviet Union. Gulag prisoners always suffered the most from resource shortages. Prisoners were at the bottom of the ration list for centrally planned allocations. Although German POWs had their own forced-labor camps, they were frequently treated like Gulag inmates. Much like the initial prisoners sentenced to the Gulags in the early 1930s and the early stages of the war, many of the German prisoners died in the disease-ridden conditions of transport.[41] Once they arrived in the camps, prisoners underwent delousing and medical inspections. Both Gulag and GUPVI camp staff sorted the prisoners by their ability to work. One prisoner wrote of the experience: "After the official delousing we weren't allowed to get dressed until we were paraded stark naked in front of three Russian doctors who would determine our fitness for work. . . . Each prisoner was pinched in the buttocks to determine how much meat was left. Then the doctors would assign a classification to determine their ability to work."[42] Those who were strong enough began working immediately on the camps' assigned labor projects to earn their rations. Gulag directives mandated that every person sentenced to a labor camp had to work if able. This rule also applied to German POWs in forced-labor camps.

However, production expectations, work assignments, and rations were not the same for all POWs or Gulag inmates. Each prisoner in the Gulag was rated by a medical commission, which determined his labor output capability. Created in 1931, the "medical-labor commissions" comprised doctors who biannually examined all prisoners and classified them by their labor capacity. For those in the Gulag, the potential economic return from one's labor determined one's physical ranking. The commissions assigned prisoners to one of three labor capability categories and to categories of illness or weakness. In the first category of labor capability were placed prisoners capable of heavy labor. These prisoners were engaged in the most physically demanding tasks such as mining, timber, or construction. Those deemed to be in labor category two, or capable of moderate labor, generally performed the same tasks as those cleared for heavy physical labor but with reduced quotas. The third labor category, or those capable only of light labor, performed ancillary or support service jobs.[43]

Prisoners found to be too weak even for light labor received rankings based on their prognosis for recovery. When doctors thought prisoners could recover

41. Beevor, *Stalingrad*, 414–415; Oleg V. Khlevniuk, *The History of the Gulag: From Collectivization to the Great Terror* (New Haven: Yale University Press, 2004), 77, 251–252, 321–322.

42. Hans Gruber, *My Odyssey thru Hell* (Bloomington, IN: AuthorHouse, 2013), 38.

43. Dan Healey, "Lives in the Balance: Weak and Disabled Prisoners and the Biopolitics of the Gulag," *Kritika: Explorations in Russian and Eurasian History* 16, no. 3 (August 29, 2015): 538–540.

their labor potential after a period of reduced work or complete rest with improved rations and anti-scurvy medication, those prisoners experienced a temporary reprieve to recover. After their period of convalescence, they were expected to be in peak physical form and reassigned to heavy labor. Very few prisoners could benefit from opportunities to recover, however. Central government officials permitted camp officials to assign only up to 1.5 percent of their prisoners to these recovery teams, which meant that many prisoners went without the care that they needed. Thus, minor illness or injury could lead to incapacitation or death. The harsh conditions and lack of opportunity for recovery increased the death toll of the camp system. Moreover, officials rarely confused those capable of improvement with the gravely diseased or those who were too emaciated for recovery. Those deemed incapable of quick recovery often died.[44]

For the POWs, as for much of the civilian home front population, the harsh conditions of intensive labor and insufficient rations led to malnutrition and diagnoses of emaciation and starvation disease, known as "nutritional dystrophy." Camp doctors studied the disease, and it received its own classification in the Soviet medical system during World War II.[45] The accurate understanding of the disease began during the Leningrad Blockade (1941–1944). Over the course of the siege, doctors in Leningrad studied not only patients but also themselves. Because previous medical texts and studies did not accurately describe the condition, doctors coined new terms of "nutritional dystrophy" (*alimentarnaia distrofia*) and *distrofik* (one who suffers from dystrophy) to describe the disease of starvation linked to the insufficient supply of food. They noted that the severity of the disease corresponded to caloric deficits exacerbated by low temperatures, the difficulties of daily life, and heavy labor. Through trial and error, they learned how to combat the disease. Dystrophy was caused not just by a lack of food but also by nutritional deficiencies: people suffering from this condition did not just require more food. Indeed, overfeeding could even kill them. To recover, a patient needed warmth, quiet, and days of extremely limited activity and an easy-to-digest diet with additional nutrients.

Doctors from Leningrad published their findings on the disease between 1943 and 1947, and their discoveries had an immediate impact on Soviet medicine. The so-called Leningrad disease or nutritional dystrophy soon began to appear in NKVD documents as well. Beginning in 1943, the NKVD categorized dystrophy as a distinct illness, and nutritional dystrophy became an important term in Gulag documents.[46] Those diagnosed as *distrofiki* had three

---

44. Healey, "Lives in the Balance," 540–541.
45. Healey, "Lives in the Balance," 536.
46. Manley, "Nutritional Dystrophy," 206–207, 209, 216–218, 225, 231, 252.

possible fates. In rare circumstances they recovered despite the lack of neces-sary medical and nutritional support. In most cases, however, they died. Some were lucky enough to be released from the camps. Invalids were a burden on the camp economy, and the OGPU/NKVD/MVD ordered the release of in-valids or those incapable of working in various batches over the history of the Gulag.[47] Often, this was done both to decrease their drain on camp resources and to hide the real camp mortality statistics.

By the time that large numbers of German POWs entered the forced-labor system around 1943, NKVD personnel were well versed in grading inmates and assigning them work based on their labor capacity. Maximum economic productivity dictated both the organization of the Gulag and the treatment of German POWs. Like Gulag prisoners, German POWs went before medi-cal commissions to have their physical condition assessed and their labor po-tential categorized. During and after World War II, these medical inspections occurred monthly for the POWs, in contrast to the biannual inspections of the Gulag inmates; however, the POW assessments occurred less frequently than the weekly inspections of the German POWs done by the Bolsheviks dur-ing the Civil War.[48]

Although previous medical experience with Gulag prisoners informed the categories and labor assignments of POWs, the needs of the war required modifications to the system. In February 1944, V. V. Chernyshëv, the deputy commissar of the NKVD, sent an order to the heads of the NVKD and those in charge of POWs, assigning greater responsibilities to POWs in the second labor category.[49] Prior to this order, prisoners classified in this category—those who could do most physical jobs but with reduced quotas—were limited to working only within the labor camps. However, as the war progressed and the labor shortage increased, prisoners belonging to the second labor category were allowed to work in or outside the camp for either the camp or other eco-nomic ministries. A follow-up order in April from S. N. Kruglov, the deputy people's commissar of internal affairs of the Soviet Union, stressed the need to most efficiently use the labor of those fit for work.[50] Both orders empha-sized the need to maximize labor output and to set rations adequate for their physical conditions. Furthermore, the orders highlighted once again that

47. Healey, "Lives in the Balance," 540; Mikhail Nakonechnyi, "'They Won't Survive for Long': Soviet Officials on Medical Release Procedure," in *Rethinking the Gulag: Identities, Sources, Legacies*, ed. Alan Barenberg and Emily D. Johnson (Bloomington: Indiana University Press, 2022), 103–128; Golfo Alexopoulos, *Illness and Inhumanity in Stalin's Gulag* (New Haven: Yale University Press, 2017), 133.

48. RGVA, f. 1p, op. 15a, d. 68, ll. 5–6; GARF, f. 393, op. 89, d. 1, ll. 131 (ob) and 132, Hoover Insti-tution Archives Reel 3.3983.

49. GARF, f. 9401, op. 1, d. 714, l. 292–293, in Zagorul'ko, *Voennoplennye v SSSR*, 578–580.

50. GARF, f. 9401, op. 1, d. 715, l. 160–162, in Zagorul'ko, *Voennoplennye v SSSR*, 580–581.

POWs in the second labor category were to receive smaller rations than those in the first, a reminder that seemed to imply that camp commandants had been providing equal amounts of food to both groups.

Communication went in both directions between central organs and POW camps. Heads of camps sent reports to the central UPVI leadership informing them about the status of the POW population. For example, the assistant director of the Stalingrad Oblast NKVD, Lieutenant-Colonel Petrukhin, accounted for the status of the POWs in camps 50, 108, and 123 in June 1944. This report broke down how many POWs worked for each of the main camps and in which local industries, as well as how many POWs in each camp belonged to each of the three labor categories. Petrukhin also gave totals for those sick with dystrophy and those in hospitals.[51] These types of reports showed that central NKVD leaders demanded a clear accounting from regional NKVD camp officials of the labor capabilities and health of the POW population. Such reports allowed the central leadership to make their own accounting and assessment of POWs' physical standing and labor potential, which presumably informed both future deployments of POWs to particular camps and the camps' labor contracts.

Camp directors were not the only officials concerned with these labor categories. Immediately after the war, reports to top Soviet officials outlining work assignments of POWs also noted their physical condition. By 1944, the influx of prisoners into the UPVI system resulted in the NKVD changing its status from the Administration for Affairs of Prisoners of War and Internees (UPVI) to the Main Administration for Affairs of Prisoners of War and Internees (GUPVI).[52] The reports of the GUPVI went to the highest levels of the Soviet government. A May 17, 1945, memo to Beria from M. S. Krivenko, a lieutenant-general of the GUPVI, reported the total number of POWs, their work assignments, the number of POWs belonging to the three labor categories, and the percentages of the total POW labor force that represented.[53] The physical condition of the POWs was almost as important to the state as their assigned industries. Later, in June 1946, newly promoted Minister of Internal Affairs S. Kruglov sent a memo to Stalin, Beria, and Molotov in which he reported not only on the breakdown of POW labor by ministry but also on the POWs' physical condition. He accounted for those who could labor, the ill, and the dead.[54] Leading officials placed importance on being kept apprised of the breakdown not only of POW labor but also of their physical condition.

51. RGVA, f. 47p, op. 14, d. 4, ll. 6–7.
52. Kuz'micheva, Skvoz' plen, 10.
53. GARF, f. 9401, op. 1, d. 2227, l. 28–30.
54. GARF, f. 9401, op. 2, d. 137, ll. 366–377.

Modifications to POW labor assignments would mean nothing if prisoners were unfit to perform their assigned tasks. Additionally, as shown later in this chapter, at times chief Soviet officials attempted to make interventions regarding the supplies and care for POWs to maximize their labor efficiency and potential.

POW Rations

The process of dividing prisoners by physical capability not only determined their assigned labor tasks but also the food they received to sustain or improve their physical standing. Just as the GUPVI borrowed from the Gulag's system of physical ratings, so too did it employ that system's ration policies. In the Gulag, labor productivity determined rations. The labor category of a prisoner, as well as his labor assignment, dictated the ration amount. The NKVD had years of experience learning how to adjust rations, finding the minimal investment needed to sustain the inmates and stave off death. Rations also served as the motivation for captives to work.[55] Prisoners only received the full daily ration by meeting the labor quota: insufficient labor returns resulted in a reduction of the ration.

The system that applied to the German POWs, however, differed from that applied to Gulag prisoners in two respects. First, not all German POWs were equal in status. Inequality among inmates also existed in the Gulag, but generally as a result of the crime the inmate had been sentenced for and not necessarily his status outside the camps. In the GUPVI, officers and generals, as well as the ill, received higher rations. German officers and generals did not engage in physical labor, yet their ration norms called for high rations that even surpassed those of the free Soviet population. Even though the Soviet government did not sign the Geneva Convention, it abided by some of its conditions, including the stipulations prohibiting officer labor and requiring giving enemy captives rations on par with those of their counterparts in the capturing nation's military. Soviet authorities likely realized that failing to provide better conditions for captive officers and generals could result in their own officers being treated poorly in enemy hands. Better treatment for officers could benefit not only the war effort but also the restructuring of a postwar Germany. Some German officers also participated in pro-Soviet propaganda movements; those men could serve as potential recruits for the formation of

---

55. Steven A. Barnes, *Death and Redemption: The Gulag and the Shaping of Soviet Society* (Princeton, NJ: Princeton University Press, 2011), 41–42.

a Communist Party-led German state. Thus, officers required higher rations in exchange for their loyalty and assistance. Additionally, unlike in the Gulag, the German POW population became fixed after a certain point. Although Gulag officials may have had little incentive to preserve the lives of inmates because there was always a steady supply of new prisoners, GUPVI officials sought to maintain their allocated number of POWs for as long as possible after the war's end.[56]

POW rations became a matter of high importance for both camp leaders and top national leaders. All involved in the running of the nation and the camps understood the relationship between food provisioning and labor productivity. As more German soldiers were captured and mobilized into the Soviet economy in 1943, their ration norms became a closely monitored and heavily directed topic. For example, in an undated resolution from 1943, Joseph Stalin, in his role as chairman of the State Defense Committee (GKO), personally decided the labor assignments of 140,000 POWs. As chapter 2 notes, Stalin and other high-ranking officials commonly made decisions on the deployment of POW labor. Stalin also emphasized that camp and project leaders had to feed the captive laborers sufficiently.[57] After the successful mass capture of POWs after Stalingrad, as well as the failures to properly care for them, the NKVD developed a formal rationing hierarchy in April 1943. The order, No. 00683, attempted to set daily standards in grams of food per prisoner in camps and collection points for regular prisoners, officers and generals, those who were ill, and specifically for those ill with dystrophy. Although these standards more often than not denoted an ideal minimum ration that could not be filled for a series of complex reasons, especially during the course of the war, it is important to investigate what officials felt obligated to provide and to whom. Table 1.1 shows the ration norms in daily grams for prisoners, officers, generals, the sick, and those with dystrophy.[58]

As table 1.1 illustrates, there was a wide range in provisioning between enlisted men, officers, and the ill. Different groups were entitled to receive not only varying amounts of rations but also an assortment of other food sources, in accordance with contemporary Soviet theories about nutrition and medicine

---

56. On the question of Gulag rations and leaders' indifference toward death due to a steady supply of new laborers, see Alexopoulos, *Illness and Inhumanity*, 1–9.

57. RGVA, f. 1p, op. 9a, d. 8, ll. 39–40.

58. GARF, f. 9401, op. 1, d. 659, ll. 295–302, in Zagorul'ko, *Voennoplennye v SSSR 1939–1956*, 358–363. Table 1.1 shows the various norms listed in this document; it presents the approximate values of the *highest* possible caloric count based on ration norms. According to memoir accounts and information from Gulag studies, prisoners rarely received the upper bounds of the allotments, which are discussed later in this section. See appendix 1 for full information about the calculation of approximate daily calories.

Table 1.1 Daily rations and calorie calculations for German POW groups, 1943

RATION	DAILY GRAMS FOR POWS	APPROX CALORIES	DAILY GRAMS OFFICERS	APPROX CALORIES	DAILY GRAMS GENERALS	APPROX CALORIES	DAILY GRAMS SICK	APPROX CALORIES	DAILY GRAMS DYSTROPHY	APPROX CALORIES
Rye bread	600	1,500	300	750	300	750	400	1000	0	0
Wheat bread	0	0	300	726	300	726	200	484	500	1210
Flour	10	34.2	10	34.2	10	34.2	20	68.4	10	34.2
Grits/different cereals	70	239.4	100	342	100	342	70	239.4	70	239.4
Pasta	10	34.4	20	68.4	20	68.4	20	68.4	20	68.4
Rice	0	0	0	0	0	0	10	34.4	50	171
Meat	30	110.1	75	275.25	120	440.4	80	293.6	150	550
Fish	50	80.5	80	128.8	50	80.5	50	80.5	50	80.5
Butter	0	0	40	299.2	40	299.2	0	0	30	224.4
Bacon or mixed fats	3	23.91	0	0	0	0	30	239.1	20	159.4
Cheese	0	0	0	0	20	72.6	0	0	0	0
Vegetable oil	10	90	10	90	10	90	10	90	0	0
Tomato puree	10	6.6	0	0	0	0	10	6.6	7	4.62
Sugar	10	39.8	40	159.2	40	159.2	20	79.6	30	119.4
Tea substitute	2	0	0	0	0	0	0	0	0	0
Natural tea	0	0	1	0	1	0	0.5	0	0.5	0
Salt	10	0	20	0	20	0	20	0	20	0
Bay leaf	0.1	0.3	0.2	0.6	0.2	0.6	0.2	0.6	0.2	0.6
Pepper	0.1	0.25	0.2	0.5	0.2	0.5	0.2	0.5	0.2	0.5
Vinegar	0.7	0.22	1	0.32	1	0.32	1	0.32	1	0.32
Mustard	0	0	0	0	0	0	0.3	0.49	0.3	0.49
Potatoes	300	246	400	328	400	328	300	246	400	328

Dried fruit	0	0	10	26.4	10	26.4	10	26.4	10	26.4
Fresh milk	0	0	0	0	0	0	200	118	300	177
Mixed vegetables	0	0	0	0	0	0	200	62	250	77.5
Fresh vegetables	0	0	200	62	200	62	0	0	0	0
Potato flour	0	0	0	0	0	0	5	17.84	5	17.84
Baker's yeast	0	0	0	0	0	0	50	37.5	100	75
Cabbage, sour or fresh	100	100	0	0	0	0	0	0	0	0
Carrots	30	27	0	0	0	0	0	0	0	0
Beets	50	21.5	0	0	0	0	0	0	0	0
Onions	10	4.7	0	0	0	0	0	0	0	0
Root vegetables, greens, cucumbers	10	1.5	0	0	0	0	0	0	0	0
Total Daily Food	**1,315.9**	**2,470**	**1,607.4**	**3,290.87**	**1,642.4**	**3480.32**	**1,707.2**	**3,193.65**	**2,024.2**	**3,564.97**

and how they in turn affected labor productivity. For example, vitamins from vegetables came from different sources depending on one's health and rank. Enlisted men largely survived on rye bread, potatoes, and cabbage, with supplemental small rations of animal proteins and a few other vegetables. Officers, generals, and the ill were entitled to lower portions of rye bread but higher concentrations of animal proteins, vegetables, and starches. Hierarchy and illness thus dictated rations. The enlisted men, who were the primary workers, received the worst rations of all the German captives. This likely led to their weakening and subsequent placement on illness and *distrofik* ration schemes, as well as to their repatriation after May 1945.

The differentiation of rations based on rank and physical condition was not novel. In 1939, the NKVD enacted Top Secret Operation Order 00943, which attempted to standardize camp rations in the Gulag. The order resulted in twelve food norms based on a variety of factors including, but not limited to, fulfillment, under-fulfillment, and over-fulfillment of quotas, as well as illness. The daily base ration consisted of 1,100 grams of rye bread, 650 grams of potatoes and vegetables, 155 grams of fish, and small amounts of other items.[59] The German POW ration in 1943 was much lower than that of the Gulag inmates in 1939, but in practice, the conditions of the war meant that Gulag inmates received far less than they were entitled to. In 1942, the highest year of Gulag mortality, prisoners who met their labor quotas by 50–70 percent were supposed to receive only 500 grams of bread; those who met it by 70–90 percent, 600 grams; and those who met it by 90–100 percent, 700 grams.[60] Again, these rations were also the stated entitlement and not necessarily what prisoners actually received. The camps, like the factory canteens and state stores that fed the free population, frequently failed to receive the supplies they were officially allocated from state stocks. Thus, even though Gulag prisoners were to receive 100 grams more of bread than POWs for fulfilling 90–100 percent of the labor quota, it is unclear how many of the Gulag inmates were of suitable health to fulfill the quota and receive the full ration and whether there was sufficient bread to give them.

For the POWs, health and rank also factored into their eligibility to receive the scarcest items available for rationing. Only generals and the ill were eligible to receive dairy products, but the ill were entitled to receive milk while only generals received cheese. Meat and animal fats provisioning constituted the major difference between the POW groups. The GUPVI provided only

59. Bell, *Stalin's Gulag at War*, 57–60.

60. Alexopoulos, *Illness and Inhumanity*, 26. Unfortunately Alexopoulos only states the bread rations for 1942. It is unclear how drastically the other food group allotments decreased from the 1939 NKVD standards, which presents problems when comparing POW rations to Gulag rations.

30 grams of meat for enlisted men, whereas every other group got more than double this amount. Officers received 2.5 times as much meat as enlisted men, the ill 2.6 times as much, generals 4 times as much, and *distrofiki* 5 times as much. Some of these ration regulations were unique to POWs. In the Gulag, one's status based on personal connections and the type of sentence (criminal or political) created a hierarchy of provisioning. In the POW camps, military rank entitled one to rare provisions while at the same time excluded one from having to work. For both GUPVI and Gulag inmates, labor productivity entitled some to extra or special rations.

The state and camp leaders intended for base rations to keep their workers in productive form, but both parties also used the size of rations to encourage maximum labor output. The norms for April 1943 also included supplemental rations for those who exceeded labor quotas. The information displayed in table 1.1 counted as the base ration. Enlisted men who worked in heavy labor tasks could receive an additional 650 grams of bread (approximately 1,625 calories), 750 grams (approximately 1,875 calories), 850 grams (approximately 2,125 calories), or 1,000 grams (approximately 2,500 calories) based on their labor assignment and whether they exceeded their labor quota by up to 50 percent, from 50 to 80 percent, from 80 to 100 percent, and more than 100 percent, respectively. Those assigned to lighter labor assignments could receive either 500, 600, or 700 additional grams for exceeding the quota.

In special cases, other agencies intervened to ensure extra rations for heavy laborers working in the most important industrial sectors. On January 1, 1944 the GKO passed Order No. 4990s with the cooperation of the Commissariat of Coal and the Sovnarkom: it allocated a second hot meal to prisoners loading minecars in the Donbass, Ural, Kuzbass, and Karagranda coal mines.[61] In addition to the increased base ration for these specific laborers, those who worked well could also receive 100 grams of vodka daily at their lunch break as an incentive to meet and exceed the labor quota. Thus, the needs of the wartime economy dictated not only labor assignments but also labor provisions and rewards.

The ration hierarchy in GUPVI camps directly reflected the state of food provisioning in the Soviet Union as a whole. During the first few years of the war, the Soviet Union faced a food crisis. Within a month of the start of the war, the state began a complex system of food rationing. This system, however, soon faced great challenges with supply linked to the course of the war. By the fall of 1942, the Germans occupied the majority of the Soviet Union's prime farmland and had seized its food-processing plants, animal herds, and

---

61. GARF, f. 9408, op. 1, d. 30, l. 3.

collective farms. Meat, dairy products, and animal and vegetable fats were in very short supply.[62] The highest rations were reserved for the Red Army. According to the September 1941 norms, soldiers were to receive different rations based on whether they served in the rear (2,659 calories) or the front (3,450 calories) or had special roles such as airmen (4,712 calories). Moreover, commanders were entitled to an average of 450 extra calories daily from a variety of foodstuffs, including bread, meats, and higher-quality tobacco.[63] Although the base ration for enlisted German prisoners of war may not have always been fulfilled, the estimated approximate daily caloric value was not too far behind that of the Red Army rations for soldiers in the rear. This meant that Soviet authorities tried to meet the POW ration stipulation of the 1929 Geneva Convention, which stated that combatant nations were to feed their captives the same rations that they fed their troops stationed in bases.[64] According to the April 1943 norms, German POW enlisted men were to receive about 2,470 daily calories in an ideal situation, which was about 200 calories shy of the mandated 2,659 calories for Red Army rear soldiers in 1941.

The state also created a ration system for the civilian population. The Commissariat of Trade divided urban inhabitants into four groups: workers, white-collar employees, dependents, and children under twelve. It then subdivided these four groups into two categories tied to their importance to the war effort, in effect making eight ration groups. For example, those who worked for Category I—heavy labor in industries most important to the war effort, such as coal, peat, defense, and metallurgical industries—received higher rations than those working for Category II, which included transport and municipal services. As with the soldiers, however, promised ration norms differed from those received because of shortfalls in deliveries due to wastage, spoilage, theft, and unequal distribution.[65] After supplying the army and civilian populations, not much food was left for prisoners in the Gulag or the POW camps. Because the forced-labor camps focused on economic productivity, those who worked the toughest jobs and produced the most received the highest rations, regardless of whether they were a POW or a criminal. Workers who could not produce as much received smaller rations than the

62. Goldman and Filtzer, "Introduction," in *Hunger and War*, 6, 12.

63. Brandon Schechter, "The State's Pot and the Soldier's Spoon: Rations (Paëk) in the Red Army," in *Hunger and War*, 109–113.

64. "Convention relative to the Treatment of Prisoners of War. Geneva, 27 July 1929," Part 3, section II, chapter 2, "Food and clothing prisoners of war," article 11. https://ihl-databases.icrc.org/applic/ihl/ihl.nsf/States.xsp?xp_viewStates=XPages_NORMStatesParties&xp_treatySelected=305

65. Goldman, "Not by Bread Alone," 50–51, 56–57, and 71; Goldman and Filtzer, "Introduction," 25–26; Schechter, "The State's Pot," 110, all in *Hunger and War*.

most able-bodied inmates, a hierarchy mirroring that imposed on the civilian population.

Over the course of the war, and after its end, the basic ration norms for German POWs increased and then stabilized, even during times of difficulty in food provisioning around the famine of 1946–1947. Table 1.2 illustrates the standard rations for laboring POW enlisted men from 1943 to 1947.[66]

Table 1.2 shows that with the exception of the bread ration, which remained at 600 grams per day, the rations of other food groups increased slightly in 1944 and then again in 1945 for POW enlisted men. From 1944 to 1945, POW rations increased by roughly 420 grams, or an increase of 29.48 percent, resulting in a daily caloric increase of 16.35 percent. Most of these caloric increases came with the growth in rations for nutrient-rich foods such as fish, bacon, and potatoes.

As the Red Army marched ever closer to Berlin and victory, Stalin again intervened regarding POW labor. In December 1944, he ordered, as the chairman of the GKO, an increase in POW food rations and in the allotments of clothes, shoes, and trucks to ensure their increased economic productivity. By May 1945, the daily rations for fat, cereals, fish, potatoes, and cabbage increased.[67] As table 1.2 illustrates, many rations, which provided supplemental nutrients, doubled or tripled by the end of the war. These increases in 1944 and 1945 reflected the changing tide of the war and the Red Army's liberation of the nation's best farmlands. Although it would still take years for these areas to recover from the damages of the war, the return of these territories to Soviet control meant that their limited outputs could be directed back to the Soviet population and its prisoners. After the war, the basic daily ration remained at the May 1945 level.

As mentioned, ration entitlements did not always translate into the amount food received and consumed. Although the NKVD mandated strict ration requirements for Gulag inmates, memoir literature noted that a variety of factors such as theft or supply problems meant that Gulag prisoners frequently failed to receive the food stuffs to which they were entitled. Moreover, there was great variation in the rations based on the location of the camp.[68] As was the case with provisioning for Gulag inmates and the free population, German

---

66. April 1943 rations taken from GARF, f. 9401, op. 1, d. 659, ll. 295–302, in Zagorul'ko, *Voennoplennye v SSSR*, 359. October 1944 rations taken from GARF, f. 9401, op. 1, d. 703, ll. 124–129, in Zagorul'ko, *Voennoplennye v SSSR*, 371. May 1945 rations taken from GARF, f. 9401, op. 1, d. 724, ll. 257–268, in Zagorul'ko, *Voennoplennye v SSSR*, 381. November 1946 rations from GARF, f. 9401, op. 1, d. 776, ll. 22–35, in Zagorul'ko, *Voennoplennye v SSSR*, 409. December 1947 rations from GARF, f. 9401, op. 1, d. 822, ll. 107–121, in Zagorul'ko, *Voennoplennye v SSSR*, 429–430.

67. RGVA, f. 1p, op. 9a, d. 8, ll. 207, 208, and 210.

68. Barnes, *Death and Redemption*, 41–43; Bell, *Stalin's Gulag at War*, 57–60; Alexopoulos, *Illness and Inhumanity*, 15.

Table 1.2   Daily rations in grams for enlisted German POWs

ITEM	APRIL 1943	OCT. 1944	MAY 1945	NOV. 1946	DEC. 1947
Bread	600	600	600	600	600
Flour	10	10	10	10	10
Grits/different cereals	70	70	90	90	90
Pasta	10	10	10	10	10
Meat	30	30	30	30	30
Fish	50	50	100	100	100
Bacon or mixed fats	3	10	15	15	15
Vegetable oil	10	10	15	15	15
Tomato puree	10	10	10	10	10
Sugar	10	17	17	17	17
Tea substitute	2	2	2	2	2
Salt	10	10	30	30	30
Bay leaf	0.1	0.1	0.2	0.2	0.2
Pepper	0.1	0.1	0.3	0.3	0.3
Vinegar	0.7	0.7	2	2	2
Potatoes	300	400	600	600	600
Cabbage, sour or fresh	100	100	170	170	170
Carrots	30	30	45	45	45
Beets	50	50	40	40	40
Onions	10	10	30	30	30
Root vegetables, greens, cucumbers	10	10	35	35	35
Total Daily Food Grams	**1,315.9**	**1,429.9**	**1,851.5**	**1,851.5**	**1,851.5**
Approx. Daily Calories*	**2,470**	**2,636**	**3,067**	**3,067**	**3,067**
Soap (per month)	200	300	300	300	300

*See appendix 1 for full information about the calculation of approximate daily calories. Again, all calculations are the *highest* possible.

POW memoirs and repatriation accounts illustrated variations in the distribution of foodstuffs. Yet generally, the memoirs and oral and written accounts provided to German relief organizations reported that provisioning improved over the course of the war and that camp leaders attempted to ensure that POWs regularly received their base rations of bread.

Former POWs attested to the poor quality and quantity of wartime rations. Although the German POW Ernst Kehler did not state the exact amount of food he received, he wrote of his captivity in 1942 that "the experience of hunger will never be forgotten."[69] POWs continued to suffer from insufficient

---

69. Ernst Kehler, *Einblicke und Einsichten: Erinnerungen* (Berlin: Dietz, 1989), 98.

provisioning even until the last months of the war. Hans Schuetz noted that in Saratov in April 1945, he and his fellow prisoners received "half a handful each of solid, dried, aged dark bread in one-inch-square cubes. . . . The cubes were as hard as rocks. One could easily break a tooth chewing on them."[70] After the war's end, however, ration supplies improved at the camps. Multiple memoirs stated that the base ration at the camps was 600 grams of bread, provided that the men fulfilled their work quotas.[71] The memoirists also noted that the NCOs and generals received higher and supplemental rations including sugar and fat. Helmut Fuchs stated, "The ingredients for the officer's soup kettle were of better quality in some respects; for example, depending on the supply situation, yellow turnips were sometimes delivered for the officers' cauldron, while the enlisted men received rutabagas."[72] Fuchs also noted that these officers even received American canned meats, which had been provided through Lend Lease, until the supply ran out in fall 1946.

Although POW accounts noted that the men generally received the rations to which they were entitled at the war's end at least one POW reported that the food was not of good quality, something that Gulag memoirists also frequently noted. Gottfried Dulias stated that camp officials could only meet the required minimums by providing bread with an extremely high-water content. He said of the bread, "The inside remained doughy, and it must have contained about seventy percent water while the crust was of more substance. You could take the inside and squish it together. One guy even said: 'Look at what we eat, clay!' So, he squished it and threw it onto a wall, and it stuck!"[73] Additionally, Dulias complained that the "flour" used to make the bread included shells and leftovers from the processing of oats and barley, another way to supplement the flour. Yet POWs were not the only ones to receive bread baked with this modified flour. All bread, for civilians as well as prisoners, was supplemented in this way due to the shortage of flour, and Soviet civilians too missed the consistency and quality of prewar bread. Indeed, the civilian workers at the labor site received the same bread as Dulias and his fellow prisoners.[74] Dulias also criticized the quality of his morning ration, stating, "In the

---

70. A. D. Hans Schuetz, *Davai, Davai! Memoir of a German Prisoner of World War II in the Soviet Union* (Jefferson, NC: McFarland, 1997), 48.

71. Otto Rühle, *Die Ärzte von Stalingrad: Genesung in Jelabuga: Kessel Stalingrad—Antifaschule für ein neues Deutschland—Autobiographischer Bericht* (Dresden: Wünsche, 2007), 263, 271; Helmut Fuchs, *Wer spricht von Siegen: Der Bericht über unfreiwillige Jahre in Russland* (Munich: A. Knaus, 1987), 113; Willi Belz, *Soldat gegen Hitler: Ein Antikriegsbuch* (Frankfurt [Main]): Röderberg, 1987), 153.

72. Fuchs, *Wer spricht von Siegen*, 114–115.

73. Dianna M. Popp and Gottfried P. Dulias, *Another Bowl of Kapusta: The True Life Story of a World War II Luftwaffe Fighter Pilot and P.O.W. in Russia* (Bloomington, IN: AuthorHouse, 2004), 163.

74. Popp and Dulias, *Another Bowl of Kapusta*, 163.

morning our breakfast consisted of about a half-tin fill of Kapusta, which was just a greenish water (you were lucky if you found a leaf in there), and a portion of Kasha. The Kasha was made from barley and was more like a watery puree, nothing like the way it should be, as a cereal."[75] He alleged that the camp staff only used the outer leaves of the cabbage head for the soup and sold the inner leaves on the black market. Finally, Dulias stated that at times camp officials served POWs food that had spoiled. Soup, for example, contained rotten fish, which poisoned and weakened the men.[76] Although other POW memoirists generally did not give as detailed accounts of the food as Dulias, they did note that the NKVD failed to supply the mandated supplemental rations of *makhorka* (low-quality tobacco) or soap. Hans Schuetz noted that *makhorka* distributions were irregular.[77] Dulias stated that, although he and his fellow soldiers routinely received *makhorka*, they did not receive rolling papers. A nonsmoker, Dulias traded not only his *makhorka* ration to his fellow prisoners for extra food but also pages from his Bible so that they could smoke it.[78] Schuetz also noted that the lack of paper for smoking affected the Soviet workers with whom the POWs worked. Generally, both the POWs and the free population used scraps of newspaper to smoke the *makhorka*.[79]

Reports from repatriated POWs also stated that the Germans regularly received their mandated base rations while in the camp system, at least during the later stages of the war and after its end. One corporal told the Catholic relief organization Caritas on his return to Germany in August 1945 that he received 600 grams of bread, three servings of thick soup of 750 grams, and 250 grams of *kasha* (porridge, though he referred to it in German as *"Brei"*). Thus, men at Camp No. 165 at Ivanovo received a base ration of 3,100 grams of food daily. The corporal also mentioned that those who exceeded their work quotas were entitled to an additional 200 grams of bread and 250 grams of soup.[80] Other repatriates from different camps corroborated that Soviet camp officials provided their captives with the mandated base rations. One returnee reported in October 1945 that in Arkhangelsk, soldiers received 600 grams of bread, plus an additional 200 grams if they exceeded their quota, as well as an unspecified amount of kasha and thick soup.[81] Another former soldier reported in September 1946 that he received his 600 daily grams of bread as well as tea at breakfast;

75. Popp and Dulias, *Another Bowl of Kapusta*, 161.

76. Popp and Dulias, *Another Bowl of Kapusta*, 161–162, 178–179.

77. Schuetz, *Davai Davai*, 54.

78. Popp and Dulias, *Another Bowl of Kapusta*, 172.

79. Schuetz, *Davai Davai*, 62.

80. ADCV, 372.15 () Fasz. 1, "Bericht aus Russland," October 24, 1945. Here and elsewhere in the notes, the symbols () are part of the archive name.

81. ADCV, 372.15 () Fasz. 1, "Bericht über die Kriegsgefangenen in Archangelsk," October 25, 1945.

1,000 grams of kasha; and 500 grams of soup, as well as small amounts of meat, fish, and sugar at his camp near Gorky.[82] This returnee also noted that officers received 300 grams each of rye and wheat bread, as well as larger rations of sugar and fat. A repatriate interview from a former officer who returned from captivity in September 1946 from camps in Vladimir and Suzdal noted that in each camp he received 600 grams of bread, half rye and half wheat, as well as soup and kasha twice a day. He mentioned also receiving daily butter, meat, and sugar rations. Finally, he received daily allotments of 15 grams of tobacco, 30 grams of *makhorka*, 15 cigarettes, or 15 *papirosy* (nonfiltered cigarettes made with *makhorka*) depending on availability.[83]

Thus, the memoir accounts and returnee interviews denote an immediate shift in the Soviet treatment of German POWs after war's end. As the end of the war approached, officials likely scrambled to ensure that the Germans received proper treatment. After the war, the Germans no longer were enemies of the Soviet Union. Instead, Soviet officials recognized captive and free Germans alike as individuals important in the reshaping of postwar Europe. Good treatment of captive Germans suddenly became vital for the overall reputation of the Soviet Union. Soviet leaders needed former POWs to describe their humane and good treatment in captivity if they wanted to be able to persuade the German masses to establish a socialist government that would be an ally of the Soviet Union.

The importance of providing sufficient rations to the optics of good treatment increased during the 1946–1947 famine in the Soviet Union, illustrating the close relationship between labor, rations, and medical treatment for POWs. Starting in July 1946, the Soviet Union faced its fourth famine. Caused by drought and a poor harvest in 1946, the famine resulted in sharply reduced grain outputs in the second half of 1946 and over the course of 1947, peaking from February to August 1947. At the time, food rationing was still in effect in the cities. Peasants faced the double burden of having to make deliveries to the state while receiving little to no state relief. Although the 1946–1947 famine had its roots in environmental factors, it was exacerbated by improper state management. Recent scholarship estimates the number of famine deaths in the range of 1–1.5 million compounded by a demographic loss three times that of the deaths caused by the fall in birthrates, which would otherwise have been at a much higher level without famine conditions.[84]

---

82. ADCV, 372.15 () Fasz. 1, "Abschrift! Lager N. 74 Oranki Bez. Gorki," September 10, 1946.

83. ADCV, 372.15 () Fasz. 1, "Abschrift!," pages 1 and 2, 1946.

84. Michael Ellman, "The 1947 Soviet Famine and the Entitlement Approach to Famines," *Cambridge Journal of Economics* 24, no. 5 (2000): 604, 605, 607, 610–612, 617–618, 620–623; Donald Filtzer, *The Hazards of Urban Life in Late Stalinist Russia: Health, Hygiene, and Living Standards, 1943–1953* (New

Yet despite the onset of the famine in July 1946, there was a distinct monthly decrease in the number of German POW deaths and those diagnosed with dystrophy. A comprehensive medical report from January 14, 1947, presented a monthly breakdown of German POW deaths and illness diagnoses in 1946.[85] Despite the effects of the drought and poor harvest, camp directors managed to reduce POW deaths and dystrophy diagnoses quite drastically throughout the year.

Table 1.3 shows a striking reduction in POW deaths over 1946 from 7,559 in January to 875 in December, a decrease of 88.42 percent. Dystrophy diagnoses also dropped sharply from 3,918 in January to 166 in December, a decrease of 95.76 percent. As the table shows, camp leaders successfully managed to sharply decrease POW deaths and dystrophy diagnoses each month from January to May. From May to June, deaths and illness also decreased, but at a lower rate than between April and May. As the famine began to take hold in the USSR, the second half of 1946 saw monthly fluctuations between increases and decreases in death and illness rates, though the overall trend was a decrease when compared to the high numbers at the beginning of the year. In the first half of the year, 24,186 POWs died compared to 4,665 in the second half, a decrease of 80.71 percent. The first half of the year also saw 11,170 POWs diagnosed with dystrophy, whereas only 1,328 were diagnosed in the second half, a reduction of 88.11 percent.

The figures from 1946 highlight the priority the state placed on the POWs' economic contributions over punishment. When camp leaders realized that they could not maintain the health of the prisoners. they chose to drastically increase the number of repatriations to make up for the lack of food. In July 1946, when death rates began to rise and dystrophy rates increased, camp leaders responded by repatriating a massive number of POWs. Repatriation figures remained high for the rest of the year. Gulag officials followed similar practices. In some camps, local officials encouraged the early release of ill prisoners to improve a camp's mortality statistics.[86] Despite a lack of resources, the state attempted to maintain POW rations, and between proper management and increased repatriations, camp officials ensured that limited resources went to sustaining the able-bodied labor force.

York: Cambridge University Press, 2010), 163–164, 166; Nicholas Ganson, *The Soviet Famine of 1946–47 in Global and Historical Perspective* (New York: Palgrave Macmillan, 2009).

85. RGVA, f. 1/p, op. 17a, d. 1, l. 27, in Zagorul'ko, *Voennoplennye v SSSR*, 501. In Zagorul'ko, RGVA is given with its older name of TsKhIDK. There is no explanation for why the POW population increased between January and February 1946 when it should have decreased. Because of this inexplicable increase between January and February, I chose to leave these months out of my calculations for repatriations.

86. Bell, *Stalin's Gulag at War*, 61.

The German POWs, however, did not entirely escape the effects of the famine. In their accounts to staff officials before repatriation, POWs noted not only the famine and its effects but also stated that conditions improved after it ended. One prisoner, Ferdinand Bongart, stated, "Even in the winter of 1946–47, after a crop failure, our food was provided," though he did not mention whether the provided food changed in quantity or quality. Another prisoner, Gottfried Lilge, stated that the prisoners received sufficient and good food until July 1946, when the situation worsened.[87] Yet the famine's effects were limited, and the deprivation seemed to last only one week in the winter of 1946–1947. Food provisioning got a little bit better by the middle of January 1947, and by May 1947, the prisoners received excellent baked goods with berries and cream.[88] During the height of the famine, some of the suffering free citizens attempted to help the POWs. One woman from Ulyanovsk recalled the winter of 1946. "EVERYONE lived in need, there was not much bread," yet Natalya Khramtsovaya and her family gave a bit of their meager bread supply to a German POW who had helped construct their apartment building. She called him Fritz and said that he had played his harmonica for the residents in exchange for some food.[89] Not all recollections of interactions with the Germans during this period were positive, however. One Belorussian woman recounted, "After the war, the German prisoners lugged stones. Rebuilt our town. Starving. They begged us for bread. But I couldn't bear to give them even a tiny piece."[90]

The famine did affect the productivity of the POWs. A report from April 15, 1947, compared the quality and size of the POW labor force in the last quarter of 1946 to the first quarter of 1947.[91] The additional rations for camp inmates who exceeded work quotas had decreased by 40 percent as of October 1, 1946, although the drop was less severe—from 15 to 28 percent—for those assigned to hard labor, indicating the need to keep the most important laborers well fed and motivated. The decrease in extra rations took its toll on the POW population. Between January 1 and April 1, 1947, 8,175 German POWs died, a sharp increase over the much lower totals for the second half of 1946 in which 4,665 POWs died. However, these deaths constituted a considerable decrease from the same period of the previous year in which 21,720

87. RGVA, f. 1p, op. 21a, d. 62, l. 119.

88. RGVA, f. 1p, op. 21a, d. 62, l. 126–127.

89. G. A. Demochkin, *Dvadtsatyi vek Natal'i Khramtsovoi* (Ulyanovsk: Ulyanovsk State Technical University, 2015), 111.

90. Quoted from "A Woman's Story," in Svetlana Alexievich, *Secondhand Time: The Last of the Soviets*, trans. Bela Shayevich (New York: Random House, 2016), 208.

91. GARF, f. 9401, op. 2, d. 169, l. 203–212.

Table 1.3 POW totals, deaths, and dystrophy in 1946

MONTH	NUMBER OF POWS END OF MONTH	PERCENTAGE CHANGE FROM PREVIOUS MONTH	POW DEATHS	DYSTROPHY DIAGNOSES	PERCENTAGE CHANGE FROM PREVIOUS MONTH	REPATRIATIONS*
January	1,384,491	—	7,559	3,918	—	—
February	1,385,593	−21.43	5,939	3,006	−23.28	—
March	1,370,703	−12.17	5,216	2,419	−19.53	1,240
April	1,366,457	−42.37	3,006	1,141	−52.83	6,717
May	1,358,143	−46.87	1,597	447	−60.82	14,223
June	1,343,051	−45.59	869	239	−46.53	6,130
July	1,336,059	−0.81	862	251	+5.02	77,277
August	1,257,952	−3.71	830	278	+10.76	16,491
September	1,240,809	−21.45	652	245	−11.87	9,366
October	1,230,669	+18.71	774	217	−11.43	9,140
November	1,220,857	−9.68	672	171	−21.2	16,800
December	1,203,182	+30.21	875	166	−2.92	—
Total			28,851	12,498		157,384

*Repatriations were calculated by subtracting the deaths during the month from the total at the end of the month. The documents do not actually state the number of repatriations, and the calculated number may not be accurate.

POWs died. Additionally, as of April 1, 1947, only 76.3 percent of the German POW population was deemed capable of work compared to 85.5 percent on January 1, 1947. Although the report does not specify what caused these deaths, likely the decrease in the amount and variety of food exacerbated nutritional deficiencies, again indicating that local camps did not always meet the ration norms set by the central authorities. The MVD leadership realized that the delicate balance between labor productivity and resource consumption shifted during the famine. Facing stricter food shortages than before, the camps released 28,760 Germans classified as ill or unfit for labor between December 23, 1946, and April 1, 1947, so as not to burden the camp system with their support. And despite the shortages, the MVD once again reiterated that the main goal of the camps was to preserve the physical condition of POWs while increasing productivity.

Although camp leaders paid lip service to the need to feed the POWs properly, they did not always comply with the state ration norms, especially during the famine. Different ministries of the Soviet government monitored, and some caught, the misappropriation of resources meant for the German POWs. The Ministry of State Control, for example, oversaw an entity within the Ministry of the Armed Forces of the Soviet Union that tracked the resources allotted to POW camps. In a series of reports from 1947, the Ministry of State Control noted that the food shortages of late 1946 and early 1947 had significantly affected the camps. The reports stated that some camp commandants were reprimanded for failing to deliver sufficient rations. Other camp inspections found surpluses of bread by thousands of kilograms. One camp misused 2,000 kilograms of potatoes from a collective farm, and another hoarded 10,000 kilograms of potatoes meant for the POWs. All the instances suggested that camp officials appropriated food meant for prisoners to sell on the black market. In each case, the Ministry of State Control punished the camp leadership with sentences ranging from five days of work in the guardhouse for lower MVD-GUPVI officers to jail sentences of up to a month. In the case of the misuse of 2,000 kilograms of potatoes from the collective farm, the deputy minister of the MVD for the Moldovan Republic removed the head of the 8th Camp Division, Senior Lieutenant Klimenko, from his post, arrested him, and sentenced him to trial by a military tribunal.[92]

Faced with famine and food shortage, the MVD and other government officials chose to release as many physically incapable prisoners as possible to maximize the resources available for those working to build the economy.

---

92. GARF, f. 8300, op. 34, d. 11, l. 23; GARF, f. 8300, op. 34, d. 11, l. 215; GARF, f. 8300, op 34, d. 12, l. 61.

Punishment was clearly not the aim. Over the course of 1947, the MVD repatriated 247,325 POWs to Germany who were sick or physically incapable of labor. This reduced the burden on the camps and enabled their leaders to allocate scarce food resources in higher quantities to maintain the able-bodied and rehabilitate the weak and the sick. Through a program of managed release, GUPVI leaders also managed to decrease the death rates in the camps in 1947. In 1946, 2.72 percent of the population died compared to 0.61 percent in 1947.[93] Increases in repatriation meant that fewer Germans died in the camps during a time of hardship that killed many free citizens.

Although GUPVI officials managed to decrease camp death statistics by increasing repatriations, not every ill POW released made it to Germany. Enough POWs died in transit for the head of the GUPVI, Lt. General Filippov, to order the Council for Repatriation not to transfer bodies of POWs to Polish or German authorities. Those bodies were only to be surrendered to Soviet officials working for Camp No. 69 in Frankfurt (Oder).[94] GUPVI officials might have chosen to halt the transfer of remains to prevent other states from finding out about famine conditions in the USSR or to conceal the high death rates in transit.

During World War II, Soviet planners grew increasingly familiar with the necessities of food rationing. A complex provisioning hierarchy existed across the entire Soviet Union with different allotments for soldiers, civilians, and prisoners. The Gulag system already had its own system for food distribution prior to the war, although Gulag camp officials often had difficulties meeting the standards of the state; these difficulties only worsened during the war when rations were cut and labor assignments increased. The Gulag saw extremely high mortality rates in the early years of the war. German POWs also suffered from high mortality rates during the early stages of the war, but conditions slowly improved, especially after the end of the war. Although their rations were not high, comparatively German POWs received better rations than some free Soviet citizens and many Gulag prisoners. Unlike Gulag prisoners, who could and would be replaced with new prisoners, the GUPVI system had a limited number of POWs after the end of the war, and it was in the interest of camp officials and the state to maintain the health of POWs by providing sufficient rations to prolong their labor contributions. When the food situation in the nation became dire during the 1946–1947 famine, GUPVI officials increased the number of repatriations: they could not spare the extra food needed to rehabilitate POWs on the cusp of starvation disease and instead sent

---

93. GARF, f. 9401, op. 2, d. 199, l. 68–72, specifically 68–71.
94. GARF, f. 9526, op. 6, d. 385, l. 218.

these men home. Food that would have gone to these men was then redistributed among the smaller number of able-bodied workers to sustain them.

Medical Care

The priority placed on using prisoners in forced labor not only structured the rationing hierarchy in the POW camp system but also heavily influenced medical care in the GUPVI camps. As was the case with rationing, GUPVI leaders built the medical system on foundations from the Gulag, where labor needs also determined the approach to health care. Facing supply issues not only of food but also of medical supplies, clothes, and blankets, GUPVI administrators carefully attempted to balance labor needs with the inputs needed to keep their men working. Conditions slowly improved in the camps after the end of the war, but even then, POWs, like the free Soviet population, suffered from shortages of medical supplies and clothing. Camp staff weighed the costs of healing and rehabilitating their ill and injured POWs and, when it was too costly, selected those men for repatriation.

When the Politburo created the Gulag in 1929, it also laid the foundation for a medical support system for the camps. The Sanitation Department, or *Sanotdel*, served several functions in the camps. It inspected prisoners and assessed their physical standing to assign them to different labor or illness categories. The Sanotdel also administered medical care to both prisoners and camp employees. In the early years of the Gulag, camp officials worked to incorporate aspects of a nationwide public health sanitation campaign into the system. In July 1918, the Bolsheviks founded the Commissariat of Heath, which strove to fight epidemics, purify drinking water, improve sanitation, and provide health care for the nation. The state sought to provide its citizens with universal health care, but they lacked the resources to realize this goal. During the Stalinist period the Commissariat of Health continued to fight for improved health care, sanitation, and hygiene but struggled to overcome the nation's prerevolutionary underdevelopment in these sectors. Medical services overall remained inadequate. Both prisoners and camp medical staff suffered from general ignorance of the basic principles of hygiene, which caused disease to spread among prisoners.[95] Thus, the reeducation aspect of the Gulag included not only ideological and moral concepts but also those related to health and sanitation.

---

95. Healey, "Lives in the Balance," 528; David L. Hoffmann and Annette F. Timm, "Utopian Biopolitics: Reproductive Policies, Gender Roles, and Sexuality in Nazi Germany and the Soviet Union," in *Beyond Totalitarianism: Stalinism and Nazism Compared*, ed. Michael Geyer and Sheila Fitzpatrick (New York: Cambridge University Press, 2009), 97.

Moreover, the level of overall Soviet medical knowledge, coupled with an absence of standardization in diagnoses and registration of infectious diseases, meant that central sanitation departments did not receive reliable data, which complicated efforts to prevent and cure diseases across the camp system. Attempts to cure scurvy or pellagra, for example, often failed because doctors did not know their causes. Some attempts to ameliorate the situation, such as giving pine-needle drinks, only partially helped. During the early years of the war, tuberculosis, avitaminosis, and emaciation ravaged the Gulag population. It was only as more free citizens began to feel the effects of these diseases, including those doctors living through the Leningrad Blockade, that medical officials figured out how to better combat them.[96] Thus, during its first decade of operation and again during the first few years of the war, the Sanotdel struggled to properly care for Gulag inmates. Large numbers of medical personnel were sent to the front, and health care in the camps was insufficient.

The same diseases that devastated the Soviet Gulag population also greatly affected German POWs in the NKVD camps. At the end of 1943, Major General Petrov, then the head of the UPVI-NKVD, compiled a report analyzing the conditions of the camps for that year. Noting the prevalence of dystrophy, diphtheria, tuberculous, and influenza in the camps, he stated that increased medical efforts over the summer of 1943 had reduced cases of disease and death.[97] Conditions, however, varied widely across camps. POWs around Stalingrad still suffered immensely in the fall and winter of 1943–1944. Two camps in the region, Nos. 50 and 123, suffered from broken heaters and a lack of fuel. Interior temperatures in the camp buildings hovered around 42 degrees Fahrenheit. Worse, only 60–70 percent of prisoners in those camps had blankets. Camp leadership urged the staff to repair the broken heating equipment, as well as to quarantine the ill to prevent the further spread of disease. Leaders also attempted to maintain and improve the health of those German prisoners who succumbed to illness caused by the harsh conditions. The Soviet medical staff, which was likely inexperienced, soon began using the services of POW doctors as well.[98]

Indeed, many German doctors among the POWs worked in the camp medical systems. Officially, all prisoners received wages, although camp leaders retained this money to ostensibly defray the costs of feeding, clothing, and housing the prisoners. Select prisoner groups, however, did manage to obtain their wages through a system of bonuses based on output or profession. POW

---

96. Oxana Ermolaeva, "Health Care, the Circulation of Medical Knowledge, and Research in the Soviet Gulag in the 1930s," *East Central Europe* 40, no. 3 (January 1, 2013): 343, 345–349.

97. RGVA, f. 1p, op. 9a, d. 9, l. 3.

98. RGVA, f. 47p, op. 14, d. 4, ll. 1–4.

doctors, for example, received forty rubles a month, and paramedics received twenty.[99] The NKVD realized the importance of knowing the former professions of POWs and employing them in their areas of expertise. For most professions, however, work compensation did not include a pay bonus. Camps badly needed those with medical training to work in the camp hospital system, and so they rewarded medical professionals for their expertise.

Commemorative albums produced within camps for the benefit of local camp leaders provide evidence of centralized orders for the provisioning of skill-based bonuses. These albums, which recorded daily life, documented prisoners receiving medical treatment not only from Soviet staff but also from German doctors. In one case, three German doctors assisted a lead Soviet surgeon in an operation. This example was also described in a 1949 German-language book titled *Prisoners of War in the Soviet Union*. The book noted that its unnamed publisher and editor used 15,000 documents from POWs across the Soviet Union as source material.[100] The authors likely created and published this book as pro-Soviet propaganda. Families and political officials in the GDR wanted the release of their family members. To mitigate anger or angst over their prolonged captivity, Soviet propagandists produced books to show these families that their relatives received good care in the Soviet Union.

Although this book served as propaganda, the unpublished camp life albums, now in the Russian State Military Archive, were never intended for release. Rather, they were presented to camp leadership to commemorate the history of the camps. These albums generally followed a set format, which is discussed in greater detail in chapter 3's exploration of antifascist reeducation. The albums frequently included photos of soldiers receiving medical or dental care in the camps, either from Soviet or German medical professionals. Two albums from 1943 for camps in the Moscow area showed that German prisoners received proper medical care even during the height of the fighting when they were also the targets of anti-German propaganda during the most bitter battles of the war.[101]

In addition to lacking skilled medical professionals, the camp sanitary departments had few supplies to care for the ill. Again, this was a result of nationwide shortages during and after the war, rather than an intentional policy.

99. GARF, f. 9401, op. 1, d. 737, l. 180–214, in Zagorul'ko, *Voennoplennye v SSSR*, 631.

100. RGVA, f. 1p, op. 21a, d. 62, l. 66. Folder 62 contains part two of the book, where the photograph and caption about Soviet and German doctors are found; the first part is contained in RGVA f. 1p, op. 21a, d. 61. See RGVA f. 1p, op. 21a, d. 61 inside the cover and l. 3 for information about the publishing and sources of the book. Printed copies of the book list the place of publication as Berlin.

101. RGVA, f. 39, op. 7, d. 1, ll. 6ob–9ob for treatment in the Moscow Oblast or RGVA, f. 105p, op. 4, d. 15, ll. 7–11ob for treatment at Camp No. 27 in Krasnogorsk.

Indeed, when the Red Army captured German medical personnel, they also confiscated their supplies, which they then sent on to camp medical departments. One camp inventory from Camp No. 27 in Krasnogorsk listed all the medical devices and drugs in the possession of the sanitary department before the camp was closed, the majority of which had been captured German supplies.[102] Some of the captured drugs included antiseptics and antibiotics. On the camp's closing, these items were transferred to other POW camps and to MVD branches and worksites, including those in the Gulag system.

Many captured items beyond health care supplies were used to supply camps. In some camps, captured German weapons such as Walther P38 and PP pistols and the Luger Parabellum became the service weapons of camp staff.[103] German vehicles also were used in the transport and labor tasks of German prisoners. To supplement Soviet- and American-produced vehicles, GUPVI camps used captured Mercedes, Man, and Henkel trucks, as well as Opel and Mercedes sedans, some of which were the elite limousines of German generals, for their needs.[104] Distribution of seized and Lend-Lease automobiles to the camp system proved a great boon to the prisoners. The repurposing of seized or loaned technology complied with directives from top officials, such as one from Stalin in December 1944 about using POWs for forced labor in 1945.[105] In addition to setting ration standards, the directive called for clothes and shoes to be distributed so that the POWs did not weaken or fall ill. Stalin also mandated that they be given access to more cars and trucks.

After the German capitulation, Soviet officials tried to improve camp life. In August 1945, NKVD officials ordered all camp directors to take measures to prevent the outbreak of malaria and to keep the POWs healthy.[106] On November 13 of that year, Kruglov warned GUPVI directors and those in charge of construction for the NKVD not to deploy POWs to outdoor work without adequate shoes or clothes. He stated that in the long run, it would be more beneficial to their overall labor potential to keep them indoors.[107] The need for camps to fulfill production demands, however, meant that POWs were put to work despite the lack of adequate clothing. Gottfried Dulias noted having to go out during a heavy snowfall to fetch potatoes. He related that he and his fellow POWs were "dressed fairly warm with the exception of what we wore on our feet. We wore a Russian winter cap that had earflaps. The usual-issue

102. RGVA, f. 1p, op. 18, d. 3, ll. 203–210.
103. RGVA, f. 496p, op. 2, d. 60, ll. 7ob—8ob.
104. RGVA, f. 1p, op. 15a, d. 4, l. 100; RGVA, f. 505p, op. 2, d. 5, l. 13; RGVA, f. 105p, op. 18, d. 3, l. 5.
105. RGVA, f. 1p, op. 9a, d. 8, ll. 207–208, 210.
106. GARF, f. 9401, op. 1, d. 744, l. 106 (front and back).
107. GARF, f. 9401, op. 1, d. 744, l. 355–357.

shoes were not suitable for that weather. They had wooden soles and were nailed together with canvas tops."[108] In the wet snow, the shoes quickly became drenched, and the tops separated from the bottoms, exposing the men's feet to the snow. Dulias complained of having to wrap his feet with strips of cloth in place of socks, though he likely did not know that this had been standard procedure for Soviet soldiers and ordinary citizens as well. The footcloths, known as portianki, were standard issue for the Russian Army since the sixteenth century and remained so until 2013. After hours of walking in the snow, Dulias contracted frostbite, and a German medic treated his feet with a lukewarm bath.[109]

After the war's end, NKVD-MVD leaders made more concentrated efforts to heal POWs who had the potential to return to work after a period of convalescence. As previously stated, the transition of Germans from enemies to potential allies in the postwar realignment of Europe meant that Soviet authorities needed to improve conditions of captivity. On February 20, 1946, about 77,000 German POWs were in special hospitals.[110] Although not all these men were capable of recovery, some stood a chance of receiving care that would enable them to return to the workforce. Otherwise, their stays in special hospitals would be short ones before death or repatriation ensued.

Camp directors realized that certain concessions were necessary to keep prisoners healthy. On September 13, 1945, Chernyshëv sent a directive to the MVD, NKVD, and camp directors, which acknowledged the need to lighten the workload for prisoners in the third labor category.[111] This directive was an addendum to the previous instructions of August 28, 1945, which had called for coercing the maximum labor output from all POWs. It shortened the workday to four to six hours for members in the third labor category, and it stressed that they were only to perform light work within the camp. The Soviet administration had learned from experience that both weakened prisoner populations in the Gulag and civilians on the home front could provide little useful labor without proper food and care. Although reduced hours and lighter tasks meant greater costs per prisoner, in the long run, it was economically more efficient than maintaining a large, permanently incapacitated population. Soviet officials made compromises and adjustments in treating POWs to ensure their prolonged economic contribution.

---

108. Popp and Dulias, *Another Bowl of Kapusta*, 182.

109. Popp and Dulias, *Another Bowl of Kapusta*, 182–183; Kramer, "Russian Military Ordered to Switch to Socks." Catherine Merridale, *Ivan's War: Life and Death in the Red Army, 1939–1945* (New York: Henry Holt, 2007), 56–57.

110. GARF, f. 9401, op. 2, d. 142, l. 26.

111. GARF, f. 9401, op. 1, d. 744, l. 191.

Subsequent directives emphasizing the use of POW labor clearly delineated the conditions in which the POWs were expected to work and the treatment they were supposed to receive. For example, a GUPVI directive from September 29, 1945, urged local camp leaders to use POWs only "in strict accordance with their physical condition." Expanding on this point, the document outlined the three labor categories and carefully delineated the specific type of work for each. It reiterated that prisoners in the third category were to work no more than four to six hours daily, and every prisoner, regardless of labor capability, was entitled to a minimum of eight hours of nightly rest and three hot meals daily.[112]

Along with the new attention to prophylactic measures on feeding, clothing, and exposure to the elements, Soviet leaders also improved POW medical care in the months after the war. Whereas the Gulag of the 1930s suffered from the lack of an organized medical system and central reporting of disease statistics, POW forced-labor camps began to use a codified system for disease monitoring in the months following the war. By December 1945, the GUPVI issued a standardized form, No. 31 A, which required medical personnel to track twenty-five illnesses, including typhus, dystrophy, malaria, angina, tuberculosis, and influenza.[113] These forms were part of monthly inspections of prisoner health and physical standing. Although central GUPVI leaders ordered camps to produce monthly reports on their POW populations, some camps also produced annual inspection reports based on these monthly reports. These annual summaries included breakdowns of labor assignments, ill prisoners and their diseases, and the number of deaths.[114]

For some POWs, medical care consisted of release. According to state policy, only ill or incapacitated POWs went home, and some were too sick to complete their journeys. German POWs designated for repatriation traveled by rail from their camps across the Soviet Union to Camp No. 69 in Frankfurt-an-Oder, a transit camp in Soviet-occupied East Germany. Those who arrived dead at Camp No. 69 or who died while there received autopsies from Soviet doctors.[115] Generally, these autopsy reports listed cases of POW deaths as heart attacks or strokes, with contributing health complications such as cirrhosis or meningitis. Toward the end of 1949, German doctors began to assist their Soviet counterparts in performing the autopsies and providing their own reports, which generally concurred with the findings of the Soviet doctors.[116]

---

112. GARF, f. 9401, op. 1, d. 737, l. 180–214 in Zagorul'ko, *Voennoplennye v SSSR*, esp. 628–629.

113. RGVA, f. 511p, op. 1, d. 10, ll. 6 and 6ob.

114. RGVA, f. 1p, op. 15a, d. 68, ll. 5–6.

115. For POW autopsies at Camp No. 69 see, for example, GARF, f. 9526, op. 6, d. 508, l. 1; GARF, f. 9526, op. 6, d. 509, l. 117; GARF, f. 9526, op. 6, d. 631, l. 31.

116. GARF, f. 9526, op. 6, d. 635, ll. 324–328; GARF, f. 9526, op. 6, d. 636, ll. 299–308.

POW memoirs corroborate the efforts of Soviet officials to provide medical care for their German captives during and after the war. Gerhard Dengler stated that he contracted typhus around the time of his capture. He was sent to a POW camp hospital near Gorky, where the staff nursed him back to health. Dengler attested to the compassion of his Soviet caregivers, writing,

> With a severe case of typhus, I was soon quarantined in the camp hospital. . . . I also had third-degree dystrophy. . . . In the hospital we were looked after by a Soviet doctor. . . . We prisoners were not shot but treated in accordance with the Hague Convention and, despite our own nutritional difficulties, were fed and cared for with such self-sacrifice that a few of the Soviet helpers contracted the diseases we had brought in, and some succumbed.[117]

Hans Schuetz noted that after falling ill, he was downgraded to the third labor category, which allowed him to work only four hours a day at light tasks around the camp.[118] Gottfried Dulias also fell ill after months of hard labor and insufficient rations. After being assigned to a *lazarette* or hospital camp, his work assignment was to bury the dead.[119] Dulias also reported on the medical care given to a fellow prisoner who, early in the war, was in a detail cutting down trees. The men had to work only with small hand tools, which resulted in frequent injuries, some of which were quite serious. One frozen morning, his partner's hatchet bounced off a tree and back into his leg, cutting down to his shin bone. Dulias took the man to the local hospital and watched the doctor immediately apply first aid. Dulias then had to leave and return to the worksite to fulfill his day's quota. He never saw his partner again. Either the man returned home because of his injuries or died.[120]

Indeed, German POW memoirs corroborate that incurring illness or becoming injured was the most frequent means of securing repatriation. Hans Schuetz intentionally starved himself so he would be weak enough to be classified as unfit for labor and returned home. His plan almost worked; however, he was turned away from the train at the last minute because it was full. Reassigned to light labor, Schuetz regained his health and only returned home after his foot was broken when a log rolled over it in a timber accident.[121] Dulias

117. Gerhard Dengler, *Zwei Leben in einem* (Berlin: Militärverlag der Deutschen Demokratischen Republik, 1989), 92–93.
118. Schuetz, *Davai Davai*, 119.
119. Popp and Dulias, *Another Bowl of Kapusta*, 184.
120. Popp and Dulias, *Another Bowl of Kapusta*, 165.
121. Schuetz, *Davai Davai*, 113, 115–115, 118, 150–151.

returned home because he frequently fainted and was unfit for labor.[122] Accounts from POWs to relief organizations after their repatriation corroborate the correlation between poor physical standing and release. One corporal reported that he broke his leg on June 29, 1945. On July 25, doctors released him on a repatriation transport to Frankfurt an Oder, along with 449 other ill or injured Germans. During the two-week train ride from Russia to Frankfurt an Oder, the men received 600 daily grams of bread as well as two servings of soup, which was almost equivalent to the rations for those working in camps.[123]

Camp officials recognized the need to provide proper medical evaluations and care for their POWs. Lack of treatment largely stemmed from scarcities of resources and of qualified staff. When possible, medical staff worked to restore the health of the POWs so they could return to the labor force. However, camp officials also understood the economics of caring for and healing prisoners. Although they did not want to have a smaller workforce, it was in the best interest of the camps for officials to release those who were too ill or injured to quickly return to work with the minimal resource investment. Thus, one's labor potential dictated the terms of medical care and repatriation.

Leisure Activities

Although work was the *raison d'être* of camp life, it did not define the entirety of the camp experience. Camp administrators also made some effort to administer to the intellectual and emotional needs of the prisoners by creating a variety of leisure activities. Most prisoners worked six days a week, and Sunday was a universal day off.[124] The activities undertaken by the German captives during their time off were similar to those of soldiers stationed at base camps and included playing sports, reading books and newspapers, and putting on musical performances and plays. Many of these leisure activities served the dual purpose of troop entertainment and antifascist reeducation. The Gulag also had its own Cultural-Educational Department, which organized reeducation activities.[125] Both the Gulag and GUPVI attempted to refashion their prisoners into proper, socialist citizens through cultural work. In essence, the cultural work in both institutions strove to create socialist workers loyal to the Soviet Union. Gulag leisure programs were connected to the broader

122. Popp and Dulias, *Another Bowl of Kapusta*, 198.
123. ADCV, 372.15 () Fasz. 1, "Bericht aus Russland," October 24, 1945.
124. RGVA, f. 1p, op. 21a, d. 61, l. 106.
125. Bell, *Stalin's Gulag at War*, 44.

Soviet campaigns of developing socialist workers, whereas GUPVI leisure programs primarily existed to support the antifascist reeducation program.

The Gulag developed the Cultural-Educational Department in the 1930s to correct and politically educate a subgroup of prisoners in the camp system. It sorted the inmates into those who could be redeemed and those who could not. For the select few determined to be redeemable, educational officials expended resources to retrain them. The men had to be transformed from criminals into enthusiastic socialists, who would contribute to the growth of the system during their rehabilitation and after their release. In the Gulag, this cultural-educational work emphasized economic production. Gulag officials organized camp newspapers, theater troupes, orchestras, film screenings, and sports teams. Camp newspapers, for example, urged inmates to increase their labor contributions. Soccer teams and matches aimed to bring the Stalinist emphasis on physical culture to the captives. As it did for the free population, improved physical fitness increased productivity in the workplace and prepared citizens to defend the country in the event of war. Soccer matches and theater productions also served to entertain not only the captives but also camp staff members and their families. Many of these camps existed in remote locations, and the cultural work with the prisoners also served to keep the workers and nearby free citizens amused.[126]

Although the GUPVI again borrowed from the Gulag experience when it came to entertaining and reeducating POWs through cultural work, the GUPVI had its own challenges rooted in overcoming the anti-Soviet Nazi propaganda that the troops had encountered during the war. Much of the POW cultural work was documented in camp albums created by the Antifascist Reeducation Department. As mentioned, these POW camp albums, which chronicled daily life, frequently included sections about labor, medical treatment, and leisure time. They showed POWs occupying themselves with playing sports and chess, reading newspapers, and performing in or listening to musical bands.[127] The German-language book about camp life, *POWs in the Soviet Union*, included a 95-page chapter on camp life and leisure activities.[128] One prisoner contributor noted that his camp included a soccer field, a running track, and long and high jump spaces.[129] The book also included photos of

126. Barnes, *Death and Redemption*, 57–58; Bell, *Stalin's Gulag at War*, 44; Barenberg, *Gulag Town, Company Town*, 82–83; Steven Maddox, "Gulag Football: Competitive and Recreational Sport in Stalin's System of Forced Labor," *Kritika: Explorations in Russian and Eurasian History* 19, no. 3 (2018): 510.

127. RGVA, f. 39p, op. 7, d. 1, ll. 14–16ob; RGVA, f. 105p, op. 4, d. 15, ll. 17–21.

128. RGVA, f. 1p, op. 21a, d. 61, ll. 45–139.

129. RGVA, f. 1p, op. 21a, d. 61, l. 106.

prisoners playing chess, as well as information about an exhibition of prisoner-produced art.[130] Prisoners at some camps viewed films, others had their own orchestras, and in some soldiers performed plays, such as *Macbeth*, and even ballets. The lack of women to fill roles did not seem to bother the troops. Men played the female roles and dressed as women.[131]

Select camps and prisoners close to the capital benefited from outings to major sites of Soviet culture in Moscow. Prisoners went on excursions to Red Square, the Kremlin, Lenin's Mausoleum, and St. Basil's Cathedral. Others viewed triumphs of Soviet engineering, such as the ornate Metro or the massive Gorky Central Park of Culture and Leisure. One prisoner wrote of a trip to the renowned Bolshoi Ballet, and another of walking through the halls of the Tretyakov Gallery, home to some of Russia's greatest masterpieces.[132] Prisoners in camps far from Moscow also benefited from cultural outings. In Ulyanovsk, a small group of German prisoners visited a local branch of the Central Museum of V. I. Lenin on February 22, 1947, and signed the guestbook, noting how the museum's collection impressed them and inspired them to work for the future of Europe.[133] These cultural outings to important sites of Russian and Soviet culture and history clearly aimed to impress the German captives and serve as pro-Soviet propaganda efforts. Although the goal of these excursions was to develop a German appreciation of Soviet culture, politics, and people, the highly visible visits of captive Germans could have served an equally important reverse effect on the Soviet population. Free citizens engaging with these German captives could have helped disassociate the men from the former fascist ties. It could have been important to the Soviet government to have Soviet citizens support Soviet-German friendship and new and improved relations between the states in the postwar era.

The cultural facilities, resources, and excursions described in the preceding two paragraphs likely were not found in every camp. These tours of cultural sites and the higher quality of facilities often were provided by centers of antifascist reeducation, which were directed to officers first and foremost. Better treatment of officers during the war aimed to bring more officers into the effort to end the war. After the war, the superior facilities aimed to convince officers to return to Germany with a positive attitude toward both the Soviet Union and socialism.

However, as chapter 3 discusses, antifascist reeducation programs extended to much of the camp system, regardless of rank or class. The most common

130. RGVA, f. 1p, op. 21a, d. 61, ll. 114, 117, 100.

131. RGVA, f. 1p, op. 21a, d. 61, ll. 209, 223, 258, 260.

132. RGVA, f. 1p, op. 21a, d. 62, ll. 202–210.

133. GANI UO, f. 441, op. 1, d. 13, l. 110.

leisure and antifascist activity was reading the newspaper, especially after 1945. Prisoners noted their access to Izvestiia in Russian and to select German-language publications produced either by the Soviet government or the East German regime, including *Die Morden Tribune, Tagliche Rundschau, Neues Deutschland*, and *Berliner Zeitung*.[134] Soviet officials restricted access to mass-produced print material on an ideological basis. German prisoners could read the news a few days after it had been published abroad but only those articles written from the pro-Soviet standpoint. At times, censors working for the camps intercepted mail that contained newspapers from the West. Some con-fiscated publications included a White emigrant and staunchly anti-Soviet pub-lication known as "At the Turning Point" (*На Переломе*; *Na Perelome*) and a Catholic newspaper, "Belief and Life."[135] Even though the Soviet Union was officially an atheist state, Soviet officials did not prevent Germans from express-ing their religious beliefs. At Christmas, for example, prisoners had their own concerts and celebrations.[136] One returnee noted in his memoir that the pris-oners held a Christmas celebration at his camp, including a celebration of mass.[137] Another stated, "We had succeeded in persuading the Russians to provide a little tree that has been adorned with home-made Christmas deco-rations. Some of us saved a little from our rations to have at least something for Christmas Eve. I too have put aside 300 grams of bread and sliced it with prayers, as one does at home with Christmas stollen."[138]

As well as circulating Russian and East German newsprint publications among the German POWs, individual NKVD-MVD camps produced their own newspapers. POWs produced handwritten and illustrated newspapers, which camp leadership displayed on large bulletin boards. In the camps of the Stalin-grad Oblast, for example, soldiers and camp leaders produced such newspapers from 1946 to 1949.[139] Article headlines included "Our Work—A Building Ground for Peace!" and "Our Work in the Soviet Union Serves to Secure Peace." Themed issues were devoted to the lives of Vladimir Lenin, Karl Liebknecht, and Rosa Luxemburg, as well as Joseph Stalin's sixty-ninth birthday in 1949.[140]

---

134. RGVA, f. 1p, op. 21a, d. 61, ll. 87 and 125; RGVA, f. 53p, op. 7, d. 4, ll. 106–107; RGVA, f. 39p, op. 7, d. 69, l. 1.

135. RGVA, f. 1p, op. 21a, d. 5, ll. 1–2.

136. RGVA, f. 1p, op. 21a, d. 62, ll. 2 and 32; Giusti, *Stalin's Italian Prisoners of War*, 117.

137. August Halbe, *5 Jahre kriegsgefangener Priester im Ural: Ein Erlebnisbericht von Vikar August Halbe* (Bochum-Weitmar: Pfarramt Heilige Familie Heimkehrer-Dankeskirche, 1959), 37–44.

138. Adelbert Holl, *After Stalingrad: Seven Years as a Soviet Prisoner of War*, trans. Tony Le Tissier (South Yorkshire, UK: Pen and Sword Military, 2016), 62.

139. RGVA, f. 47p, op. 7, d. 29 through 65. Folders 29–31 covered 1946, folders 32–46 covered 1947, folders 47–58 covered 1948, and folders 59–65 covered 1949.

140. RGVA, f. 47p, op. 7, d. 59, ll. 1, 2, 6, 7, and 13.

POWs engaged in other forms of creative writing to occupy their free time. These writings also fell under the jurisdiction of the antifascist educational programs in the camps, but the soldiers could write more creative pieces in these activities, rather than just reporting accounts of their biographies and life in the camps. Soldiers produced a variety of written pieces, including poetry, short stories, and plays.[141] The central antifascist department of the GUPVI even held competitions for the best antifascist play. One play submitted to the competition, "The Deserter"—written by the prisoners of Camp No. 215 in Ulyanovsk—described their antifascist conversion. In the first act, a group of German soldiers at the front listen to a news broadcast and realize that they are fighting for the wrong side. The soldiers flee, only to be captured but treated well by the Red Army. In the second act, the soldiers work on construction tasks in the Soviet Union and yearn to return to their homeland, where they want to build a socialist state. In the final act, the soldiers reflect on their lives three years after returning to Germany, where they swear to keep working until the goal of socialism is achieved.[142] One prisoner, Heinrich Gerlach, wrote a 614-page novel called *Breakthrough at Stalingrad* in 1944 about his experiences in the fateful battle.[143] Other prisoners wrote a musical piece for drums, trumpet, trombone, and violins with lyrics called "March of the Antifascists."[144] The lyrics of the song go as follows:

Antifascists
Fight for democracy
No path should be hard
To win the victory:
Freedom, equality, honor
Should be the battle cry.
Beat the Nazi,
So that the world—of it—is free!

Work of the fist (*Faust*) and forehead (*Stirn*)
Shake hands
Liquidate the fascist,
Who burned the world:
Freedom, equality, honor

---

141. RGVA, f. 1p, op. 21a, d. 61, l. 247.

142. RGVA, f. 4p, op. 22n, d. 195.

143. RGVA, f. 4p, op. 22n, d. 132. For more information about the novel see, Jochen Hellbeck, "Breakthrough at Stalingrad: The Repressed Soviet Origins of a Bestselling West German War Tale," *Contemporary European History* 22, no. 1 (February 2013): 1–32.

144. RGVA, f. 4p, op. 22n, d. 174, ll. 1–7.

Should be the battle cry.
Beat the Nazi,
So that the world—of him—is free!

Not only did the soldiers write performance pieces but they also performed them for each other. In Camp No. 193 in Vologda, prisoners wrote a play called *Secret Plan Ro-Vu-La*, which they performed on stage.[145] Although some soldiers may not have enjoyed taking part in the antifascist reeducation program, its purpose was not only didactic, and many took part in the entertainment it offered.

A final, and important, form of POW leisure activity and writing was corresponding with family members at home. During the war, captured German soldiers did not have the right to send and receive letters. Similarly, Gulag prisoners rarely had the opportunity to correspond with those outside the camps. When they could write, their writings were limited and censored. Many prisoners resorted to smuggling letters out to remain in contact with their families.[146] The lack of communication presented hardships for both the captured Germans and their families back home. The chaotic nature of the war, as well as the lack of reporting of casualties and captures, meant that German families did not necessarily know the fates of their loved ones. Germans in Soviet captivity also did not know the conditions of their family members during the Allied campaigns in Germany nor the status of relatives serving in other units. The lack of direct news likely caused low morale among German citizens and captured soldiers alike.

Beginning in June 1945, however, the Soviet government permitted German POWs to write home and receive mail. The only prisoners who remained without the right to correspondence were convicted war criminals: these men had to receive special permission from the Ministry of Foreign Affairs to write home.[147] Again, the end of the war signaled a shift for Germans from enemies to potential allies. Free Germans, as well as those returning to Germany from the Soviet Union, needed to have as good an opinion as possible about the Soviet Union if Soviet authorities hoped to garner support for their actions in Europe after the war. Moreover, banning correspondence after the war's end would have provided the other Allied powers with another reason to publicly decry the leadership of the Soviet Union.

Over the years, German POWs actively corresponded with their relatives at home. In 1948, for example, prisoners sent 10,110,185 letters to Germany.

145. RGVA, f. 1p, op. 21a, d. 61, l. 246
146. Barnes, *Death and Redemption*, 13; Bell, *Stalin's Gulag at War*, 69.
147. RGASPI, f. 82, op. 2, d. 1168, l. 113; RGVA, f. 1p, op. 3t, d. 10, l. 225.

In the same period, the MVD received 33,932,620 letters for former soldiers of the German, Austrian, Hungarian, and Romanian forces. However, the right to correspondence did not entail the right to free and open communication. Of the roughly 43,000,000 letters exchanged in 1948, MVD officials confiscated 114,188 incoming and 64,238 outgoing letters for all former Axis armies. Most confiscated letters from abroad included information about the difficulties of life in the Soviet zone of occupation, in contrast to the British, American, and French zones. Letters seized from POWs disclosed information about MVD camp locations, the nature of work performed, deaths of fellow prisoners, and "slanderous fabrications about the conditions of detention."[148] Soviet officials attempted to hide any evidence of bad conditions under their control, which served as a passive form of propaganda. Both free and captive Germans alike only received good news about their relatives living under Soviet jurisdictions, which could reinforce more overt pro-Soviet propaganda efforts.

Generally, Soviet officials limited German POWs' correspondence to the mailing of Red Cross postcards. The front of the postcard had standardized information for the address. The other side provided a small space to inform family members about a prisoner's status or life in the camps.[149] In an early postwar postcard that was successfully delivered to Germany, one prisoner wrote on October 6, 1945, "Since June 28, 1944 I have been a Russian prisoner of war. It is not like how the Nazis told us, that everybody gets shot. I am well and in good health, we have enough to eat."[150] Hans Schuetz noted in his memoir that he and his fellow prisoners received the right to correspondence and were astounded that they were able to send and receive mail, writing, "We got postcards nearly every other month to write our loved ones. We didn't believe it at first—mail actually arrived at our camp! The return cards we sent many months ago came back to us and there even a few letters!"[151]

Starting in 1951, German relief organizations and families obtained the right to send packages to POWs in the Soviet Union. The receipt of packages had been a long-standing privilege and saving grace in the Gulag. Camp officials used the threat of not being allowed packages to coerce or punish their prisoners. Prisoners also heavily relied on the packages and their food contents for lifesaving extra calories, especially during provisioning shortages.[152] In 1951, POWs could receive packages weighing up to four kilograms. The German

148. RGVA, f. 1p, op. 21a, d. 5, ll. 1–2.
149. Red Cross Postcard, undated, Josef Kayser papers, box 1, folder 2, Hoover Institution Archives.
150. ADCV, 372.15 () Fasz. 1, "Auszug aus dem Schreiben des Kriegsgefangenen," October 6, 1945.
151. Schuetz, *Davai Davai*, 94.
152. Barnes, *Death and Redemption*, 42–43; Bell, *Stalin's Gulag at War*, 42–43; Alexopoulos, *Illness and Inhumanity*, 26, 40.

Catholic relief organization Caritas organized a campaign to send a minimum of six thousand Christmas packages to POWs that would include milk, meat, lard, honey, nuts, figs, dates, cookies, and candles.[153] Caritas broadcast the announcement of the Christmas packages on the radio. They also stated that the Protestant Relief Service and the German Red Cross also hoped to make at least 6,000 packages each, with a goal of between 20,000 and 25,000 Christmas packages to be sent to the Soviet Union for Christmas 1951. The packages were a success, and families were eager to send supplies to their relatives. By 1952, Caritas alone sent three thousand packages monthly to the Soviet Union.[154]

The number of packages only increased as time went on, even as the remaining number of POWs in the USSR decreased. Between October 1954 and March 1955, Caritas sent 24,499 packages, although some went to internees or people held within the Soviet Occupation Zone.[155] For those in captivity, the packages not only brought needed food supplements but also feelings of joy and hope. On their return home, former POWs sent letters of gratitude to Caritas thanking the organization and its directors. One returnee wrote, "Since 1951, I regularly awaited your monthly package. Sometimes I received two. Please be assured that without this selfless and self-sacrificing help, half of us would have starved."[156] Another former POW wrote in November 1955 that he had just received his final package at home in Berlin. It had been forwarded home after his repatriation. He stated that he was nonetheless happy to receive the goods, which were still in good condition despite weeks of transport from Germany to the Soviet Union and back. He concluded his letter this way: "The Caritas association in Freiburg has given me such much joy over the last few years and saved me from many a nutritional problem. Please accept my heartfelt thanks again for all the kind assistance you have given me during my stay in Russia."[157] These packages truly improved the lives of POWs still held in Soviet captivity. They enabled the men to supplement their standard rations and to have a taste of home. Those who received packages vividly remembered not only their arrival but also the effect they had on morale.

The GUPVI did not limit prisoner correspondence to friends and relatives at home. Prisoners were also permitted to write to each other in different camps. Frequently this occurred on special occasions, such as correspondence

153. ADCV, 372 + 063, "Kriegsgefangenhilfe. Paketinhalt," November 11, 1951.
154. "Monatlich 3000 Lebensmittelpakete an russische Kriegsgefangene," *Badische Neuste Nachrichten*, August 5, 1952, as seen in ADCV, 372 .059 Fasz. 1.
155. ADCV, 372.059 Fasz. 2, "Bericht der Caritas-Kriegsgefangenenhilfe für das Halbjahr Oktober 1954 bis März 1955."
156. ADCV, 372.2.095, pages 11 [sic] and 2, November 22, 1955.
157. ADCV, 372.2.095, page 42, November 29, 1955.

with Father Josef Kayser, a priest held captive in Camp No. 27 in Krasnogorsk. During captivity, he belonged to the National Committee for a Free Germany (Nationalkomitee Freies Deutschland, NKFD), an organization of officers formed in 1943 that promoted surrender among German fighting forces. As a member of the NKFD, Father Kayser could correspond with members of antifascist organizations within the GUPVI system. He also received permission to perform pastoral care while writing to prisoners in other camps, in line with the policy of allowing prisoners some freedom of religion. Often, however, writing paper was scarce in the camps, and prisoners had to write to each other on whatever scraps of paper they could find. For example, they would write on the backs of tobacco cartons.[158]

Although most POWs spent their leisure time in their assigned labor camps, some privileged prisoners spent time at special relaxation camps akin to the sanatoria where Soviet citizens spent their vacations. These small vacation camps housed fifteen to twenty-five men for ten days at a time. The *Politotdel*, or Political Department, of the GUPVI intentionally created these camps for the purpose of dispelling anti-Soviet propaganda and fostering good relations between the POWs and the Soviet Union. In them, prisoners read books and newspapers, watched films and theater productions, and went to parks and museums. Prisoners even went on excursions to local shops. These camps aimed to create, to a limited degree, a sense of normal life and even a vacation atmosphere in the Soviet Union.[159] Although very few POWs were given the opportunity to go to these leisure camps, the Soviet political officers did attempt to create a system for instilling fond memories in the hope that the former POWs would return to either East or West Germany with pro-Soviet feelings. The GUPVI documents reporting on the leisure camps note that they were extremely successful and popular.

Although labor conditioned most aspects of camp life, Soviet officials realized the need to provide leisure activities for the German captives. Leisure activities served the twofold task of giving the men some respite and generating pro-Soviet sentiments. Increased morale would help the men be better workers. Positive attitudes toward Soviet captors would also help the Soviet Union when it came time for the men to return home. The returnees would be able to temper their stories of work with accounts of intellectual progress, their rights to correspondence and pastoral care, and the cultural and economic successes

158. Assorted correspondence, Nationalkomittee Freies Deutschland, 1943–1945, Josef Kayser papers, box 1, folder 2, Hoover Institution Archives; correspondences, Prisoner of war camp pastoral care, 1943–1945, 1 and 2, Josef Kayser papers, box 1, folders 3 and 4, Hoover Institution Archives.

159. RGVA, f. 39p, op. 7, d. 69, ll. 2–5.

of the socialist state. Cultural work with POWs existed to support their antifascist reeducation.

Although experiences from World War I and international law informed how Soviet officials treated German captives, labor needs ultimately shaped much of the POW camp life experience. NKVD officials applied the parameters established in the Gulag system to derive the maximum labor output from the POWs with the minimum economic investment. GUPVI leaders used the Gulag's system of grading the physical condition of POWs to deploy their captives throughout the wartime economy. Indeed, the experiences of Gulag labor and medical care dictated how GUPVI leaders attempted to care for and mobilize the German captives. The medical infrastructure developed in the Gulag gave Soviet administrators the ability to readily sort POWs by labor potential and integrate them into the Soviet economy. The camp labor hierarchies were scaled to get the most out of every prisoner based on his physical capabilities. Food policy toward the POWs was based on overall national conditions, rather than the intentional starvation of prisoners, which was Nazi policy toward Red Army captives during the war. As the tide of the war turned and the food supply improved, conditions for the POWs also changed for the better. The state sometimes expended resources to try to improve the health of ill POWs in hopes of returning them to the physical capacity to work for eight or ten hours a day.

As was the case with the Gulag, conditions in GUPVI camps changed frequently. Officials consistently modified camp conditions based on the status of the war and overall national conditions. After the war, the state repatriated POWs too ill or injured to recover to lessen the resource burden on the USSR, especially during the famine of 1946–1947. The war's end also ushered in an increase in leisure and propaganda activities for the POWs. Generally, these activities helped contribute to the labor output as well. Overall, the state of the Soviet economy and the drive to restore it became the leading determinants of the conditions of German POWs. As the next chapter shows, the Soviet economy relied heavily on the labor of the POWs, especially during the immediate postwar era. Camp life, then, affected the Soviet national economy. Thousands of POW forced-labor camps operated across the territory of the Soviet Union with the goal of restoring the nation's economy amidst a dire labor shortage. Effectively managing the POWs on a camp-by-camp level contributed directly to the national economy. World War II's tremendous human and physical toll on the Soviet Union made these contributions possible.

CHAPTER 2

German POWs and the Postwar Reconstruction of the USSR

"A period of 25 years—that is the time Russia will need to restore what has been destroyed," the Nazi general Stülpnagel told Hitler.[1] Leonid Brezhnev alleged that Stülpnagel said this sometime in the late fall of 1943, after the Red Army had driven the Wehrmacht out of the Dnieper region. Stülpnagel's predictions were certainly in line with Nazi war aims, and many Soviet officials believed the damages in the Dnieper region alone would take a quarter-century to repair.

According to one contemporary scholar, the destruction was so severe that the Soviet Union resembled a "defeated power" rather than the victor that it was.[2] A Soviet state commission calculated the cost of war damages at 2,569 billion rubles.[3] Damage included the ruining or burning of 1,710 cities and 70,000 villages and settlements. Major industrial centers such as Stalingrad,

---

A shortened version of this chapter appeared as Susan Grunewald, "Applying Digital Methods to Forced Labor History: German POWs during and after the Second World War," in *Rethinking the Gulag: Identities, Sources, Legacies*, ed. Alan Barenberg and Emily D. Johnson (Bloomington: Indiana University Press, 2022), 129–154.

1. Leonid Brezhnev, *How It Was: The War and Postwar Reconstruction in the Soviet Union* (Oxford: Pergamon, 1979), 59.

2. Donald A. Filtzer, *Soviet Workers and Late Stalinism: Labour and the Restoration of the Stalinist System after World War II* (Cambridge: Cambridge University Press, 2002), 13.

3. Elena IU. Zubkova, *Russia after the War: Hopes, Illusions, and Disappointments, 1945–1957* (Armonk, NY: M. E. Sharpe, 1998), 20.

Sevastopol, Leningrad, Kiev, Minsk, Odessa, Smolensk, Novgorod, Pskov, Oryol, Kharkov, Voronezh, and Rostov-on-Don lay in ruins: 31,850 factories and industries had been obliterated; 65,000 kilometers of railways and 4,100 train stations, as well as 36,000 post stations, telephone stations, and other communications infrastructure, were destroyed. Forty thousand hospitals, 84,000 schools, and 43,000 libraries were ruined. Ninety-eight thousand kolkhozy (collective farms), 1,876 sovkhozy (state-owned farms), and 2,890 machine-tractor stations were destroyed. More than seven million horses were either killed or taken back to Germany. The Germans also robbed Soviet agriculture of a vast quantity of livestock, including 17 million cattle, 20 million pigs, 27 million sheep, and 100 million chickens: all these animals were transported to Germany to support its home front.[4] All totaled, the Soviet Union lost around 25 percent of its physical assets during the war.[5]

Compounding the physical damages was the loss of life. The top-secret report for the prosecutor of the USSR that described the physical and asset damages also included an estimate of 25 million Soviet deaths during the war.[6] Recent calculations place the number of Soviet dead at 26.6 million, though it could be much higher, perhaps even more than 30 million. Roughly 20 million, or 76 percent of those killed, were men, most of whom were born between 1901 and 1931, meaning that the Soviet economy lost a considerable portion of its most capable laborers.[7] Soviet war deaths were especially staggering when compared to those of other Allied nations. The United States lost 418,500 citizens; the United Kingdom and its colonies, 450,700; and France, 567,000. Axis deaths were much higher, though there are wider ranges in reported losses. Japan lost between 2,600,000 and 3,100,000 people, and Germany between 6,600,000 and 8,000,000.[8] The death statistics become more shocking when seen as a percentage of the prewar populations. Taking 1939 population statistics into account, the United States lost 0.32 percent of its total population, the United Kingdom 0.94 percent, France 1.35 percent, Japan 3.67 percent, and Germany 7.9 percent.[9] The Soviet Union lost between 13.9 percent and 15.6 percent of its total 1939 population.[10] Even

---

4. GARF, f. 17, op. 125, d. 410, l. 72.

5. Filtzer, *Soviet Workers and Late Stalinism*, 13.

6. GARF, f. 17, op. 125, d. 410, l. 72.

7. Zubkova, *Russia after the War*, 20.

8. "By the Numbers: World Wide Deaths," National WWII Museum, accessed October 8, 2020, http://www.nationalww2museum.org/learn/education/for-students/ww2-history/ww2-by-the-numbers/world-wide-deaths.html.

9. Peter Doyle, *World War II in Numbers: An Infographic Guide to the Conflict, Its Conduct, and Its Casualties* (Richmond Hill, Ontario: Firefly Books, 2013), 206–209.

10. For this calculation, I use Zubkova's estimate of 26.6 million Soviet civilian and military deaths during the war. Zubkova, *Russia after the War*, 20. A team of Russian military scholars has noted that this accepted figure could be too low, given the chaos and poor record keeping in the early stages of the war.

using the lower estimate, the Soviet Union lost more than double the numbers of the other major combatant nations. Indeed, the USSR lost more of its total pre-war population than the rest of the major combatant nations combined. After the war, the Soviet Union needed to rebuild a ruined economy amid a dire labor shortage. As it did during the great industrialization drive of the 1930s, the Soviet state turned to forced labor to carry out very many construction projects in a short period of time.

Scholars emphasize various functions of the Gulag system and differ about its main purpose. Some contend it was economic, whereas others prioritize political repression.[11] There is also little agreement about the driving impera-tives behind its expansion. Although prisoners of war were generally held in their own forced-labor camp system, the German POWs represent one group of Soviet inmates of the NKVD/MVD who were initially held for economic reasons. Political repression did not serve as a guiding principle for the GUPVI: instead, its major objective was economic production. Thus, GUPVI officials drew on the experiences of the Gulag labor camp system to use POWs for their maximum labor potential. Gulag inmates had contributed a great deal to the war effort, and the lessons learned during the mobilization of Gulag inmates were applied to those in the POW labor camp system. Until 1949, when political considerations relating to the Cold War surpassed economic ones, German POWs were retained to help with the postwar reconstruction of the Soviet Union. Over time, however, as the nation began to recover from the war and the Cold War intensified, political and diplomatic factors also began to figure prominently in the continuing incarceration of the German POWs.

See G. F. Krivosheev et al., *Soviet Casualties and Combat Losses in the Twentieth Century* (London: Greenhill, 1997), 83–84. The two percentages—13.9% and 15.6%—represent two different figures from the 1939 Soviet Census. The lower total population figure was 170,600,000 million citizens in the pre-September 1939 territory of the Soviet Union. The higher total population figure was 190,700,000, which reflected territorial gains after September 1939. The census figures are reported in Roger A. Clarke, *Soviet Economic Facts 1917–1970* (London: Macmillan, 1972), 3.

11. For scholars who argue that the Soviet authorities created the Gulag to enact political repression, see Aleksandr Isaevich Solzhenitsyn, *The Gulag Archipelago, 1918–1956: An Experiment in Literary Investiga-tion* (New York: Harper & Row, 1974); Robert Conquest, *Kolyma: The Arctic Death Camps* (New York: Vi-king, 1978); and Anne Applebaum, *Gulag: A History* (New York: Doubleday, 2003). For scholars who argue that there was a complex relationship between economics, politics, and ideology, see Lynne Viola, *The Unknown Gulag: The Lost World of Stalin's Special Settlements* (Oxford: Oxford University Press, 2007); Oleg V. Khlevniuk, *The History of the Gulag: From Collectivization to the Great Terror* (New Haven: Yale University Press, 2004); Paul R. Gregory and Valery V. Lazarev, *The Economics of Forced Labor: The Soviet Gulag* (Stanford, CA: Hoover Institution Press, 2003); Steven Anthony Barnes, *Death and Redemption: The Gulag and the Shaping of Soviet Society* (Princeton: Princeton University Press, 2011); Julie Draskoczy, *Be-lomor: Criminality and Creativity in Stalin's Gulag* (Brighton, MA: Academic Studies Press, 2014); Alan Barenberg, *Gulag Town, Company Town: Forced Labor and Its Legacy in Vorkuta* (New Haven: Yale Univer-sity Press, 2014); and Wilson T. Bell, *Stalin's Gulag at War: Forced Labour, Mass Death, and Soviet Victory in the Second World War* (Toronto: University of Toronto Press, 2018).

In the decade after the war, Soviet authorities held up to 3,180,000 German POWs, who were released in waves up through 1956.[12] Punishment was not the prime motivating factor behind the use of German POW labor, although their contribution to the reconstruction process was also seen as punishment for the destruction Germany had inflicted on the country. However, Soviet officials were most concerned with getting the maximum economic output from their prisoners. Facing an acute labor shortage, the government desperately needed every able-bodied man it could get to rebuild what the Nazis destroyed. Thus, at least until 1949, at which time most of the POWs had already returned to Germany and the economy had almost reached its prewar levels, the Soviet government detained able-bodied POWs for their labor contributions.

The War Years

In the year or so after the invasion on June 22, 1941, the Red Army captured few German soldiers. As tide of the war changed, however, and the Soviet forces switched from defensive to offensive fighting, they captured an ever-increasing number of Germans. The Soviet government followed precedents from both World War I and the Gulag forced-labor system for organizing and mobilizing its captured Germans into the national economy. Whereas the population of the Gulag decreased over the war due to deaths and amnesties, the number of Germans in Soviet captivity increased, and they assumed a vital place in the Soviet national economy.

The Gulag system had grown considerably from its inception in 1929 to the outbreak of World War II. The Soviet economy relied heavily on forced labor for large-scale construction projects, the cutting of timber, and mining. In 1940, forced labor produced 60 percent of the nation's gold, almost 80 percent of its tin, and about 50 percent of its nickel.[13] By 1941, the Gulag, under NKVD control, also produced 12 percent of all Soviet lumber.[14] Thus, by the time of the German invasion on June 22, 1941, the national economy was relying heavily on the contribution of the Gulag's forced labor. The role of Gulag labor remained vital during the war. From 1941 to 1944, Gulag prisoners laid 2,143 miles of new railroads, paved 2,820 miles of highways, and constructed 634 miles of oil pipeline. They

---

12. Michael Borchard, *Die deutschen Kriegsgefangenen in der Sowjetunion: Zur politischen Bedeutung der Kriegsgefangenenfrage 1949–1955* (Düsseldorf: Droste, 2000), 43.

13. Paul Gregory, "An Introduction to the Economics of the Gulag," in *The Economics of Forced Labor: The Soviet Gulag*, ed. Paul Gregory and Valery Lazarev (Hoover Press, 2003), 8.

14. Otto Pohl, *The Stalinist Penal System: A Statistical History of Soviet Repression and Terror, 1930–1953* (Jefferson, NC: McFarland, 1997), 40.

produced 70,700,000 rounds of ammunition, 25,500,000 M-82 and M-120 shells, 35,800,000 hand grenades, 9,200,000 antipersonnel mines, and 100,000 bombs. Additionally, they produced other vital goods for the war effort, including ration kits, field telephone cable, rafts, mortar tubes, gas masks, cloth, and uniforms. These industrial successes, however, came at great cost. The inefficiencies of the Gulag system continued during the war, and death rates shot up. From January 1, 1941, to January 1, 1946, 932,000 Gulag prisoners died: more than half of all the deaths throughout the Gulag's entire existence.[15]

By 1943, when the Soviet Union began to capture large numbers of German soldiers, the Gulag system was fully entrenched as a vital component of the Soviet economy. Indeed, the destruction caused by the war only increased the state's reliance on forced labor. For the Soviet economy, the capture of German soldiers provided a timely new source of labor amid growing labor shortages. The deaths in the Gulag system caused by terrible wartime conditions and the mass release of Gulag prisoners to fight for the Red Army meant that the forced-labor system was in especially great need of workers.[16] An increase in the forced-labor system was directly tied to the Battle of Stalingrad, which resulted in a new conceptualization of the role of POWs in the Soviet Union. Lasting from August 23, 1942, to February 2, 1943, the Battle of Stalingrad marked a turning point in the war. After its decisive victory at Stalingrad, the Red Army began fighting its way back west, winning battle after battle and liberating the occupied territories. Prior to Stalingrad, there were only 10,528 POWs in the Soviet Union.[17] After the battle, 91,000 Germans, including 22 generals, were taken captive.[18]

Although a significant number of these prisoners died due to harsh conditions, frostbite, wounds, and the initial chaos of captivity, those who remained healthy were immediately mobilized for the war effort and reconstruction. On August 21, 1943, the Soviet government issued the decree, "On Urgent Measures to Restore the Economy in the Regions Liberated from German Occupation." The decree stated that the reconstruction of Kalinin, Smolensk, Tula, Kursk, and Orlov Provinces, all previously occupied by the Germans, was to begin no later than September 1943 and that the reconstruction of the Sta-

15. Pohl, *The Stalinist Penal System*, 40; Edwin Bacon, *The Gulag at War: Stalin's Forced Labour System in the Light of the Archives* (New York: New York University Press, 1994), 134–137; Barnes, *Death and Redemption*, 108–109; Bell, *Stalin's Gulag at War*, 4–9, 49.

16. Bell, *Stalin's Gulag at War*, 8; Barnes, *Death and Redemption*, 115.

17. I. P. Kuz'micheva, *Skvoz' plen: Nemeckie voennoplennye v Sovetskom Sojuze 1941–1956* (Moscow: Sabasnikovych, 2007), 12.

18. Antony Beevor, *Stalingrad: The Fateful Siege, 1942–1943* (New York: Penguin, 1999), 396.

lingrad, Rostov, and Voronezh Provinces and Krasnodar and Stavropol territories was to begin no later than October 15, 1943. In addition, the decree noted
which industries were to be prioritized for reconstruction. It highlighted the
importance of restoring machine-tractor stations and shipping tractors, farm-
ing machinery, horse plows, and material and technical supplies in the newly
liberated territories to support the revival of agriculture there.[19] Additionally, the German POWs were assigned specific labor tasks in the reconstruc-
tions of these regions. In Stalingrad and Kharkov, the majority of German
POWs worked in the tractor factories and for the weapons and chemical production industries; smaller numbers worked for the oil, coal, and timber industries.[20] In 1943, one-quarter of all POWs worked in the timber industry, a
sector in desperate need of labor. Those assigned to coal mining were either
deployed to the Donbass region of Ukraine or Karaganda and the Lenger areas of Kazakhstan.[21]

As the Red Army marched westward toward Berlin, it continued to capture
soldiers, who were subsequently mobilized throughout the Soviet economy.
The POWs constituted an ever-growing labor source of a scarce resource in
wartime. By the end of 1944, there were more than 300,000 German POWs
in Soviet hands.[22] The increase in the number of POWs also resulted in an administrative change in the NKVD. The Administration of Prisoners of War and
Internees (UPVI; Upravlenie po delam voennoplennykh i interovannykh)—a
branch of the NKVD that was in control of the POWs—was created in November 1939 and by 1943 had a staff of eighty-five people.[23] In 1944, the UPVI became the Main Administration of Prisoners of War and Internees (GUPVI;
Glavnoe upravlenie po delam voennoplennykh i interovannykh).[24] The transition from administration to main administration signified its greater size and
importance within the NKVD, resulting in a larger budget and more staff
members. By February 1945, 295 administrators were working for the GUPVI.[25]
A month later, the administrative staff increased to 315; the size of the administration staff reached its height of 371 people in January 1946.[26]

---

19. GARF, f. 9504, op. 1, d. 1, ll. 200-185. Delo numbered backward.
20. GARF, f. 9414, op. 1, d. 328, ll. 27-21. Delo numbered backward.
21. GARF, f. 9414, op. 1, d. 328, l. 33-28. Delo numbered backward.
22. GARF, f. 9414, op. 1, d. 328, ll. 51 and 51ob.
23. Kuz'micheva, *Skvoz' Plen*, 10, 26; GARF, f. 9401, op. 4, d. 2889, l. 6.
24. Kuz'micheva, *Skvoz' Plen*, 10.
25. GARF, f. 9401, op. 4, d. 2889, l. 60.
26. GARF, f. 9401, op. 4, d. 2889, ll. 78 and 89.

Stalin Decides and Postwar Reconstruction

Although German POWs had contributed to the wartime forced-labor system, their real economic contribution was in postwar reconstruction. Even after the return of demobilized Red Army soldiers after Germany's surrender on the night of May 8–9, 1945, the Soviet Union still faced a dire labor shortage. As the war drew to a close, Soviet leaders decided the fate of the German POWs. Realizing both the monumental task of rebuilding that lay ahead and the lack of workers, the Politburo made the decision to use the labor of POWs.

During the war, Stalin had personally intervened a few times to decide work assignments for the POWs. In February 1943, Stalin, as chairman of the State Defense Committee (GKO), sent 40,000 men to work on the reconstruction of the ruined Donbass and Rostov coal mines, ordered an additional 15,000 men to construct coal mines in the Moscow region, and allotted 20,000 men to rebuild Stalingrad. He established groups of 3,000–15,000 to work in construction industries, factories, power plants, and hydroelectric stations across the Soviet Union in places such as Russia, Uzbekistan, and Kazakhstan.[27] In December 1944, Stalin issued the decree, "On the Material Provisioning of Prisoners of War in the First Quarter of 1945 and Their Labor Exploitation," which ordered that POWs be supplied with adequate rations, clothes, shoes, and trucks.[28] This order made Stalin's intent clear that POW labor would continue to be an important and valued facet of the Soviet economy, one that needed to be properly maintained.

Over the course of 1945, Stalin refined the Soviet government's approach to the German POWs. This was a matter of the highest importance. In April 1945, Lavrentii Beria, the commissar of the Ministry of Internal Affairs (MVD) and State Security, wrote a letter to Stalin asking what to do with the 97,487 German POWs captured on sections of the Belorussian and Ukrainian fronts. Stalin replied that these POWs were to be transferred to the control of the NKVD, which would then be responsible for assigning them to various economic commissariats for deployment in their respective industries. During the war, Stalin had played a role in determining labor allocations as the chairman of the State Committee of Defense, and in 1945 he personally ordered 37,600 and 28,000 POWs, respectively to coal and construction, two commissariats vital for postwar reconstruction. In other words, roughly 67 percent of the group was assigned to those two industries. Additional POWs were allocated to metallurgical, power, and other heavy and light industrial commis-

---

27. RGVA, f. 1p, op. 9a, d. 8, ll. 39–40.
28. RGVA, f. 1p, op. 9a, d. 8, 11. 207, 208, and 210.

sariats in smaller numbers, mainly in groups of five thousand and fewer. Stalin also ordered a final group of 250 POWs to munitions commissariats.[29] Postwar planning continued with the aim of reconstruction.

Less than a month later, and just a few days before the final German capitulation, Soviet officials drew up more definitive plans for the use of the POWs. As of May 5, 1945, Beria followed the precedent set forth by Stalin and sent the majority of POWs to the Russian Soviet Federative Russian Republic (RSFSR), with additional large numbers distributed throughout Ukraine, Belorussia, Lithuania, Estonia, Karelo-Finland, Moldova, Armenia, Azerbaijan, Uzbekistan, and Georgia.[30] In addition to sending POWs to work in coal and construction, they were also assigned by the tens of thousands to aid in the reconstruction of specific cities—including Sevastopol, Orel, Bryansk, Riga, Minsk, Kiev, Stalingrad, Saratov, Taganrog, Zaporozhe, and Moscow—where they lived in camps within and just outside them.[31]

The war's end resulted in a new shift in POW labor assignments, reducing the burden on the GUPVI system. The cessation of hostilities between the Soviet Union and Germany allowed Soviet officials to begin the process of returning captured Germans, particularly those who were too ill or injured to work. In an economy of shortages, the state was not interested in allocating precious resources to support injured or weak German prisoners who would need care but were unable to work. The first major wave of POW repatriations occurred immediately after the war. On May 4, 1945, the Red Army High Command stated that Russia had captured 3,180,000 German POWs.[32] By May 17, 1945, there were only 2,090,661 German POWs mobilized by more than 34 commissariats and living in 107 NKVD camps throughout the country.[33]

Not every ill or injured German POW returned home: many died in Soviet camps or during transit back to Germany. In March 1947, Soviet foreign minister Vyacheslav M. Molotov stated that the USSR had returned 1,003,974 POWs, which was fewer than the decrease in the German POW population between May 4 and May 17, 1945, leaving 85,365 unaccounted for.[34] Molotov's repatriation figure covered the period from May 1945 to March 1947, almost two additional years of repatriations. The majority of deaths may have occurred from May 4 to May 17, 1945, a chaotic period during which many

29. GARF, f. 9401, op. 2, d. 95, l. 36–38.

30. GARF, f. 9401, op. 2, d. 95, l. 366–367; GARF, f. 9401, op. 1, d. 2226, l. 199; GARF, f. 9401, op. 1, d. 2227, ll. 152–153.

31. GARF, f. 9401, op. 2, d. 95, l. 369.

32. Borchard, Die Deutschen Kriegsgefangenen, 43.

33. GARF, f. 9401, op. 1, d. 2227, l. 31–32; GARF, f. 9401, op. 1, d. 737, l. 239–241; f. 9401, op. 1, d. 2227, l. 100.

34. "890,532 Kriegsgefangene in der UdSSR," Neues Deutschland, March 16, 1947, 1.

men were wounded and captured in the last weeks of the war. An accurate assessment of the numbers is difficult because of the nature of Soviet repatriation and camp death statistics, which are fractured, incomplete, or still classified. The available numbers and explanations present their own challenges for analysis. According to scholars of the Gulag, for example, camp administrators frequently attributed deaths of prisoners to "death in transit," a method for lowering the death statistics of their own camps. A person who died in transit between camps did not show up on the death records for either the camp of origin or of destination.[35] Similar tactics may have been used to obscure POW mortality rates.

Although Soviet leaders such as Stalin and Beria decided where POWs would be deployed, it was up to local camp leadership to facilitate and organize the labor assignments. POWs were sent from filtration camps to the main camps, where local leadership housed and assigned them to work details based on contracts negotiated with local industries. The contracts outlined strict conditions for their labor and treatment. For example, a contract dated December 20, 1944, was concluded between Camp No. 27 in Krasnogorsk, on the outskirts of Moscow, and the nearby "Victory of Labor" Textile Factory. It stated that the textile factory could make use of fifty POWs until December 31, 1945. The factory would, at its own expense, arrange for daily transport between the camp and the factory and provide the POWs with a one-hour lunch break and food. It would also pay a salary for the POWs' work, which would go to the camp and not the POWs themselves. If the prisoners exceeded their quotas, the factory would also pay the standard bonuses, which would also accrue to the camp to help with its operating costs.[36] Industrial enterprises would thus assume the expenses of POW labor, although the camp administration would realize the value. Wages would be pooled to support the camp and the prisoners within it. Thus, individual commercial enterprises, not the NKVD/MVD, absorbed a significant portion of the costs of the camp. From the point of view of the camps, loaning out labor defrayed the high costs of incarceration and may have allowed camp accountants to demonstrate camp efficiency and profitability. No scholar has found any evidence of the Gulag system ever being economically profitable; even leading Soviet officials knew of the Gulag's unprofitability. The inefficiencies of the Gulag motivated Stalin's successors to reform the system immediately after his death.[37]

---

35. Khlevniuk, *History of the Gulag*, 78.

36. RGVA, f. 105p, op. 8, d. 16, ll. 7 and 7ob.

37. Barnes, *Death and Redemption*, 38–39; Amy Knight, *Beria: Stalin's First Lieutenant* (Princeton, NJ: Princeton University Press, 1995), 185; Miriam Dobson, *Khrushchev's Cold Summer: Gulag Returnees, Crime, and the Fate of Reform after Stalin* (Ithaca, NY: Cornell University Press, 2009), 7–8; Jeffrey S. Hardy,

In the process of formalizing another labor contract in 1946, leaders of Camp No. 27 negotiated with those of the Minister of Defense Factory No. 393 over the number and conditions of workers assigned to it. One stipulation was that the factory had to erect barracks for the workers on loan from the camp.[38] Thus, prisoners were not only paid and fed by the factories or industrial enterprises but also often housed by them. Although there were camps enclosed by gates, walls, and barbed wire, the "loaning" of POWs to industry meant that prisoners interacted with free Soviet labor. Labor needs outweighed the fears of having Soviet citizens interact with former Germany enemies or of prisoners escaping from housing beyond camp walls. The loaned POWs may have had their own barracks, but they were still living beyond the confines of major camp settlements.

This contract, like many others, illustrated the permeability of camp boundaries as POWs moved easily back and forth from camps to worksites. It also revealed Russian industries' desperate need for workers. Factory No. 393 already employed 300 POWs, but leaders asked for an additional 700–800. Factory officials even stated that up to 20 percent of the POWs could be those in the third labor category; that is, those who could only work short hours at light tasks due to physical impairment.[39] Any labor contribution, no matter how small, in the estimation of the factory's managers, was better than nothing.

It is unclear how camp leaders chose which POWs to loan to local industry or to live outside the camps. POW memoirs frequently detailed the work assignments of the men, but they rarely provided the rationale behind their labor assignments. One POW worked at a nearby sawmill, a yeast factory, and later a tannery.[40] He suggested that his assignments depended on the labor needs of a particular enterprise at any given time. In other cases, assignments were based on skill. One POW stated that he was placed in a local factory after pretending that he spoke Swedish. The factory needed to install turbines purchased from Sweden in 1929, and all the manuals and supporting documents were in Swedish. He managed to translate and speak Swedish well enough because of the similarities between German and Swedish.[41] Officials at another camp recruited a Russian-speaking POW to the camp's antifascist effort. At times, he served as an interpreter between POWs and Russians at local worksites. When not

The Gulag after Stalin: Redefining Punishment in Khrushchev's Soviet Union, 1953–1964 (Ithaca, NY: Cornell University Press, 2016), 22–23.

38. RGVA, f. 105p, op. 10, d. 8, l. 68.

39. RGVA, f. 105p, op. 10, d. 8, l. 68.

40. A. D. Hans Schuetz, *Davai, Davai! Memoir of a German Prisoner of World War II in the Soviet Union* (Jefferson, NC: McFarland, 1997), 53–54, 61–62, 81–82.

41. Hans Gruber, *My Odyssey thru Hell* (Bloomington, IN: AuthorHouse, 2013), 44–45.

making propaganda materials or translating, he did whatever tasks needed more men on a given day. For example, one day he drove a truck to a nearby riverport and helped unload sacks of cement from a ship.[42]

The loaning of laborers to enterprises also ensured frequent contact between German POWs and the local free population. Generally, memoirs portray these interactions as friendly.[43] The memoirs even tell of the generosity of the local population toward the POWs. One POW earned a card for an extra ration at the tannery cafeteria after completing the unpleasant task of cleaning out a lye pit. The cook took pity on him and filled his bowl to the brim with *kasha* (porridge), giving him in one serving more than his week's allotment in the camp.[44] Another POW, Horst Zank, earned the trust of his captors while working as a translator and propagandist. On his rare days off, he was permitted to walk in the woods surrounding the camp. While walking in the forest one day, he came across an elderly woman picking berries with her grandson. The woman asked whether he was a POW and then asked many questions about his family back home. When Zank said that he had not had any communication with them for more than 2.5 years, the women took pity on him, grabbed his cap, filled it with berries, and wished him luck. However, some of the people of Tatarstan, the republic in which Zank's camp was situated, did not all respond so kindly to his presence. At times, children and the elderly taunted Zank and his fellow prisoners. They shouted "Gitler kaput" (literally "Hitler is broken," but really meaning "Hitler is defeated") or called them fascists. Occasionally, the elderly or children would throw stones.[45]

The labor shortages of the war and postwar years led to numerous labor disputes between the commercial enterprises: the German POWs were a highly sought-after resource. A variety of camps and commissariats wrote to the central GUPVI leadership begging for additional POWs. Throughout 1944, for example, the National Commissariat of Coal Production pled for more POWs to work in their mines. However, all the able-bodied POWs were already deployed, and GUPVI officials had to deny many of the requests for additional laborers.[46]

When possible, the GUPVI tried to fill the gaps, but it often could not come close to meeting the demand. In March 1946, for example, the commissar of

42. Horst Zank, *Stalingrad: Kessel und Gefangenschaft* (Hamburg: E.S. Mittler, 1993), 164–165.

43. For evidence of routine, cordial interactions between German POWs working alongside the free Russian population see Schuetz, *Davai Davai*, 61; Helmut Fuchs, *Wer spricht von Siegen: Der Bericht uber unfreiwillige Jahre in Russland* (Munich: A. Knaus, 1987), 137–138; and Dianna M. Popp and Gottfried P. Dulias. *Another Bowl of Kapusta: The True Life Story of A World War Ii Luftwaffe Fighter Pilot and P.O.W. in Russia* (Bloomington, IN: AuthorHouse, 2004), 169.

44. Schuetz, *Davai Davai*, 81–82.

45. Zank, *Stalingrad: Kessel und Gefangenschaft*, 164, 166.

46. RGVA, f. 1p, op. 2i, d. 13, ll. 2–3, 5, 6, and 13–15.

Civilian Housing implored the GUPVI for one thousand laborers in Crimea but received only one hundred.[47] At other times, the GUPVI was so overwhelmed with requests that it took months to respond. Even the intervention of high-level ministers could not guarantee that factories received workers or even replies to their requests. In December 1945, the deputy minister of Civilian Housing Construction of the RSFSR contacted V. V. Chernyshëv, deputy head of the MVD. The letter requesting five hundred POWs to work on a housing construction project went unanswered, and another one was sent in May 1946.[48] Two weeks later, the deputy head of the GUPVI, Major-General Ratushchnyi, replied that the leaders of Camp No. 319, the closest one to the housing project, had already assigned all its POWs to the Ministries of Aviation, Ferrous Metallurgy, Lumber, and Communications, there were no additional laborers, and he could not deliver the requested five hundred POWs to the Ministry of Civilian Housing Construction.[49] The repeated requests for POWs reflected the extreme labor shortages of the postwar years, and the failure to supply the POWs to civilian housing construction attests to the continuing priority of heavy industry over consumer needs.

In addition to deciding where to send the POWs and what tasks they would do, Soviet leaders also emphasized the importance of economic productivity. On July 2, 1945, Beria sent a directive to camp directors stressing that prisoners must be compelled to fulfill production targets. He also ordered camp directors to submit monthly reports detailing the physical conditions of POWs, their labor assignments, plan fulfillment, and expenses and profits to Stalin, Molotov, Beria, Georgii Malenkov, Nikolai Bulganin, Lazar Kaganovich, and the NKVD.[50] Thus, Soviet officials closely tracked the labor contribution and costs of the POWs, suggesting that they were making continuing calculations about the worth of the prisoners to economic reconstruction.

Indeed, memos and directives from officials to camp directors repeatedly emphasized the importance of labor productivity and cost effectiveness. On September 29, 1945, Lieutenant General I. A. Petrov, deputy chief of the GUPVI, released a comprehensive thirty-four-page plan detailing the NKVD's position on the use of POW labor.[51] It outlined NKVD's basic approach to the prisoners: they were to work to their maximum potential and, thereby

47. RGVA, f. 1p, op. 4i, d. 36, l. 13.

48. RGVA, f. 1p, op. 4i, d. 36, l. 34.

49. RGVA, f. 1p, op. 4i, d. 36, l. 33.

50. GARF, f. 9401, op. 1, d. 744, l. 27, in Maksim Matveevich Zagorul'ko, *Voennoplennye v SSSR 1939–1956: Dokumenty iMmaterialy* (Moskow: Logos, 2000), 618; GARF, f. 9401, op. 2, d. 139, l. 105–111; and GARF, f. 9401, op. 2, d. 235, l. 340–348.

51. GARF, f. 9401, op. 1, d. 737, l. 180–214, in Zagorul'ko, *Voennoplennye v SSSR*, 628–641.

cover the costs of their incarceration through their "salaries." The document stressed that "the camp administration is obliged to seek maximum labor productivity and to provide reimbursement to the state for the cost of the camp."[52] Although the document contained more detailed sections for various subdivisions within the camp, each subheading reiterated the priority placed on the maximization of output. All prisoners were to be used "to their maximum according to their specializations and qualifications"[53]—to work and to produce as much as possible to aid the recovery of the country.

As time progressed, reports on German POWs began to assess their specific contributions to the Soviet economy. These reports were of two types: ones for internal GUPVI leadership and ones from GUPVI leaders to other Soviet officials and organizations. The head of the GUPVI, S. Kruglov, for example, sent a top-secret report to Stalin, Molotov, and Beria in June 1946 on the number and physical condition of the German POWs.[54] It included information about how many POWs were ill, repatriated, or had died, as well as detailed breakdowns of their labor deployments. According to the report, 1,408,817 German POWs were sent to forty-two of forty-three possible labor assignments across a variety of industries. The roughly 1.4 million working German POWs represented 4 percent of the total free state-employed national population.[55]

As table 2.1 shows, most of the POWs were assigned to either the MVD, defense industries, or fuel and heavy industries. Roughly 17 percent of all POWs, or 239,510 men, worked for the fuel and power industries. These deployments aimed to restore the power grid throughout the liberated territories and in the energy sector as a whole. Nearly the same percentage of POWs—16.9 percent of POWs, or 238,540 men—worked in defense-related industries in June 1946. Close to 180,000 POWs worked for heavy industry and metallurgy, comprising 12.6 percent of the working German POWs. Both the MVD and transport industries each employed roughly 10 percent. The POWs working for the MVD completed tasks within the camps, awaited new assignments for other ministries and industries, or labored on specific MVD economic projects such as the Volga-Don Canal and the Baikal-Amur Mainline (BAM) railroad.[56] Nearly 7 percent worked for a variety of construction

52. GARF, f. 9401, op. 1, d. 737, l. 180–214 in Zagorul'ko, *Voennoplennye v SSSR*, 628.

53. GARF, f. 9401, op. 1, d. 737, l. 180–214 in Zagorul'ko, *Voennoplennye v SSSR*, 628.

54. GARF, f. 9401, op. 2, d. 137, ll. 366–377.

55. Clarke, *Soviet Economic Facts*, 23. Clarke gives a figure of 32 million state-employed workers in 1946. This does not account for unfree labor.

56. Edeltraud Maier-Lutz, *Flußkreuzfahrten in Rußland. Unterwegs auf Wolga, Don, Jenissej und Lena* (Berlin: Trescher Verlag, 2005), 235; RGVA, f. 1/p, op. 10i, d. 1, l. 3; Nicholas Stargardt, *The German War: A Nation under Arms, 1939–1945* (New York: Basic Books, 2015), 556.

Table 2.1   List of German POW work assignments, June 1, 1946

NO.	NAME OF MINISTRY	GERMAN ARMY POWS
1	Ministry of Internal Affairs	15,4216
2	Ministry of the Armed Forces	15.9120
3	Ministry of Construction of Heavy Industry Enterprises	10,6248
4	Ministry of Construction of Fuel Enterprises	82.567
5	Ministry of Railways	74.627
6	Ministry of Coal Industries of the Eastern Regions	19.844
7	Ministry of Coal Industries of the Western Regions	74,467
8	Ministry of Construction of Military and Naval Enterprises	46,638
9	Ministry of Electric Power Stations	54,444
10	Ministry of Nonferrous Metallurgy	29,151
11	Ministry of the Timber Industry	23,224
12	Ministry of the Building Materials Industry	42,212
13	Ministry of the Airplane Production Industry	30,079
14	Ministry of Iron and Steel Industry	28,066
15	Ministry of Transport Machine-Building Industry	20,644
16	Ministry of Civilian Housing Construction	31,567
17	Ministry of the Food Industry	24,611
18	Ministry of Tractor and Agricultural Machinery	18,908
19	Ministry of the Navy	16,487
20	Ministry of Armaments	16,295
21	Ministry of Chemical Production	11,789
22	Ministry of the Petroleum Industry of the Eastern Regions	1,255
23	Ministry of the Petroleum Industry of Western Regions	1,459
24	Ministry of the Paper Industry	37,279
25	Ministry of the Motor Vehicle Industry	15.174
26	Ministry of the Textile Industry	12,503
27	Ministry of the Shipbuilding Industry	6,244
28	Ministry of the Heavy Machine Building Industry	8,431
29	Ministry of Light Industry	9,680
30	Ministry of the River Fleet	5,226
31	Ministry of Local Industry	5,562
32	Ministry of Agriculture and Livestock Farming*	8,640
33	Ministry of the Electronics Industry	5,292
34	Ministry of the Machine-Tool Industry	6,511
35	Ministry of the Fishing Industry of the Western Regions	5,705
36	Ministry of the Fishing Industry of the Eastern Regions	0
37	Ministry of Mechanical Engineering and Instrumentation	2,907
38	Ministry of the Local Fuel Industry	5,474
39	Ministry of Meat and Dairy Industry	2,881
40	Ministry of (Grain) Procurement	2,718
41	Ministry of the Rubber Industry	809
42	Ministry of Finances	294
43	Other local organizations	199,569
	TOTAL	**1408817**

Source: GARF, f. 9401, op. 2, d. 137, ll. 370–371.

*In other years, this was known as the Ministry of Agriculture.

industries, and 4.5 percent worked for food industries including fishing and grain procurement. The remaining 20 percent of the POW workforce were assigned to a variety of tasks, including producing chemicals, paper, and textiles, as well as to local organizations and light industries. Thus, 89 percent of the German POWs worked for various economic ministries, all in vital sectors of the economy.

The POW labor assignments for June 1946 illustrate the state's needs and priorities for postwar reconstruction at that time: power, defense, heavy industrial construction, civilian housing construction, and transportation. The largest percentage of the POWs worked in coal and the construction of electric power stations. Many other POWs worked for metallurgical enterprises or in the construction of heavy industry, fashioning machine tools and building heavy machinery. These industries were essential to the development of light industry and the consumer sector. Numerous German captives also worked to make building materials, construct housing, and build various forms of transportation in the USSR. Although some produced motor vehicles, ships, or airplanes, 50 percent of POWs working for transportation-related industries were deployed to the Ministry of Railways, which faced the great challenge of repairing and replacing railway tracks. These 74,627 POWs accounted for 5 percent of all German POW workers in June 1946. One prisoner described working to replace railway ties for one line, writing, "Thousands of people were working on the huge construction site, Russians and German prisoners of war."[57] Finally, a small subset of the POWs worked for a variety of food-related industries. The largest number of these POWs worked for the Ministry of the Food Industry, and the second-largest group worked for the Ministry of Tractor and Agricultural Machinery that produced agricultural machinery and equipment. These labor assignments correlated directly to damages sustained during the war.[58]

In addition to tracking the physical conditions and labor assignments of the POWs, the GUPVI reports to Soviet leaders also detailed the financial costs of the camps.[59] In September 1946, GUPVI officials sent a report to Stalin, Molotov, and Beria.[60] As well as providing updated totals on working, ill, deceased, and repatriated POWs, the report summarized the labor efforts of the POW camp system for the first quarter of 1946. The total earnings of the POW camps were 1,156,000,000 rubles, and total expenditures were 1,134,000,000 rubles.[61] Thus,

---

57. Fuchs, *Wer Spricht von Siegen*, 189.
58. GARF, f. 17, op. 125, d. 410, l. 72.
59. GARF, f. 9401, op. 2, d. 137, ll. 366–368, 374.
60. GARF, f. 9401, op. 2, d. 139, ll. 105–111.
61. GARF, f. 9401, op. 2, d. 139, l. 111.

the camps were not only self-sustaining but also profitable. However, Soviet statistics regarding forced labor cannot be taken at face value. Although the MVD reported the camps to be profitable, suggesting that earnings created by the camp labor exceeded expenditures, expenses for many workers may have been offloaded to other economic ministries. It is impossible to determine whether the camps were profitable, as the MVD claimed, without also consulting the costs for POW labor expended by other industries. Studies of the Gulag also note the rampant use of *tufta*, or the falsification of a wide variety of camp statistics from work norms to mortality rates.[62] Given the ubiquity of statistical padding, GUPVI officers likely followed the same techniques as their fellow Gulag MVD officials.

Reports from the GUPVI to Stalin, Molotov, and Beria continued over the course of 1947 and into 1948, indicating that for several years after the war, the economic contribution of the POWs was still deemed of highest importance.[63] The GUPVI also circulated reports internally. One such report from March 5, 1947, revealed that POWs also formed a significant percentage of the postwar labor force in several major industries.[64] They represented 20.1 percent of the workers in the Ministry of the Construction of Heavy Industry Enterprises, 31 percent in the Aviation Industry, 16.8 percent of the Ministry of Power Plants, 27.7 percent of the Ministry of the Construction of Fuel Industries, 24.1 percent of the Ministry of Building Materials, and 27.2 percent of the Ministry of Pulp and Paper Industries. After deaths and repatriations, 772,351 German POWs remained in the Soviet Union as of January 1, 1948.[65] Even with a reduced labor force, German POWs still contributed around ten million rubles to the growth of the national economy.[66]

---

62. Bell, *Stalin's Gulag at War*, 94; Oleg Khlevnyuk, "The Economy of the OGPU, NKVD, and MVD or the USSR, 1930–1950," in *The Economics of Forced Labor: The Soviet Gulag*, ed. Paul Gregory and Valery Lazarev (Stanford: Hoover Press, 2003), 64–65; Leonid Borodkin and Simon Ertz, "Coercion versus Motivation: Forced Labor in Norilsk," in *The Economics of Forced Labor*, ed. Paul Gregory and Valery Lazarev, 90; Barnes, *Death and Redemption*, 182; Mikhail Nakonechnyi, "'They Won't Survive for Long': Soviet Officials on Medical Release Procedure," in *Rethinking the Gulag: Identities, Sources, Legacies*, ed. Alan Barenberg and Emily D. Johnson (Bloomington: Indiana University Press, 2022), 103–128; Golfo Alexopoulos, *Illness and Inhumanity in Stalin's Gulag* (New Haven: Yale University Press, 2017), 133.

63. GARF, f. 9401, op. 2, d. 169, ll. 203–212, and d. 199, ll. 75–79.

64. TsKhIDK, f. 1/p, op. 9a, d. 9, l. 183–184, in Zagorul'ko, *Voennoplennye v SSSR*, 679–680. The Center for Storage of Historical Documentary Collections (TsKhIDK) was renamed the Russian State Military Archive (RGVA) in 1999. This citation represents the way in which the document was cited in the published collection of primary sources.

65. GARF, f. 9401, op. 2, d. 199, l. 78.

66. GARF, f. 9401, op. 2, d. 199, l. 76.

By 1950, the GUPVI began to produce comprehensive reports assessing the overall contribution of German POWs to the Soviet economy. On January 17, 1950, Major N. N. Chernov, head of the Fourth Division of the First Department of the GUPVI, summarized the use of all POW labor in the Soviet Union from 1941 to 1949. According to Chernov, from 1944 to 1949 POWs produced 98,500,000 tons of coal and accounted for 25.9 percent of the labor force in the coal industry, with a total production valued at almost six billion rubles; this amounted to 10.5% of the total coal production of the USSR from 1945 to 1949. From 1946 to 1949 POW labor accounted for 25 percent of the value of all construction and installation work. In the same period, POWs also constructed 450 kilometers of the BAM railroad. They paved 2,100 kilometers of roads and bridges, for a value of 1.6 billion rubles. POWs also produced seven million cubic meters of wood that translated into 760 million rubles worth of building and construction materials.[67] This contribution to the timber industry was minor, however. From 1946 to 1949, the Soviet Union produced 463 million cubic meters of timber. The POW-produced timber, then, accounted for only 1.5 percent of the national production in those years.[68] Additionally, POWs totaled somewhere between 40 and 60 percent of the labor force for the construction of power plants. The Ministry of Power Plants reported to Chernov that POWs made up 80–90 percent of the labor force for the Sevanskaya and Dzaudzhikauzskaya Power Plants, located, respectively, in Sevan, Armenia, and Vladikavkaz, Russia.[69]

Over the course of 1950 and 1951, the regional heads of the MVD produced multiple reports for Colonel-General S. N. Kruglov, the minister of internal affairs. Within the Soviet Union, thirteen economic regions contained camps. Each of these thirteen regions was divided into subregions that housed anywhere from one to twenty or more camps. The Moscow region alone contained twenty-three camps, second in the nation only to the twenty-six camps of the

---

67. RGVA, f. 1/p, op. 10i, d. 1, l. 127–138. The total figure of POW contribution to the national coal industry in these years is slightly skewed. The available statistics for All Union coal production provide annual totals for 1945 to 1949. The POWs are reported to have produced 98.5 million tons of coal from 1944 to 1949. Presumably, their coal production figures were lower in 1944 than in later years because they first had to rebuild the mines destroyed during the war. Annual coal production figures also rose steadily over the years. According to Clarke, the coal industry produced 149.3 million tons in 1945, 164.1 million tons in 1946, 183.2 million tons in 1947, 208.2 million tons in 1948, and 235.5 million tons in 1949 for a total of 940.3 million tons over those years. See Clarke, *Soviet Economic Facts*, 53. Although the date ranges do not perfectly line up, it is safe to say that German POW coal mining was significant to that industry toward the end of the war and in the early years of postwar reconstruction.

68. U.S.S.R. Council of Ministers, Central Statistical Administration, *The U.S.S.R. Economy: A Statistical Abstract* (London: Lawrence & Wishart, 1957), 79.

69. RGVA, f. 1/p, op. 10i, d. 1, l. 3.

Sverdlovsk region.[70] In his report to Colonel-General Kruglov, Lieutenant-General N. K. Bogdanov, head of the MVD of the Moscow region, provided an account of the total number of POWs in the Moscow system from 1945 to 1949, along with a breakdown of the number of prisoners working for various commissariats in each year.[71] In the Moscow region alone, POWs contributed almost three billion rubles worth of work and materials to the national economy between 1946 and 1949.[72] Furthermore, over this period the state gradually reduced subsidies to the camps for ill or weak prisoners. By 1950, all camps were required to support their POW populations by balancing their own budgets. In the Moscow region, this saved the state roughly three million rubles.[73] With the exception of the immediate postwar release of ill and weak prisoners, the second-largest number of POWs were released from the Moscow region in 1948 and 1949.[74] Lacking state subsidies, camps were even less inclined to support weak or ill prisoners than they were in the past. For a prisoner, the fastest way out of a camp was to prove himself unable to work.

The summer of 1950 signaled the end of the POWs' economic importance and, with that, the end of the GUPVI. By May 1950, the majority of the German POWs in the Soviet Union had either returned home or died. The roughly 26,000 German POWs who remained in labor camps or the Gulag were considered to be war criminals.[75] As the camps closed, the MVD reassigned staff from the GUPVI to the Gulag. For example, in February 1950, the officers of MVD Camp No. 108 in the Stalingrad province were transferred to several Gulag camps, including Karaganda and Vorkuta.[76] The decrease in the number of POWs also led to the downgrading of the GUPVI to the UPVI of the MVD on June 20, 1951.[77] At its height in January 1946, the staff of the central

70. Maksim Matveevich Zagorul'ko, *Regional'nye struktury GUPVI NKVD-MVD SSSR, 1941–1951: otchetno-informatsionnye dokumenty*, Vol. 1 (Volgograd: Izdatel', 2005), 530 and Maksim Matveevich Zagorul'ko, *Regional'nye struktury GUPVI NKVD-MVD SSSR, 1941–1951: otchetno-informatsionnye dokumenty*, Vol. 2 (Volgograd: Izdatel', 2005), 452.

71. RVGA, f. 1, op. 15a, d. 385, l. 79–129, in Zagorul'ko, *Regional'nye struktury GUPVI NKVD*, Vol. 1, 538–539.

72. RVGA, f. 1, op. 15a, d. 385, l. 79–129, in Zagorul'ko, *Regional'nye struktury GUPVI NKVD*, Vol. 1, 542.

73. RVGA, f. 1, op. 15a, d. 385, l. 79–129, in Zagorul'ko, *Regional'nye struktury GUPVI NKVD*, Vol. 1, 543.

74. RVGA, f. 1, op. 15a, d. 385, l. 79–129 in Zagorul'ko, *Regional'nye struktury GUPVI NKVD*, Vol. 1, 549.

75. Frank Biess, *Homecomings: Returning POWs and the Legacies of Defeat in Postwar Germany* (Princeton, NJ: Princeton University Press, 2006), 45. For more information on this topic, see chapter 4.

76. RGVA, f. 47p, op. 22, d. 1, l. 146.

77. GARF, f. 9401, op. 4, d. 2889, l. 208.

GUPVI administration was 371 employees, but by September 1948, it employed only 76 people. With the downgrade in June, the MVD cut the UPVI's staff to only 39 employees.[78] Both the economic priorities of state leaders and the GUPVI's overall trajectory are well illustrated by focusing on one camp, as shown in the next section.

POW Camp No. 215

Although POWs were put to work during the war, their use drastically increased after the war ended. The Red Army captured hundreds of thousands of German soldiers in the last months of the war, and once Soviet leaders turned from war to reconstruction, these POWs needed to be mobilized. As the mapping section of this chapter shows in greater detail, the POWs were deployed primarily in places that had been occupied and destroyed by the Nazis or in major sites of industrial production or resource extraction. During the war, Soviet leaders ordered the evacuation of large sectors of Soviet industry to the east—the Urals, Siberia, or Central Asia—and after the war they sent POWs to these growing industrial centers such as Ulyanovsk.

Formerly known as Simbirsk, Ulyanovsk had been a sleepy provincial town in the years leading up to the Nazi invasion. Its major claim to fame was that it was the hometown of both Vladimir Ilyich Lenin, born Ulyanov, and one of his political rivals Alexander Kerensky. The city was renamed in honor of Lenin after his death. In 1941, the Stalin Automobile Factory (*Zavod Imeni Stalina*; ZIS) had been evacuated to Ulyanovsk, which housed numerous warehouses and was served by two railway lines. In October 1941, 1,500 workers arrived from Moscow to reconstruct the evacuated ZIS factory in customs warehouses. This factory produced the ZIS-5 truck, a workhorse of Soviet industry and the Red Army. It delivered supplies on the "Road of Life" to besieged Leningrad over the frozen Lake Ladoga and served as the platform for the famed *Katyusha* mobile rocket launchers. Indeed, the ZIS-5 truck was the second-most important vehicle for the war effort after the T-34 tank. By July 1942, Ulyanovsk had become the center of production of the ZIS-5 truck, and the factory was known as UlZIS, or Ulyanovsk ZIS. In September 1944, the factory was renamed the Ulyanovsk Automobile Factory (Ul'ianovskii Avtomobillnyi Zavod; UAZ). It was decided that the factory would continue to manufacture trucks after the war. Production of the ZIS-5 truck soon ceased,

---

78. GARF, f. 9401, op. 4, d. 2889, ll. 89, 165, and 211.

but designers replaced it with the GAZ-AA truck, which the factory began producing by October 1947.[79]

For Ulyanovsk, the war served as the impetus both for the creation of its automobile industry and the importation of a labor force. NKVD/MVD POW Camp No. 215 operated in Ulyanovsk from October 1944 to April 1949.[80] After the war, the camp helped in the transition from a wartime to a peacetime economy. ZIS-5 trucks were no longer needed for military purposes, but light trucks were still needed for industrial tasks. Rather than moving the UAZ factory back to Moscow, it was decided to rebuild the ZIS factory in Moscow and to keep an additional truck factory in Ulyanovsk. POWs played a major role in the industrial growth of the city, contributing both to the construction of the Ulyanovsk Automobile Factory and of a large district of civilian housing for the factory workers. Initially, local leaders assigned the POWs to the construction of the thermal power station, which would power the assembly lines of the factory.[81] The secondary labor task for the POWs at the factory was to construct a foundry.[82] Smaller contingents of POWs were also assigned to working in a quarry and in road and sewer construction.[83] The other major contribution to the automotive factory was building Avtozavodskaia Ulitsa (Auto Factory Street) in an undeveloped area near the UAZ. All the houses were built in the same style by German POWs from plans drawn up by German architects. Construction began in 1944 on the grounds of the former collective farm, "Birthplace of Ilych."[84]

As figure 2.1 shows, the German POWs constructed houses in styles more akin to those in their homeland than to those in the USSR. The homes they erected near the UAZ factory had a two-story design, generally with sloped roofs, small, ornate balconies, and some stylistic embellishments in the ma-

---

79. Andy Thompson, *Cars of the Soviet Union: The Definitive History* (Yeovil, Somerset: Haynes Publishing, 2008), 36–37.

80. RGVA f. 511p, op. 1, d. 1; Veronika Chvatova, Ulrich Austermühle, and Rossija Archivnoe Agentstvo, *Orte des Gewahrsams von deutschen Kriegsgefangenen in der Sowjetunion (1941–1956): Findbuch; [Standorte von Kriegsgefangenenlagern, Arbeitsbataillonen, Friedhöfen sowie Einrichtungen des Frontlagernetzes; auf der Grundlage von Dokumenten der Kriegsgefangenenverwaltung aus dem Staatlichen Russischen Militärarchiv]* (Dresden: Stiftung Sächsische Gedenkstätten zur Erinnerung an die Opfer politischer Gewaltherrschaft, 2010), 178.

81. GANI UO, f. 8, op. 3, d. 303, l. 37.

82. GANI UO, f. 8, op. 3, d. 305, ll. 44–48.

83. GANI UO, f. 8, op. 3, d. 305, ll. 44–48.

84. GANI UO, f. 5968, op. 4 contains a series of photographs, each of which is listed as a separate delo, taken in 2015 and 2016 for the historic preservation of the Avtozavodskaia Ulitsa architecture in the wake of recent teardowns of old houses and the construction of modern, high-rise apartment buildings. The information about construction dates, architectural plans, and location of the houses is listed on page 3 of the guide to the archival collection (*opis*).

FIGURE 2.1. Apartment house at 26/10 Auto-Factory Street. Photo by author.

sonry work. Although the designs had to have been approved by local leader-ship, they indicate that the POWs were allowed to work from their own architectural traditions, with the plans presumably created by the skilled de-signers and workers among them.

As with the rest of the USSR, Ulyanovsk too suffered a large labor short-age and faced continuing shortages of food, decent housing, warm cloth-ing, and footwear. Many POWs suffered from the absence of these items. In 1945, members of the Ulyanovsk provincial party committee discussed delays in the construction of the automobile factory due to the shortage of labor:

> COMRADE ISAEV: [There are plenty of supplies], but here we are restrained
> in the labor force; how to replenish it, I do not know.
> COMRADE TERENT'EV: Why do the Germans not work?
> COMRADE ISAEV: About 600 are ill, and the others are busy.
> COMRADE TERENT'EV: How many additional people do you need?
> COMRADE ISAEV: 3,500 people are needed.[85]

---

85. GANI UO, f. 8, op. 3, d. 305, l. 26.

The largest problem the Soviet Union faced in the reconstruction effort was thus not a shortage of material supplies but one of manpower. Local camp officials deployed every able-bodied POW to one task or another, and the free population had no additional workers to give. Local leaders understood that ill prisoners could not be deployed for work but instead often needed special feeding and care.

A 1947 report to the Ulyanovsk provincial party committee, which oversaw the province, showed that the POWs made up a significant portion of the automotive factory's workforce. Table 2.2 shows the breakdown of POW assignments in the city in September 1947. POWs in Ulyanovsk were predominantly assigned to construction tasks related to the automotive factory; they made up almost half the workforce. The second-largest group of prisoners performed a variety of unnamed tasks for the MVD, also likely in construction. Of the small number of POWs who worked in food industries, 50 worked in bread factories, and an additional 150 worked on the local *sovkhoz*, or state farm. Thus, construction of factories and of infrastructure were the two primary labor assignments for POWs, and some POWs were deployed in small numbers to other necessary industries, such as food, or to less demanding labor tasks. Moreover, fully 20 percent of the POWs were unable to work, of whom 12 percent were ill and 8 percent awaited repatriation. The Ulyanovsk provincial party committee was deeply involved with reconstruction, labor, and the POWs. Although the NKVD/MVD camp leadership was largely responsible for work assignments for their prisoners, they had to contend with the demands of local leaders for workers, which created tensions between camp officials and industrial managers. In turn, central leaders in Moscow were bombarded by requests from camp officials asking for large shipments of POWs to help fulfill labor quotas in industrial enterprises in a given region or city.

To ensure the maximum labor contribution from POWs, a GUPVI directive in September 1945 instructed that they be assigned to work in jobs in their professions and fields of expertise.[86] In Camp No. 215, the order was implemented through careful tracking. Over the course of 1947, camp leaders tracked monthly not only the number of POWs but also their experience working as metallurgists, builders, engineers, doctors, electricians, automobile mechanics, and tractor drivers.[87] By 1948, their records became more standardized, as officials made greater efforts to match POWs' specialties with their work assignments. The first breakdown of POW professions from January 31, 1948, was handwritten and included the age range of the prisoners: under 18, 18–25, 25–35, 35–45, 45–50, and

---

86. GARF, f. 9401, op. 1, d. 737, l. 180–214, in Zagorul'ko, *Voennoplennye v SSSR*, 628.
87. RGVA, f. 511p, op. 1, d. 5, ll. 14, 23, 48, 73, 95, 140, 166, 193, 212, 264, and 279.

Table 2.2   German POW labor deployment in Ulyanovsk, September 1947

LABOR ASSIGNMENT	NUMBER OF POWS	PERCENTAGE OF TOTAL WORKFORCE
Automobile factories	1,150	46
Misc. MVD assignments	440	17
Food industries	200	8
Other tasks	220	9
Sick	300	12
Ready for repatriation	200	8
Total	**2,510**	

Source: GANI UO, f. 8, op. 5, d. 453, ll. 7–9.

over 50.[88] By the next month, the POW profession and age report had become a standardized GUPVI document, printed and identified as "Form No. 14." Listed as top secret, it was standardized with a few blanks for camp administrations to fill in the date, camp number, and numbers of POWs by profession, military rank, military affiliation, political affiliation, and age. The first part of the form listed the professions, and there were overarching categories for work experience such as engineering, factory worker, construction, automotive specialists, and road building.[89] Thus, camp officials attempted to create work histories for the POWs that would allow them to be used most effectively in future assignments. The leadership of Camp No. 215 filled out "Form No. 14" over the course of 1948. Camp accountants generally filled them out in the first few days of each month, though in some months they produced reports both at the beginning and end, such as for October 1948. In September 1948, the supply of standardized forms appeared to run out. From September 1948 to January 1949, the leadership of Camp No. 215 continued to produce "Form No. 14" reports, though they reverted to handwritten copies of the original template.[90] POW memoirs also attest to the camps' attempts to match POWs' previous experience with camp labor assignments. Hans Schuetz wrote, "We *vojeno plenys* (prisoners of war) had to bring the mill back into operation. Mechanics worked on the machinery and the saws."[91] The overall task was to restore the sawmill, and those with training as mechanics had to put their skilled trade to use with the machinery.

---

88. RGVA, f. 511p, op. 1, d. 6, ll. 23 and 23ob.

89. RGVA, f. 511p, op. 1, d. 6, ll. 48 and 48ob.

90. RGVA, f. 511p, op. 1, d. 6, ll. 99 and 99ob, 120 and 120ob, 181 and 181ob, 200 and 200ob, 239 and 239ob, 250 and 250ob, 277 and 277ob, 303 and 303ob, 323 and 323ob.

91. Schuetz, *Davai, Davai!* 53.

Although Ulyanovsk was not necessarily the most significant location for German POWs, it serves as a good example of how national directives worked on a local level. The POWs helped construct an automotive factory, which would produce one of the major brands of the Soviet automobile industry. They also fostered the city's growth by providing the housing stock needed for those moving into the city and working in the factory after it became fully operational. The same type of construction, which helped contribute to the development of the postwar economy, took place in many other provincial cities or industrial centers in the nearby Urals or Volga region, such as Chelyabinsk, Sverdlovsk (present-day Yekaterinburg), Magnitogorsk, or Kuybyshev (present-day Samara).[92]

Mapping of German POW Camps

Although archival evidence details the assignments of POWs in the period before and after the end of the war, there is little documentation for postwar labor contributions of the POWs. Despite the Soviet Union having a centrally planned economy, there was no central repository of available and declassified documents relating to the economic contributions of the German POWs.[93] Information about POW labor is instead contained within individual folders for each of the thousands of camps that operated across the territory of the Soviet Union. For any given camp, there are either a series of yearly folders or camp histories produced after their closing.[94] None of this information has been centrally tabulated. Thus, the economic contribution of the German POWs to the Soviet economy can be difficult to assess. Geographic Information System (GIS) mapping of the locations of the POW camps has proven to be a means to work around this problem with documentary sources. This section presents a series of maps analyzing the locations of the German POW camps; they plot the intersections between camp locations, resource deposits, industrial centers, and transportation hubs in the Soviet

92. Chvatova et al., *Orte des Gewahrsams*, 84, 155, 178, 182.

93. Attempts to find central planning documents or records of POW labor contributions were undertaken in the State Archive of the Russian Federation (GARF), the Russian State Military Archive (RGVA), and the Russian State Archive of Economics (RGAE).

94. See, for example, RGVA f. 47p, op. 22, d. 1, ll. 8–122, which is a report for the history of MVD POW Camp No. 108 from 1943 to 1950 in the city of Stalingrad. This report includes a breakdown of the labor contributions of the camp during its existence. RGVA f. 511p, op. 1, d. 1, ll. 1–81 is a similar history for Camp No. 215 in Ulyanovsk. Not every camp had a central history file such as this. For example, RGVA f. 496, op. 1, d. 6, ll. 1–26 discusses the labor contributions of POW Camp No. 315 in the Dnepropetrovskaya Oblast' of Ukraine for 1945.

Union. Appendix 2 provides a full explanation of the steps taken to produce the maps, including the choices made when cleaning the data and attempting to find coordinates for the nearest settlements associated with a given camp.

POW Camps in the Entire Soviet Union

During and after World War II, 4,313 German POW camps operated throughout the territory of the entire Soviet Union, in every republic with the exception of Tajikistan. Most of these camps operated in the republics that had seen the fiercest fighting of the war. As figure 2.2 illustrates, many of the German POW camps were concentrated in areas formerly occupied by the Wehrmacht, indicating that Soviet officials deployed German POWs to rebuild what they had destroyed. It must be noted that all camp locations are approximate in

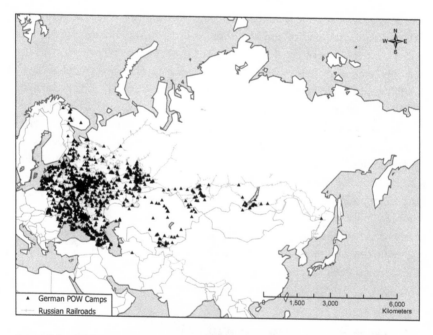

FIGURE 2.2.   POW camps in the entire USSR, 1941–1956. I used the camps from Chvatova et al., *Orte des Gewahrsams von deutschen Kriegsgefangenen in der Sowjetunion (1941–1956)*, 12–247, to look up approximate camp locations based on the villages or cities given. The railroad lines for Russia are modern, although the basic rail lines, including the main lines of the Trans-Siberian railway, existed long before the start of World War II. I downloaded the railroad information from "Transportation," Land Resources of Russia, last modified 2002, http:// webarchive.iiasa.ac.at/Research/FOR/russia_cd/trans.htm. Note that the All-Union maps in this series represent 4,266 camps of the 4,313 listed in the book. Some camp locations were unfindable.

Table 2.3   German POW camps USSR, 1941–1956

REPUBLIC	CAMPS	OPEN YEAR	CLOSE YEAR	TOTAL YEARS OF OPERATION
Armenia	18	1944	1949	5
Azerbaijan	56	1944	1950	6
Belarus	199	1944	1951	7
Estonia	66	1944	1950	6
Georgia	70	1941	1950	9
Kazakhstan	102	1943	1950	7
Kyrgyzstan	16	1945	1948	3
Latvia	102	1943	1949	6
Lithuania	42	1944	1949	5
Moldova	19	1944	1948	4
Russia	2858	1941	1956	15
Tajikistan	0	–	–	–
Turkmenistan	4	1943	1948	5
Ukraine	699	1942	1954	12
Uzbekistan	62	1943	1949	6

Source: Chvatova et al., *Orte des Gewahrsams von deutschen Kriegsgefangenen in der Sowjetunion (1941–1956)*, 12–247.

these maps. They are not indicative of where each camp was located. Camps could have been contained within the city or on the outskirts.

Of the 4,313 camps located throughout the Soviet Union, 3,986 were in Belarus, Estonia, Latvia, Lithuania, Moldova, Russia, and Ukraine, all republics that were either wholly or heavily occupied by the Nazis. Of the total number of camps, 2,858, or 66 percent, were in the Russian Republic. Although these camps were sited throughout both European and Asiatic Russia, they were concentrated primarily in the following areas: those that had seen fighting during the war, those in the industrial centers in the Ural Mountain range, and those along the Trans-Siberian Railroad as figure 2.2 illustrates. The republic that had the highest number of camps outside fighting territories was Kazakhstan, where POWs worked in the coal industry.[95] Table 2.3 presents the data for the number of camps per republic, their opening and closing dates, and their total years of operation.

As table 2.3 shows, many of the camps opened in republics during or after 1944 as the Red Army was marching toward Berlin. The vast majority of camps did not open until after the Battle of Stalingrad (1942–1943), when the Red Army began capturing large numbers of POWs. The republics of Belarus, Kazakhstan, Russia, and Ukraine had both the greatest number of camps and the longest-running ones. This is likely because Belarus, Russia, and Ukraine

---

95. GARF, f. 9414, op. 1, d. 328, ll. 28–33.

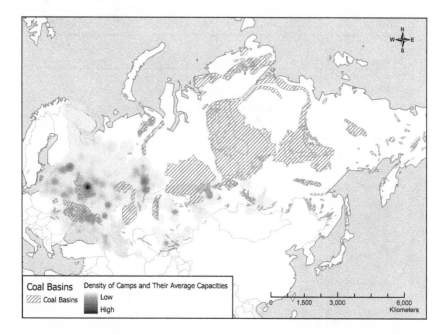

FIGURE 2.3.   Soviet coal basins and German POW population densities, 1941–1956. Coal data from Michael Brownfield et al., "Coal Quality and Resources of the Former Soviet Union: An ArcView Project," last modified 2001, accessed October 24, 2017, https://pubs.usgs.gov/of /2001/ofr-01-104/readme.htm. A color version of this map is in appendix 2.

were heavily damaged by fighting, and Ukraine, Russia, and Kazakhstan were the central sites of the Soviet coal industry. Figure 2.3 depicts coal basins in relation to the density of camps.[96] Republics such as Armenia, Kyrgyzstan, Moldova, Turkmenistan, and Uzbekistan all had small numbers of camps that generally did not run for more than five years. The industries in these regions were less vital to the long-term restoration of the national economy.

Most of the camps closed between 1948 and 1950, which indicates that their use was largely related to postwar reconstruction and the Fourth Five-Year Plan of 1946–1950, aimed at economic restoration.[97] Although the economy was only fully restored by 1953 at the time of Stalin's death, efforts were well underway by 1950, and a considerable portion of the damage had been repaired. By

---

96. For figure 2.3, density was calculated by taking the average of a camp's minimum and maximum capacity as listed in Chvatova et al., *Orte des Gewahrsams.* Some camps grew over time, whereas others shrank. It is unclear whether camps tended to operate at, under, or over capacity. Of the 4,313 German POW camps listed in Chvatova et al., 76 had no information related to their capacity; thus, those camps are not represented in the capacity heatmap.

97. Eugène Zaleski, Marie-Christine MacAndrew, and John Hampton Moore, *Stalinist Planning for Economic Growth, 1933–1952* (Chapel Hill: University of North Carolina Press, 1980), 347.

this point, POW numbers had dwindled. Their labor was still used, but they had become pawns in diplomatic negotiations as the Cold War began to intensify.

The need to hold the POWs as a captive labor force also decreased in these later years as the Gulag population grew amidst a new wave of postwar crackdowns. During the war years, many Gulag inmates either were freed to fight for the Red Army or died. As the Gulag population decreased, the increasing POW population filled the labor gap. After the war, the opposite held true. With the cessation of hostilities, the number of newly captured German soldiers could only decrease, whereas arrests led to the increase in the Gulag population. The Gulag population increased from 601,000 at the beginning of 1946 to 809,000 in 1947, and then to 1.1 million in 1948. These increases in the population coincided with a wave of arrests and sentencings for "counterrevolution" and for various violations of the draconian labor laws still in place.[98]

The distribution of camps across the Soviet Union also corresponded to population centers, to territories that saw the fiercest fighting and destruction, and to centers of Soviet industry in the Urals region. The siting of POW camps followed a very different pattern from that of Gulag camps that tried, although unsuccessfully, to geographically isolate their captives from the free population.[99] A comparison of the sites of German POW camps from 1941 to 1956 with the locations of Gulag camps in 1945 and 1946 illustrates this difference. Figure 2.4 shows the locations of headquarters of Gulag camps, around which hundreds of subcamps could be associated with each main camp. Gulag camps tended to cluster more in the north of the RSFSR and in remote regions of western Siberia. In general, POW camps did not operate in these inhospitable areas. For example, Soviet authorities did not place any German POW camps in the vicinity of two of the most notoriously harsh Gulag settlements, Vorkuta in the north and Kolyma in western Siberia.

Digital mapping has altered many of the commonly held notions about both the Gulag system and the POW camps. The formative study on Gulag maps, *Mapping the Gulag*, challenges the notion that the Gulag only existed in the frozen reaches of Siberia. Many Germans also associated the GUPVI camp system with Siberia and snow, although mapping shows that most GUPVI camps operated outside Siberia. Those that did operate in Siberia did not experience the region's harshest climate extremes. Whereas some Gulag camps existed in the Soviet Union's coldest places, figure 2.5 shows that this was not the case for the GUPVI system.

---

98. Barnes, *Death and Redemption*, 157–159; Barenberg, *Gulag Town, Company Town*, 59–63.

99. Bell, *Stalin's Gulag at War*, 7, 63, 69; Barnes, *Death and Redemption*, 7, 14; Barenberg, *Gulag Town, Company Town*, 41, 97.

FIGURE 2.4. The distribution of gulag camps in USSR, 1945–1946. Judith Pallot et al., "1945–1946," Mapping the Gulag, last modified December 9, 2009, http://www.gulagmaps.org /maps/map.php?series=1&map=4546.

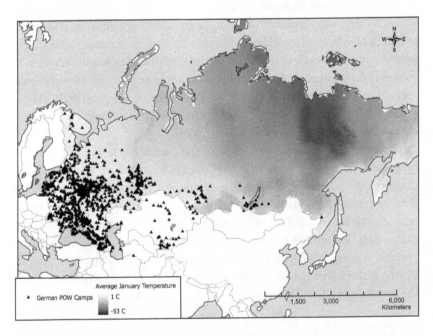

FIGURE 2.5. German POW camps 1941–1956 and average January temperature. Temperature data from "Climate," Land Resources of Russia, last modified 2002, http://webarchive.iiasa.ac .at/Research/FOR/russia_cd/climate.htm. Color version of map is in appendix 2.

Although German POW camps did expose their inmates to temperatures more extreme than those of Germany, most of the camps existed in the more temperate European regions of the Soviet Union and Russia.

Herein lies one of the greatest differences between the GUPVI and Gulag systems. As Wilson Bell, Steven Barnes, and Alan Barenberg point out, Soviet authorities tried, although often failed, to isolate Gulag inmates from the free population geographically because of concerns about the potential for prisoners to corrupt free populations.[100] However, Soviet authorities did not randomly choose the locations for Gulag camps. In his study of Vorkuta, Barenberg shows that a mix of factors determined the camp's location, including the need to develop a rich coal basin in an inhospitable area and to support internal colonization of the vast expanses of the Soviet Union. For Vorkuta and other Gulag locations, forced prison labor enabled the state to address labor shortages in these remote regions while simultaneously isolating perceived internal enemies from potential bases of support.[101] Although the locations of Gulag camps correlated to the harshest climates and most remote regions of the Soviet Union, the need to develop important extractive industries directed their placement, rather than the desire to punish.

The difference in the locations of Gulag and GUPVI forced laborers likely stems from the conditions of the war. The German POWs needed to rebuild what they had destroyed, both from an economic standpoint and to fulfill notions of postwar justice. Employing them in the industrial and population centers of the Soviet Union accomplished both tasks. Soviet authorities also recognized that the POWs would either die or return to Germany. Unlike Soviet citizens, who could remain in remote regions around the camps after their release, the Germans could not be used to colonize the internal expanses of the Soviet Union. Although a handful may have remained, the overwhelming majority returned to the places in Germany where they had either enlisted in the army or been drafted.[102] Memoir accounts and returnee interviews also overwhelmingly state that the men wanted to go home as soon as possible.[103]

100. Bell, *Stalin's Gulag at War*, 7, 63, 69; Barnes, *Death and Redemption*, 7, 14; Barenberg, *Gulag Town, Company Town*, 41, 97.

101. Alan Barenberg, "'Discovering' Vorkuta: Science and Colonization in the Early Gulag," *Gulag Studies* 4 (2001): 25–28.

102. See GARF, f. 9526, op. 6, d. 508, ll. 66–68, for an example of how Soviets tracked not only the number of those repatriated in a given convoy or period but also how many Germans returned to which occupation zone of Germany.

103. See GARF, f. 9401, op. 2, d. 169, ll. 367–76, for examples of German POW reactions in May 1947 to the news that they would be held in Soviet captivity until December 1948. Soviet authorities polled the POWs to assess their reactions and presented this information to Stalin, Beria, Molotov, and Zhdanov. Learning about their continued incarceration depressed most of the Germans. Memoir accounts vary drastically in terms of tone, composition, and reaction to captivity, but every memoir is

FIGURE 2.6.   German POW camps in the USSR, December 1942.

Even if more had been given the opportunity to stay, it is unlikely that many would have chosen to do so. Thus, employing the POWs in the population-rich and previously more developed regions of the Soviet Union outweighed concerns of escape, fraternizing with Soviet citizens, and punishment.

A temporal analysis of the GUPVI camp system also supports the argument that labor needs shaped the initial organization of POW camps. Figure 2.6 shows those camps operating in December 1942.[104] At this time, there were only a handful of POW camps, primarily in the European parts of the RSFSR and in the industrial center of the Urals. After the major victory at Stalingrad and the subsequent increase of German captives, the camp system rapidly increased in size. Figure 2.7 shows the growth in the camp system by June 1943.

The continued success of the Red Army on the battlefield resulted in the vast expansion of the GUPVI camp system, which peaked after the war's end. Figure 2.8 shows the extent of the camp system in June 1945 when camps operated across

---

most descriptive in two parts: capture and release. Many memoirists expressed elation when given the news that they will be returned to Germany. See Ernst Kehler, *Einblicke und Einsichten: Erinnerungen* (Berlin: Dietz, 1989); Schuetz, *Davai, Davail*; Otto Rühle, *Die Ärzte von Stalingrad: Genesung in Jelabuga: Kessel Stalingrad—Antifaschule für ein neues Deutschland—autobiographischer Bericht* (Berlin: Wünsche, 2007); or Popp and Dulias, *Another Bowl of Kapusta* for examples of positive attitudes regarding release.

104. See appendix 2 for a full series of maps from December 1942 to December 1955.

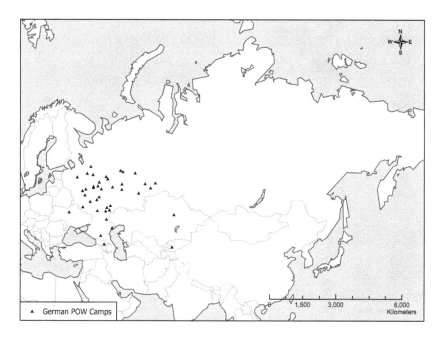

FIGURE 2.7. German POW camps in the USSR, June 1943.

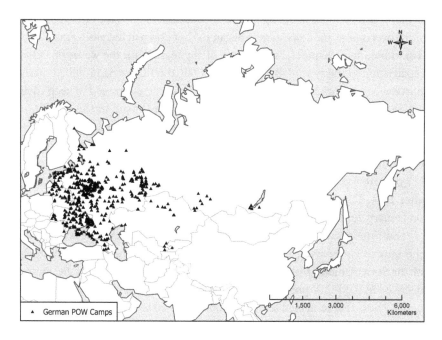

FIGURE 2.8. German POW camps in the USSR, June 1945.

FIGURE 2.9.   German POW camps in the USSR, December 1950.

almost the entirety of the Soviet Union, though they were densely concentrated in places that had seen active fighting or in industrial or resource centers.

Between 1945 and 1949, camps began to shut down in increasing numbers. The subsequent chapters discuss some of the reasons for the waves of POW repatriation in this period. By the end of 1949, the POWs had fulfilled many postwar economic tasks. Soviet authorities, however, continued to keep their German captives after 1949 for diplomatic reasons linked to the Cold War rather than economic ones. Figure 2.9 illustrates the much-reduced camp system in December 1950, showing that by this point the small number of camps could only have had a minimal economic impact. From 1950 to 1955, the number of camps kept decreasing. Only one GUPVI forced-labor camp remained after 1954. This last remaining camp, that of Kirsanov near Tambov, closed on January 28, 1956. Figure 2.10 shows its location.

Thus, the growth of the camp system over the course of the war and in the immediate postwar era corresponded directly to the economic needs of the Soviet Union. With each passing year after the war's end and the annual decrease in the POW population, the camps provided less and less economic utility. Those that remained served to house the final few thousand POWs who had not been sentenced in war tribunals. Chapter 4 discusses the release of these last prisoners from the Soviet Union in 1955 and 1956.

FIGURE 2.10.   German POW camps in the USSR, December 1955.

POW Camps in the Ukrainian Soviet Socialist Republic

A close examination of the POW camps that operated in the Ukrainian SSR emphasizes the economic contribution of the German prisoners in a contained geographic area that was severely damaged by the war.[105] According to Chvatova and colleagues' published list of camps created from documents from the Russian State Military Archive, 699 POW camps operated in the Ukrainian SSR from 1941 to 1956.[106] Of these, 672 were mapped in the USGS survey on coal resources of the former Soviet Union and the ArcGIS World Cities map layer.[107] As figure 2.11 shows, the largest group of camps were located around Kiev, the republic's capital; Kharkov, a major industrial center; and Stalino and

---

105. These maps denote camps that were in the Ukrainian SSR at the time. They do not account for Crimea becoming part of the Ukrainian SSR in 1954. Those camps are listed and accounted for under the RSFSR in both Chvatova et al. and my maps. This was pointed out on November 10, 2017, by Karl Qualls while a portion of this chapter was presented at the ASEEES annual convention. This is by no means a political statement on the part of the author; rather, it is a choice to use and account for camps according to contemporary Soviet borders.

106. Chvatova et al., *Orte des Gewahrsams*, 198–235.

107. The GoogleMaps script and hand cleaning of data returned approximate locations for only 672 of the 699 camps. A number of camps were excluded from these visualizations because they were listed as mining settlements around certain cities. These mining settlements were removed from the dataset because there was no way of knowing where exactly they were located outside the nearest major city.

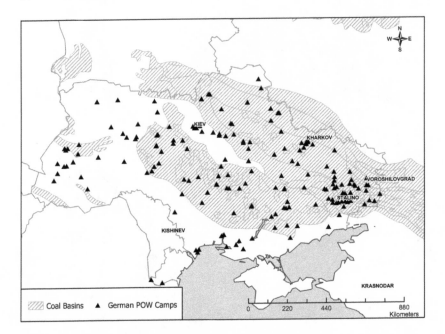

FIGURE 2.11. German POW camps and coal basins in Ukraine, 1942–1954. Chvatova et al., *Orte des Gewahrsams von deutschen Kriegsgefangenen in der Sowjetunion (1941–1956)*, 198–235, and Brownfield et al., "Coal Quality and Resources of the Former Soviet Union: An ArcView Project," last modified 2001, accessed October 24, 2017, https://pubs.usgs.gov/of/2001/ofr-01-104/readme.htm.

Voroshilovgrad, powerful centers of coal and metallurgical production. For republican and city-level Ukrainian officials, the POWs provided a perfect solution to a lack of local laborers for reconstruction tasks ranging from housing construction and restoring factories to mining coal.[108]

Figure 2.11 also illustrates that almost three-quarters of all the POW camps were in the coal-rich regions of Ukraine. Furthermore, large concentrations of POW camps were located near cities whose economies revolved around coal extraction, such as present-day Donetsk or Luhansk, previously known as Stalino and Voroshilovgrad. Ukraine's rich coal fields were a major source of production for the entire Soviet Union, and many of the POWs incarcerated in this republic worked in the coal industry. The coal mines had initially been flooded or blocked by party activists as the Red Army retreated to deprive the invading Germans of their use.[109] Later, the Germans in retreat destroyed

---

108. Martin Blackwell, *Kyiv as Regime City: The Return of Soviet Power after Nazi Occupation* (Rochester: University of Rochester Press, 2016), 54–56.

109. Wendy Z. Goldman and Donald A. Filtzer, *Fortress Dark and Stern: The Soviet Home Front during World War II* (New York, NY: Oxford University Press, 2021), 17–18.

whatever sites they had restored. Coal was one of the foundational resources for the reconstruction effort. Coal mining was also one of the most dangerous occupations in the Soviet Union. In 1943, workers in the coal mines in the Kuzbass region suffered one accident for every six workers. The Soviet authorities had a very hard time finding voluntary free workers, due in part to the danger and the strenuous nature of coal mining.[110] German prisoners served as a ready labor source to circumnavigate some of these labor issues in the nation's most important coal basins. As previously noted, Beria and Stalin closely tracked the totals of German POWs and personally assigned them to specific commissariats, industries, and cities, viewing coal mining as a priority.[111]

As figure 2.11 highlights, there were a large number of POW camps in the Luhansk and Donetsk regions. The camps cluster near the increased concentration of black bands on the map, which indicates a higher concentration of coal deposits. POWs in these camps were clearly employed in coal mining, which is also indicated by GUPVI documentation that lists camps in those regions not only by the cities but also by the mines they served. For example, there were camps at mines 5, 6, 7, 8, 12, and 31 in Stalino (Donetsk) alone.[112] POW memoirs also note the importance of the Donetsk coal basin. Ernst Günther Schenck, who served as a doctor at a Moscow hospital for POWs, wrote that many POWs in that hospital "stayed together until the fall of 1947, when the great upheaval began again: some of the sick were transported home, the majority to the coal mines in the Donets Basin."[113]

A temporal analysis of the POW camps in Ukraine reveals that most of the camps were opened in 1944 and 1945 as the Red Army advanced westward into Europe, and most closed between 1945 and 1949. Table 2.4 presents the opening and closing years of the 693 POW camps in Ukraine.

Again, the trends in the opening and closing of camps denote the relationship between the military progress of the war and the needs of postwar reconstruction. Once Ukraine was liberated and large numbers of German soldiers were captured, the NKVD had both the opportunity and the need to open camps in the territory. The successful military campaigns on the road to Berlin continued to result in an increasing number of prisoners. These men were then put to work on reconstruction projects already underway. For

---

110. Goldman and Filtzer, *Fortress Dark and Stern*, 276.

111. GARF contains a number of documents in which Stalin himself ordered or tracked the assignments of the German POWs. See, for example, f. 9401, op. 2, d. 137, ll. 366–377; f. 9401, op. 2, d. 95, ll. 36–38; and f. 9414, op. 1, d. 328, ll. 21–27, 28–33, and 51 front and back.

112. Chvatova et al., *Orte des Gewahrsams*, 224.

113. Ernst Günther Schenck, *Woina Plenni: 10 Jahre Gefangenschaft in sowjetischen Lagern* (Stockach: Bavarian Connection, 1985), 57.

Table 2.4   POW camps opening and closings in
Ukraine, 1941–1956

YEAR	NUMBER OF CAMPS OPENED	NUMBER OF CAMPS CLOSED
1941	0	0
1942	1	0
1943	3	0
1944	183	4
1945	391	201
1946	20	84
1947	53	40
1948	31	186
1949	8	128
1950	1	43
1951	0	1
1952	0	2
1953	0	0
1954	1	4
1955	0	0
1956	0	0

Source: Chvatova et al., *Orte des Gewahrsams von deutschen Kriegsgefangenen in der Sowjetunion (1941–1956),* 198–235.

Ukraine, and for the camps across the USSR, the largest number of camps were
opened in 1945 when the highest number of newly captured Germans became
available as workers. Not everyone, of course, was able to work. After the cessation of hostilities in 1945, illness, injury, the restoration of the economy,
and growing Cold War tensions caused camp populations to decrease and
camps to shut down. In general, the large-scale closing of camps between 1946
and 1949 coincided with the country's Fourth Five-Year Plan, which ran from
1946 to 1950 and aimed to restore the nation to its prewar economic level.[114]

Over the course of the 1930s, the Gulag system had become an important part
of the Soviet economy, which relied on forced labor for large-scale construction projects and the extraction of raw materials. Although scholars continue
to debate the economic effectiveness of prison labor, as well as the larger purpose of the Gulag, this chapter shows that one important subset of the Soviet
state's forced labor population, the German POWs, were consciously deployed
by the state to serve economic goals of reconstruction. Moreover, the data

114. Zaleski et al., *Stalinist Planning for Economic Growth,* 347.

reveal that German POWs provided significant contributions to the Soviet economy.

From their initial mass captures in 1943 through 1950 and the fulfillment of the Fourth Five-Year Plan, German POWs played an important role in the Soviet economy. After Germany's capitulation on May 9, 1945, German POWs actively worked to repair the massive wartime destruction, helping offset the enormous Soviet death toll. Although forcing German prisoners to rebuild the nation that they had destroyed was a distinct form of punishment with political meaning, the use of forced labor of German POWs was primarily motivated by economic needs. After releasing the ill or those incapable of physical labor, the NKVD distributed the remaining 1,666,391 German POWs within an already established and functioning forced-labor system, where they made definitive contributions to the Soviet economy. Soviet leaders such as Stalin, Beria, and Molotov were deeply involved in the deployment of the POWs, choosing their labor assignments and closely tracking their contributions. The POWs were viewed as an important labor resource for the Soviet economy. Their significance is further substantiated by the competition over, and requests for, their services. Appeals for workers by a variety of ministries. as well as the details of labor contracts between camps and local industries, reveal how necessary the POWs were to the economic projects of the country. Indeed, administrative directives regarding the German POWs were consistently motivated by economic concerns. The NKVD/MVD sought to extract the highest possible levels of production from their POW population with the lowest resource investment. The camps were expected to become self-sustaining.

Mapping analysis reinforces and details the economic contributions of the POWs. The geographic placement of the camps corresponded both to what had been occupied territories that had been ravaged by the war and to key industrial and resource centers. Camps were not placed in harsh regions to punish or exterminate the POWs, but rather where they could make a substantial contribution to the economy. Although forced labor may not have been as productive or cost effective as free labor, it contributed vitally to postwar reconstruction, especially amid the terrible shortage of men and women caused by war losses. The process of reconstruction was largely completed by 1950. Only after the economy had stabilized, and Soviet officials had repatriated most of the POWs, did the Soviet government hold the remaining prisoners for political rather than economic reasons. While economics primarily determined camp conditions and POW incarceration, politics also played an important role in the POW experience. Camp officials expended considerable effort to reeducate German POWs and use them for propaganda efforts on repatriation after exhausting their economic utility.

Chapter 3

Antifascist Reeducation and Germans as Propaganda Agents

Although the focus on labor productivity primarily dictated POW life and conditions, political education also played an important role in camp life and repatriation. Previous experience with Gulag camps not only shaped POW labor assignments but also reeducation. The Cultural-Education Department of the Gulag sought to instill proper socialist values among those believed to be redeemable through cultural means such as newspapers, theater troupes, film screenings, and sports competitions.[1] In the GUPVI, the Antifascist Reeducation Department used the same types of resources as did the Gulag administration in attempting to transform former German soldiers into antifascists and socialists. The regimented structure of the camps provided Soviet officials with a large-scale mechanism to reshape Germans both during and after the war for different goals: inducing the surrender of German soldiers and reeducating them to bring about a transformation of the German nation.

During the war years, the GUPVI Antifascist Reeducation Department provided the Red Army with propaganda to be distributed among soldiers on

---

1. Steven A. Barnes, *Death and Redemption: The Gulag and the Shaping of Soviet Society* (Princeton, NJ: Princeton University Press, 2011), 57–58; Wilson T. Bell, *Stalin's Gulag at War: Forced Labour, Mass Death, and Soviet Victory in the Second World War* (Toronto: University of Toronto Press, 2018), 44; Alan Barenberg, *Gulag Town, Company Town: Forced Labor and Its Legacy in Vorkuta*, (New Haven: Yale University Press, 2014), 82–83; Steven Maddox, "Gulag Football: Competitive and Recreational Sport in Stalin's System of Forced Labor," *Kritika: Explorations in Russian and Eurasian History* 19, no. 3 (2018): 510.

the German frontlines. From 1942 until May 8, 1945, all political work with POWs had as its aims ending the war with Hitler and making peace with the USSR. This work included arranging meetings between exiled German communists and sympathetic captured Germans, especially high-ranking officers, and producing leaflets and radio broadcasts geared to encouraging members of the Wehrmacht to surrender, denounce Hitler, and end the war. Although not inconsequential, this wartime antifascist work with POWs paled in comparison to the massive propaganda efforts targeted at POWs and implemented after war's end.

In addition to exposing all returnees to some antifascist reeducation, Soviet leaders enrolled smaller numbers of men in intensive antifascist programs in both the Gulag and POW camps. Criminals and political prisoners in the Gulag experienced different lives in the system. Generally, political prisoners did not belong to the category of prisoners who could be reeducated through labor and cultural activities. As Steven Barnes notes, "Educational activities in the Gulag were never uniform. They always served to further distinguish prisoners from one another."[2] Likewise, not every prisoner in the GUPVI system received the same antifascist education or associated privileges such as early release. Although most POWs returned to Germany after the war because they were ill or injured, select groups of specially trained, actively antifascist POWs returned to all four occupation zones of Germany to engage in agitation and propaganda (agitprop) work. Before these men returned home, the Soviet leadership assumed that they needed to be properly reeducated and refashioned into antifascists. As was the case in the Gulag camps, corrective training would be provided to make this possible. Once they had undergone a significant transformation, the POWs could return home and help their fellow citizens develop a proper prosocialist and pro-Soviet worldview.

The ideological training of German POWs constituted a critical part of the POW experience. Experiences of former POWs attest to the prevalence of these antifascist activities; after being repatriated, they often described the reeducation system to the staff of Caritas, the German Catholic relief organization. They also wrote extensively in their memoirs about their experiences with political reeducation. The tone and content of these memoirs changed over time as political and cultural environments changed. Those returnees who resettled in the former GDR commonly wrote narratives about antifascist transformation, and the East German regime publicly lauded these men as antifascist heroes. After reunification, some of these men were demoralized by the collapse of the GDR and revised earlier narratives to reflect a more critical stance toward their

---

2. Barnes, *Death and Redemption*, 58.

antifascist reeducation in the Soviet Union.[3] Not surprisingly, memoirs written by those who returned to West Germany and those written after German reunification in 1990 generally did not write about antifascist reeducation positively, but the schooling left an impact on these men as well. Two memoirs written after reunification, Schuetz's *Davai Davai!* and Gruber's *My Odyssey thru Hell*, include detailed accounts of antifascist work among POWs.[4]

The West German government also acknowledged the centrality of the antifascist program to the POW experience in the Soviet Union when it created the Maschke Commission, the Scientific Commission for the History of the German Prisoners of War, in 1957 to study POW captivity in Allied hands.[5] The commission acquired much of its information from questionnaires completed by returnees. These questionnaires included space for the former POWs to describe their experiences with the antifascist organization in the Soviet camps.[6] Unpublished archival collections also include recollections of the antifascist apparatus.[7] Although the returnees may not have accomplished all the prosocialist goals that Soviet and East German leaders first set forth, the memory of the reeducation program stayed with the men long after they returned home.

Repatriation of men who had received antifascist training after the war occurred in three major waves. The first wave took place in summer 1945, immediately after German capitulation. The next wave occurred throughout 1949 and early into 1950 in response to the formal establishment of the Federal Republic of Germany (FRG; West Germany) and the German Democratic Republic (GDR; East Germany) in May and October 1949, respectively. The final wave of repatriation occurred in 1953 in response to amnesties and releases of prisoners following Stalin's death in March and a major uprising in East Germany in June.

3. Christiane Wienand, *Returning Memories: Former Prisoners of War in Divided and Reunited Germany* (Rochester, NY: Camden House, 2015), 4, 87, 136–148.

4. A. D. Hans Schuetz, *Davai, Davai! Memoir of a German Prisoner of World War II in the Soviet Union* (Jefferson, NC: McFarland, 1997); Hans Gruber, *My Odyssey thru Hell* (Bloomington, IN: AuthorHouse, 2013).

5. Jay Lockenour, *Soldiers as Citizens: Former Wehrmacht Officers in the Federal Republic of Germany, 1945–1955* (Lincoln: University of Nebraska Press, 2001), 204n32; Rolf Steininger, "Some Reflections on the Maschke Commission," in *Eisenhower and the German POWs: Facts against Falsehood*, ed. Günter Bischof and Stephen E. Ambrose (Baton Rouge: Louisiana State University Press, 1992), 171–173.

6. "Plan der Wissenschaftlichen Kommission," BA-M, B 205/1771, S. 13

7. Josepf Kayser papers, assorted letters in folder 3 (POW camp pastoral care correspondences, 1 of 2), Hoover Institution Archives and Walter Kraemer typescript: And hell on earth, page 138, Hoover Institution Archives.

Antifascist Training during World War II

The capture of German soldiers and their long-term detainment as prisoners of war led quickly to the establishment of an antifascist reeducation program within Soviet POW camps. During the war, its focus was to develop a group of antifascist pro-Soviet Germans who would later help produce propaganda materials that urged German surrender. These German-language materials would then be disseminated among the frontline troops of the Wehrmacht.[8] Even though these efforts had little impact on the war itself, the structure of the GUPVI camp system, like that of the Gulag camps, provided a conducive environment for mass reeducation programs. German POWs were quite literally a captive audience: they had no choice but to participate in GUPVI's antifascist programs. The antifascist reeducation system grew and became increasingly important in the postwar years.

The UPVI-NKVD centralized its wartime antifascist efforts in Camp No. 27 in Krasnogorsk, located twenty-seven kilometers from the center of Moscow; it opened on June 5, 1942.[9] Although a formal curriculum for antifascist training had yet to be standardized in the camps, Camp No. 27 had its own political apparatus, which engaged in mass political work among the POWs. Camp officials crafted a program for reeducation based on interviewing their captives and assessing their political leanings.[10] The Soviet leadership understood that some of the POWs could be former communists or left-wing party members. Not all of them had fled Germany or been persecuted within Germany. Characteristic interview responses of prisoners with different political leanings were collected and sent for review to the head of the UPVI-NKVD in both July and December 1942. The July report listed those POWs who saw themselves as actively antifascist and provided an in-depth discussion of morale among the German forces.[11] As the war progressed and the Red Army began to mount successful offensives on its home territory, the population of Camp No. 27 grew. In December 1942 alone, the camp nearly doubled in size, from 482 prisoners to 747.[12] When 316 prisoners arrived at

---

8. Allied forces extensively used aerial propaganda leaflets for psychological warfare. Brian S. Gunderson, "Leaflet Dropping Operations in World War II," *Air Power History* 45, no. 1 (Spring 1998): 28–39.

9. Veronika Chvatova, Ulrich Austermühle, and Rossija Archivnoe Agentstvo, *Orte des Gewahrsams von deutschen Kriegsgefangenen in der Sowjetunion (1941–1956): Findbuch; [Standorte von Kriegsgefangenenlagern, Arbeitsbataillonen, Friedhöfen sowie Einrichtungen des Frontlagernetzes; auf der Grundlage von Dokumenten der Kriegsgefangenenverwaltung aus dem Staatlichen Russischen Militärarchiv]* (Dresden: Stiftung Sächsische Gedenkstätten zur Erinnerung an die Opfer politischer Gewaltherrschaft, 2010), 110.

10. RGVA, f. 105p, op. 2, d. 11, ll. 40–54 and ll. 1–9.

11. RGVA, f. 105p, op. 2, d. 11, 40–54, esp. ll. 40–41 and 44.

12. RGVA, f. 105p, op. 2, d. 11, ll. 1–9, esp. ll. 2–4.

the camp between December 21 and 22, camp staff conducted individual conversations with 183 of them: of that subset, 24 claimed to be antifascists, 63 reported being on the side of antifascism, 20 described themselves as fascists, 5 said they were on the side of fascism, and 71 deemed themselves to be apolitical. Unsurprisingly, those who identified as antifascist felt that Hitler was responsible for the war, that Germany would lose, and that the fighting would end very badly for their nation. Those who remained staunchly fascist in captivity told their captors that morale at the front and on the home front was high and that Germans both on the frontlines and at home were well supplied, implying that they were capable of fighting for a long time. The fascists felt that ultimately Germany would triumph in the war.

Much of the initial antifascist work done with POWs centered on the production of leaflets or of radio broadcasts, forms of psychological warfare that sought to motivate Wehrmacht soldiers to desert and surrender to Red Army forces. Walter Ulbricht and Wilhelm Pieck, socialists exiled in Moscow who would become two of East Germany's most important political officials, worked to create materials that would undermine the morale of the German forces. Ulbricht personally oversaw German-language programming for Radio Moscow and drove loudspeaker trucks in the line of fire at the Battle of Stalingrad.[13] Exiled German communists worked with captured German soldiers to create anti-Nazi propaganda for dissemination to the German Army.

Initially, as the Nazis advanced far into the territory of the Soviet Union and were convinced they would quickly destroy the USSR, the German military leadership dismissed Soviet propaganda efforts as desperate and outright lies. These early wartime materials consisted of either signed written testimonies or recordings of captive Germans describing the good conditions of their captivity. The Wehrmacht Information Office (Wehrmachtsauskunftstelle, WASt) acknowledged the existence of these materials but considered them to be inaccurate.[14] Wehrmacht officers were convinced that Germans in Soviet camps received poor treatment, little to no medical care, and very small rations. They denied the veracity of any signed accounts or radio broadcasts from German POWs. Moreover, according to the information bureau, there was no assurance that the men named in Soviet captivity reports were still alive. That is, Soviet propagandists could have taken names of real troops from deceased soldiers' identification tags to create these materials. One internal memo from late October 1942 stated that the claim of Soviet propaganda that

13. Catherine Epstein, *The Last Revolutionaries: German Communists and Their Century* (Cambridge, MA: Harvard University Press, 2009), 83–84.
14. Herrn Oberst Sonntag, October 7, 1942, BA-M, RW 48/10.

the Red Army did not shoot its captives was unbelievable.[15] The Red Army produced many leaflets for the German forces with assurances that it did not, and would not, shoot any German captives. WASt officials claimed these leaflets were full of lies and relayed to the upper command of the German Army their opinion on the matter.

The reluctance of the Wehrmacht and WASt to believe Soviet assurances of fair treatment on surrender likely stemmed from two causes: Germany's own anti-Soviet propaganda and its poor treatment of captured Red Army soldiers. The Nazi propaganda machine successfully influenced the minds of its soldiers and officers. Hitler's race war on the *Ostfront* targeted both Jews and Slavs. German troops believed that surrender to Soviet forces and Soviet victory would mean the end of civilization.[16] They also feared being killed by their Red Army counterparts on capture. In addition to the anti-Bolshevik and anti-Slavic worldview of the Nazis, German soldiers undoubtedly feared retribution for their murder of Soviet citizens and captured Red Army soldiers. The Wehrmacht allowed millions of captive Soviet soldiers to starve to death or even shot them outright.[17] These fears of Soviet retribution and the successes of the German propaganda machine applied to both soldiers on the Eastern Front and to WASt intelligence officers in Germany.

The wartime German propaganda machine, then, was more effective in influencing the Wehrmacht troops than Soviet counterefforts. Until the last days of the war, German soldiers felt that it was safer to surrender to Western allies than to the Soviets because doing so would give them higher chances of survival.[18] Having been told by his officers that the Red Army would shoot all German prisoners, L. D., who entered Soviet captivity in late June 1944, was astounded that he and his comrades were treated well and had plenty to eat in captivity.[19] Another former soldier, Günter Koschorrek, wrote when describing the final months of the war in his memoir, "We have only one wish—to get as

15. "Abschrift" to the Oberkommando des Heeres, October 29, 1942, BA-M, RW 48/10.

16. Omer Bartov, *Hitler's Army: Soldiers, Nazis, and War in the Third Reich* (Oxford: Oxford University Press, 1992), 34–35.

17. See chapter 1 for more details or the following sources: Wolfram Wette, *The Wehrmacht: History, Myth, Reality* (Cambridge, MA: Harvard University Press, 2009), 17; Oksana Nagornaya, "Drugoi Voennyi Opyt": Rossiiskie Voennoplennye Pervoi Mirovoi Voiny v Germanii, 1914–1922 (Moscow: Novyi Khronograf, 2010), 20; David Stahel, *The Battle for Moscow* (Cambridge: Cambridge University Press, 2015), 41; Karsten Linne, "Hunger und Kannabalismus bei sowjetischen Kriegsgefangenen im Zweiten Weltkrieg," *Zeitschrift für Geschichtswissenschaft* 58, no. 3 (March 2010): 248; Rebecca Manley, "Nutritional Dystrophy: The Science and Semantics of Starvation in World War II," in *Hunger and War: Food Provisioning in the Soviet Union during World War II*, ed. Wendy Goldman and Donald Filtzer (Bloomington: Indiana University Press, 2015), 5–6.

18. Bartov, *Hitler's Army*, 35.

19. ADCV, 372.15 () Fasz. 1, "Auszug aus dem Schreiben des Kriegsgefangenen L.D."

far away from the Russian front. Even if we have to be taken prisoner, then we'd much rather it was by the British or the Americans."[20] After being captured by the Americans, Koschorrek still feared a transfer to Soviet captivity at the end of the war. To prevent this from happening, Koschorrek reopened an old grenade shrapnel wound with a rusty nail and stuffed a length of gauze bandage into the opening, intentionally giving himself a fever and an infection. He wrote, "I would rather die from blood poisoning than be sent to the hell of Siberia."[21] Waking two days later in a hospital, Koschorrek described speaking with the doctor, who had managed to save his life. The doctor stated that he would not be transferred and that he knew exactly why Koschorrek had risked his life.[22]

Even though propaganda produced by Soviet officials, exiled German communists, and German POWs for the German frontlines did not greatly help the Soviet war effort, the materials did result in one unintended consequence: German families received closure about the status of their relatives. The names published or read aloud in the wartime propaganda materials served as the only means of identifying Germans in Soviet captivity because the Red Cross and other neutral parties were forbidden to inspect POW camps and Soviet officials did not release lists of those captured. These propaganda releases enabled German military officials to move names of soldiers from lists of MIAs to confirmed POWs, though they had no assurances that these men were still alive in captivity. At times, however, Wehrmacht officials caught Soviet propaganda agents engaging in deception. Some leaflets and radio broadcasts contained falsified material meant to misinform German troops. Soviet propagandists cited German soldiers as the sources of the information used in their psychological materials. They used information from real army units but often used fake names of soldiers. When the information did include accurate personal information, the Wehrmacht relayed it to German families.[23] In some sense, then, initial Soviet propaganda efforts brought closure to German families.

Despite Soviet propaganda's lack of influence on active soldiers at the front, the Soviet antifascist program became meaningful among the captured Germans once the tide of the war began to turn. After the Battle of Stalingrad (August 23, 1942—February 2, 1943), Germany military victory began to look less assured. The Soviet success at Stalingrad also saw an influx of German

20. Günter K. Koschorrek, *Blood Red Snow: The Memoirs of a German Soldier on the Eastern Front* (London: Greenhill, 2005), 306–307.
21. Koschorrek, *Blood Red Snow*, 314.
22. Koschorrek, *Blood Red Snow*, 314–315.
23. "Aktenvermerk über Besprechung bei Chef AWA am 15.10.43," BA-M, RW 48/10; "Täuschungsversuche der Feindpropaganda," October 1942, BA-M, RW 48/10; and "Anlage: 1 Merkblatt des OKW," BA-M, RW 48/10.

POWs into the camp system. As Soviet forces captured ever-larger numbers of German soldiers, Soviet leaders saw the need to develop a school for antifascist reeducation among the POWs. The camps provided a perfect setting to undertake this work. Through the camps, agitprop workers could educate captured Germans en masse and work to create a sizable, pro-Soviet cohort by the end of the war. In March 1943, the Central Committee of the Communist Party decreed the creation of a formal antifascist school with input from the Central Executive Committee of the Communist International (Comintern); it charged the UPVI-NKVD with its administration. The central committees of the Party and the Comintern decided that the school curriculum would include four main thematic units: Germany as the epicenter of imperialist war, the Soviet Union as a country of socialism, World War II and the inevitability of the defeat of Hitler's Germany, and basic concepts of state and society.[24]

By April 1943, these broad themes for the antifascist school, along with a relationship between the Comintern and the UPVI, were established. Political work among POWs in the USSR had three main goals: (1) to transform POWs into antifascists, who would later publicize the importance of friendship with the Soviet Union; (2) to prepare antifascist cadres who would assist the Red Army in its mission to liberate Germany politically and remove Hitlerism from its territories; and (3) to train some POWs to become active antifascists on their return home after war's end, where they would work to promote antifascism and support for the Soviet Union. Ideally, the schooling would last for two or three months. It would include individual and group talks; lectures, gatherings, and conferences on the discussion of contemporary political topics; the publication and distribution of newspapers, magazines, and political and artistic literature in the native language of the POWs, as well as camp wall newspapers; group listening sessions of antifascist radio programs; film screenings; question-and-answer nights; POW labor conferences; and gatherings in which POWs would write letters home or to fellow active soldiers.[25]

The Central Executive Committee of the Comintern had the task of organizing the cadres and work among the POWs, as well as finding teachers for the schools and literature for the camps. The Main Political Administration of the Red Army (GlavPU RKKA) was responsible for providing materials for publications, radio programs, film screenings, and libraries. The UPVI-NKVD was to coordinate all the political work among POWs and the involvement of the Comintern and the GlavPU RKKA. It also would enact any directives of the Central Committee of the VKP(b) regarding the antifascist reeducation of

---

24. RGVA, f. 4p, op. 2, d. 3, ll. 19–21.
25. RGVA, f. 4p, op. 2, d. 3, ll. 22–27.

POWs. The involvement of the Comintern did not last long, however. On June 10, 1943, it disbanded because of the changing tide of the war. As the Red Army prepared to march westward into the heart of Europe, Stalin encouraged the national independence of communist movements to negate the Hitlerite claim that Moscow controlled all communist parties abroad.[26]

A milestone in the development of the antifascist programs occurred on July 12 and 13, 1943, at Camp No. 27 in Krasnogorsk when the camp hosted a conference for the National Committee for a Free Germany (Nationalkomitee Freies Deutschland; NKFD). The NKFD included exiled German communists, soldiers, and officers. Its chair, Erich Weinert, was a German communist writer, and the vice chairmen were Major Karl Hetz and Lieutenant Count Heinrich von Einsiedel, prisoners of war. Together, the committee crafted a program that called for the end of the war and the overthrow of Hitler and German fascism. It advocated the creation of a Free Germany, which is what they also titled their newsprint publication, *Freies Deutschland*. The newspaper became a device for agitation and propaganda work not only behind Soviet lines but also for distribution among active German forces. The Soviet government printed thousands of copies of the NKFD's call to depose Hitler, as well as the newspaper in leaflet form to be dropped from planes to the German forces. It also broadcast six daily radio programs of the NKFD over twelve wavelengths to Germany and Austria, in addition to regular German-language propaganda radio transmissions.[27]

To the dismay of Soviet political officers, however, no German generals joined the NKFD, even though thirty were in Soviet captivity during the time of its convening.[28] Many German higher officers refused to join it because exiled German communists spearheaded it and they themselves were anticommunist. They wanted a group that would be anti-Hitler and antifascist, but not overtly communist.[29] An alternative, noncommunist group for organizing officers opposed to Hitler—the League of German Officers (Bund Deutscher Offiziere; BDO)—was formed two months later in September 1943: The most important officer in the BDO was Field Marshal Friedrich Paulus, the com-

26. RGVA, f. 4p, op. 2, d. 3, ll. 22–27; Kevin McDermott and Jeremy Agnew, *The Comintern: A History of International Communism from Lenin to Stalin* (London: Macmillan, 1996), 205.

27. RGALI, f. 3175, op. 1, d. 35, l. 18; Kuz'minykh, *Voennyi plen i internirovanie v SSSR (1939–1956 gody): Monografiia.* Vologda: Drevnosti Severa, 2016, 312; V. P. Galitskii, "Antifascistskoye dvizheniye nemetskikh voennoplennykh v sovetskikh lageryakh dlya voennoplennykh v 1941–1945 gg, i ikh znacheniye v bor'bye protiv fashizma," in *70 let Natsional'nomu komitetu "Svobodnaya Germaniya" Sbornik materialov,* ed. I. P. Kuz'micheva (Moscow: Sabashnikovykh, 2014), 17–23; Who's who of prominent Germans in the U.S.S.R. mimeograph, page 4, Hoover Institution Archives; Karl-Heinz Frieser, *Krieg hinter Stacheldraht: Die deutschen Kriegsgefangenen in der Sowjetunion und das Nationalkomitee "Freies Deutschland"* (Mainz: Hase & Koehler, 1981), 71–73.

28. RGVA, f. 4p, op. 3, d. 3, ll. 4 and 8.

29. Frieser, *Krieg hinter Stacheldraht,* 78–79.

mander of the Nazi 6th Army at Stalingrad. By August 1944, Paulus was actively engaged in antifascist propaganda campaigns geared mostly to German soldiers and the home front population; he eventually expressed his public support for the NKFD in a leaflet for distribution to Germans.[30] Paulus wrote that the war was a "senseless sacrifice" and that "the war is lost for Germany." He stated that he and his fellow POWs believed that Germany must "break away from Hitler and give itself a new governance" so it could "enter into peaceful, even friendly relations with our present opponents."[31]

Both the NKFD and the BDO worked hard to produce materials to undermine morale in the Wehrmacht. Leaflets, including those written by Paulus, urged an end to the war and became the basis for a massive and growing propaganda campaign at the front. Soviet officials did not uniquely employ POWs for wartime propaganda efforts, but they used them earlier in the war than the other Allies and to a much larger extent. The Soviet propaganda machine produced millions of leaflets to distribute. Actively antifascist German POWs produced additional leaflets and were placed close to the frontlines to give statements and lectures via megaphone. In the Battle of Berlin, almost five thousand antifascist POWs engaged in such activities.[32]

In addition to producing materials urging the end to the war, the NKFD membership and resources provided the foundation for an antifascist reeducation program for POW camps throughout the USSR. This program grew considerably after late 1943. In December 1943, the head of the UPVI-NKVD, Major-General Petrov, reported that two cohorts of POWs had completed antifascist training courses and that the number of antifascists in the camps had increased.[33] The manifesto and theses of the NKFD became a centerpiece for antifascist training in more remote camps. The assistant director of the UPVI-NKVD, Colonel Yakovets, realized the propagandistic importance of the NKFD writings. In 1944, he sent materials from their conference to remote camps, such as No. 215 in Ulyanovsk, to inspire antifascist agitation and propaganda work among the German soldiers and officers held there.[34]

As the war progressed, routine antifascist activities took place in remote camps to expose as many POWs as possible to pro-Soviet and antifascist modes of thought. In smaller camps, the majority of the antifascist training consisted

---

30. Who's who of prominent Germans in the U.S.S.R.

31. Aufruf des Generalfeldmaschalls Paulus, Klaus Kirchner Collection, box 3, folder 3118–3138, Hoover Institution Archives.

32. Kuz'minykh, *Voennyi Plen*, 312–313; V. P. Galitskii, "Antifascistskoye dvizheniye nemetskikh voennoplennykh," 22–25; Clayton David Laurie, *The Propaganda Warriors: America's Crusade against Nazi Germany* (Lawrence: University Press of Kansas, 1996), 201–201, 226.

33. RGVA, f. 1p, op. 9a, d. 9, ll. 1ob and 23ob.

34. RGVA, f. 511p, op. 1, d. 8, l. 2.

of either discussions or lectures.[35] Small groups of roughly twenty POWs gathered for discussions on topics ranging from the contents of the *Free Germany* newspaper and camp life to world affairs after capitulation. Larger groups of anywhere from one to five hundred POWs gathered to hear lectures about the surrender of the German government or the first laws in the German occupation zones. Political officers also encouraged POWs to join the ranks of the National Committee for a Free Germany. After attending the antifascist lectures and discussions, POWs could sign up for membership.[36]

Some POWs even traveled to other nearby camps for reeducation courses, which increased in frequency after the end of the war. Those from Camp No. 215 in Ulyanovsk went to the nearby Camp No. 234 in Kuybyshev (present-day Samara) for antifascist courses.[37] Former POWs also recounted in memoirs that they traveled as representatives from their main camps to nearby camps that hosted either months-long antifascist courses or shorter conferences. One POW described how he and a fellow prisoner traveled to another nearby camp for a conference: "There were six of us, and we walked through the [camp] gate without a guard. We were allowed to leave by ourselves! . . . Hundreds of people were coming and going. . . . I don't think they noticed that we were WPs [POWS]."[38] Hans Schuetz and his fellow prisoners walked across the frozen Volga amid hundreds of Russians without anyone caring who they were or guarding them. They were trusted to make this journey to the other camp and back on their own. Another POW detailed the nomination process and travel to another camp for a four-month long course.[39]

Hans Gruber, writing under a pseudonym, testified to the intensity of the reeducation program. The students took classes six days a week, attending lectures from 8:00 to 11:00 A.M. After that, the men spent thirty minutes jogging or lifting weights before lunch and a rest period. From 2:00 to 5:00 P.M., students engaged in a question-and-answer section. Gruber stated that the courses required considerable dedication and concentration. Each man had to participate actively, and those who did not show enough commitment were sent back to their labor camps.

---

35. A sample of all of the antifascist meetings in Camp No. 215 in Ulyanovsk for 1945 can be found in RGVA, f. 511p, op. 1, d. 8, ll. 4–10ob.

36. RGVA, f. 511p, op. 1, d. 8, ll. 14–48, 49–65, and 66–79.

37. RGVA, f. 511p, op. 1, d. 6, l. 327 and RGVA, f. 511p, op. 1, d. 7, l. 6.

38. A. D. Hans Schuetz, *Davai, Davai,* 129.

39. Gruber, *My Odyssey thru Hell,* 117–123.

Antifascist Training after the German Capitulation

After the war ended, antifascist reeducation in the Soviet Union became increasingly important as the four Allied Powers deliberated over the nature of a postwar Germany. The Soviet Union was committed to the creation of an antifascist Germany. Transitioning from Nazi Germany to an antifascist country, however, would require much work. One key source of manpower for the process of German denazification would be the returnee POWs who had undergone antifascist reeducation programs in the USSR. These men could give testimony to counteract the anti-Soviet and antisocialist propaganda of the Nazi years. Thus, Soviet leaders worked to expand the reach and scope of the antifascist reeducation program in the years after the war.[40] They wanted to expose as many German POWs as possible to antifascist reeducation in the hope that, on their repatriation, they would build support for positive relations with the Soviet Union and influence their fellow citizens in an unofficial capacity. The use of the antifascist POWs in the Soviet occupation zone constituted a different approach to denazification than in the American zone.

Not surprisingly, in May 1945 the antifascist program's preeminent goal of helping end the war dropped off its agenda, and the NKFD ceased to exist.[41] The goal of Soviet–German peace and friendship, however, continued and grew more important in the postwar era of antifascist reeducation of German POWs. Soviet political officers wanted to ensure that any repatriated POWs would return home with positive attitudes toward the Soviet Union. After the war, many exiled German communists, including Wilhelm Pieck, Walter Ulbricht, and Anton Ackermann, who had organized the Free Germany movement, returned to the Soviet occupation zone to become political leaders.[42] Their main goal on return was to stabilize Germany on a new antifascist basis.

How a socialist Germany would be formed was initially unclear. Members of the former Social Democratic Party of Germany (SPD) and the Communist Party of Germany (KPD) had spent years in exile in the Soviet Union during the war. Before the war, the SPD and KPD were rivals. After the end of the war, the exiled members of these parties returned to Germany where they competed for control. Eventually, in April 1946, the two parties agreed to merge to form the Socialist Unity Party of Germany (SED). The SED presented itself

40. Jörg Morré, "Umerziehung in der sowjetischen Kriegsgefangenschaft Deutsche und Österricher in der Antifa, " in *Kriegsgefangene des Zweiten Weltkrieges: Gefangennahme, Lagerleben, Rückkehr*, ed. Günter Bischof, Stefan Karner, and Barbara Stelzl-Marx (Vienna: Oldenbourg, 2005), 152–166.

41. "Betr.: Antifa," BA-SAPMO, DY 34/16519, S. 102.

42. RGALI, f. 3175, op. 1, d. 35, l. 18.

not as a Leninist party committed to Sovietization but as a Marxist party that promoted parliamentary democracy. Initially, it was to be a compromise between communist and social-democratic traditions, although it increasingly grew to become Stalinist, modeled on his interpretation of Marxism-Leninism and the organization of the Communist Party of the Soviet Union. Party discipline became increasingly important, and the party apparatus was the focal point of power in the state.[43]

Yet the return of German communists to form a new socialist government did not guarantee pro-Soviet sentiment in what would become East Germany. The German postwar population was resentful of all its occupiers, but they were especially hostile toward the Soviets. The Germans had lived through twelve years of anti-Bolshevik propaganda under the Nazis, and they were reluctant to accept Soviet-style socialism.[44] The POW question also created problems for the burgeoning SED regime. Women, who became more politically active in the postwar era regarding issues such as food policy and women's rights, attacked the SED for the slow return of their men. The women also aggressively denounced the SED and the Soviet government for the widespread violence against women committed by Soviet soldiers and ex-POWs toward the end of the war and in the years thereafter.[45] Gathering support for a socialist Germany, then, would be an uphill battle.

Given the German population's anti-Soviet and antisocialist resistance, Soviet officials assumed that former POWs who spoke positively of socialism and the Soviet Union could help increase popular support for the USSR and a postwar socialist German state. To promote this aim, Soviet leaders and political officers released specially trained pro-Soviet, antifascist POWs not only to the Soviet occupation zone but also to the other three allied sectors to do agitprop work among the German population. Soviet leaders also decided that most repatriated POWs should have some basic antifascist training so that they could promote antifascism in a more organic and less official fashion. Leaders of the Soviet occupation zone hoped these men would influence the local population

---

43. Peter Grieder, *The East German Leadership, 1946–73: Conflict and Crisis* (Manchester: Manchester University Press, 1999), 8–12; Hermann Weber, *Die DDR 1945–1990* (Munich: Oldenbourg Verlag, 2006), 15.

44. Epstein, *The Last Revolutionaries*, 85. Donna Harsch notes in her book *Revenge of the Domestic* that this widespread hatred toward Russians lasted at least until 1954 in East Germany. Harsch, *Revenge of the Domestic: Women, the Family, and Communism in the German Democratic Republic* (Princeton, NJ: Princeton University Press, 2007), 73.

45. Donna Harsch, "Approach/Avoidance: Communists and Women in East Germany, 1945–1949," *Social History* 25, no. 2 (May 2000): 163. For more details on the role of women pressuring the East German government with questions about their husbands in Soviet captivity, see Ann-Kristin Kolwes, *Die Frauen und Kinder Deutscher Kriegsgefangener: Integriert, ignoriert, und instrumentalisiert, 1941–1956* (Bielefeld: transcript Verlag, 2021), esp. chapters 3 and 4.

and be members of the new administration. Many former officials were tainted by Nazism, and there was a shortage of trained personnel. On March 30, 1946, the head of the Political Head Office of the USSR Armed Forces, I. Sikin, wrote to the head of the Propaganda and Agitation Administration of the Central Committee of the Soviet Union about the work of the Propaganda Administration of the Soviet Military Administration in Germany (SVAG, also known as SMAD in German).[46] Sikin informed his Moscow superiors that SVAG needed an additional two thousand antifascist POWs to work in municipal authorities and democratic organizations.

Reeducation of POWs was also a goal of the other Allies. U.S. authorities also attempted to retrain their German captives. During the war, they had realized the value of offering broader education about American values in hopes of denazifying their captives and fostering a pro-American attitude among the German population in peacetime. The Americans allowed German captives to graduate high school and take practical courses in engineering, economics, and agriculture. Some German POWs even took extension courses from U.S. universities, including University of California Berkley and the Universities of Minnesota, Chicago, and Wisconsin.[47] The United States also operated a major reeducation program out of Fort Eustis, Virginia, known as the "Eustis Program."[48] The program could train two thousand men at a time in a six-day course that had twelve key topics: "1. The Democratic Way of life; 2. The Constitution of the United States; 3. Political Parties, Elections, and Parliamentary Procedures; 4. Education in the United States; 5. American Family Life; 6. The American Economic Scene; 7. American Military Government; 8. Democratic Traditions in Germany; 9. Why the Weimar Republic Failed–I; 10. Why the Weimar Republic Failed–II; 11. The World of Today and Germany; 12. New Democratic Trends in the World Today." The American denazification units, then, stressed U.S. democracy and the failures of the German system that led to Nazism. In this sense, the Americans already had a plan for the postwar transition of Germany into an anti-Nazi and antifascist state. Although Soviet authorities would later follow a similar method of broadly educating POWs in Soviet culture, values, and a prescribed interpretation of the war, they did so much later than the Americans. The Soviet leaders did not plan for the postwar transition of Germany with the same urgency.

---

46. RGASPI, f. 17, op. 125, d. 392, ll. 37–45 (cited as RCChIDNI), in *Sowjetische Politik in der SBZ 1945–1949*, ed. Bernd Bonwetsch, Gennadij Bordjugov, and Norman Naimark (Bonn: Dietz, 1998), 221–225. See page 224 for information about the antifascist POWs.

47. Camp-School POW-Camp Breckinridge, Stephen M. Farrand Papers, box 2, folder 3, Hoover Institution Archives.

48. Arnold Kramer, *Nazi Prisoners of War in America* (New York: Stein and Day, 1979), 222.

Soviet leaders did not want a divided Germany but wanted to accomplish two goals in the immediate future that would benefit the Soviet Union: to help the USSR rebuild after the war and to ensure that Germany would not attack it again. To meet these objectives, the Soviet authorities wanted access to the coal fields of the Ruhr and either access to or control of German scientific and military knowledge and industrial assets. The Soviet acquisition of German industry, technology, and intelligence would ensure that Germany could not again wage war and would serve as recompense for the damages that Germany had inflicted on the USSR. Soviet leaders also sought to reform German society. The majority of the German military leaders came from the families of Junker landowners and industrial magnates. Thus, Soviet leaders believed that land reform and the expropriation of factories would destabilize the upper classes and reduce their influence and ability to wage war. Additionally, the SVAG, the body tasked with organizing and running the Soviet Occupation Zone, saw itself as a liberator and not an occupier. As such, it was tasked with rebuilding German society and helping it make the transition from Nazism and militarism to an antifascist and "democratic" state. The Soviet authorities saw their mission as rebuilding the cultural foundations of Germany and erasing all traces of Nazi ideology. German citizens had to be reeducated. Much of this work fell to the head of the Propaganda, and later Information, Department of the SVAG, Major General Sergei Tiul'panov, who worked to prevent or disband, often by force, any groups that would undermine the socialist, anti-Nazi transformation of the Soviet Occupation Zone between 1945 and 1949. Soviet and East German policies rapidly and greatly changed over this period, but the ultimate goal remained the denazification and refashioning of German society.[49]

Like the Soviets, U.S. officials began denazification in 1945 and set about removing Nazi officials from their positions. Rather than instituting large-scale economic and bureaucratic reforms, however, the U.S. occupying government tried to expand denazification across its zone by having citizens fill out ques-

---

49. Norman M. Naimark, *The Russians in Germany: A History of the Soviet Zone of Occupation, 1945–1949* (Cambridge, MA: Belknap Press, 1995), 2, 10, 141, 251, 352, 456, 467; Norman Naimark, "Die Sowjetische Militäradministration in Deutschland," in *Sowjetische Politik in der SBZ 1945–1949*, ed. Bernd Bonwetsch, Gennadij Bordjugov, and Norman Naimark (Bonn: Dietz, 1998), xv–xvi; Jan Foitzik, "Organisation der Sowjetischen Besatzung in Deutschland und Auswirkungen von kompetenzieller Diffusion auf die Rekonstruktion der Besatzungspolitik," in *Sowjetisierung oder Neutralität? Optionen sowjetischer Besatzungspolitik in Deutschland und Österreich 1945–1955*, ed. Andreas Hilger, Mike Schmeitzner, and Clemens Vollnhals (Göttingen: Vandenhoeck & Ruprecht, 2006), 97–99, 105–106; Mike Schmeitzner, "'Die Kommunistische Partei will nicht Oppositionspartei sein, sondern sie will Staatspartei sein': Die KPD/SED und das politische System der SBZ/DDR (1944–1950)," in *Sowjetisierung oder Neutralität?* ed. Andreas Hilger, Mike Schmeitzner, and Clemens Vollnhals (Göttingen: Vandenhoeck & Ruprecht, 2006), 271–273.

tionnaires (*Fragenbogen*) to assess their allegiance to Nazism and so determine the appropriate level of punishment they deserved. The Americans had too little personnel to process the large number of questionnaires, and this method of vetting citizens failed. U.S. leaders also failed to reform the German civil service, which traced its roots to the Napoleonic era in the western parts of Germany. Instead of abolishing that Napoleonic structure, U.S. occupiers chose instead to bring the civil service under democratic control. American denazification was not a comprehensive process: it failed in some cases but succeeded overall due to the sheer force of the occupying power and the willingness of Germans citizens themselves to partake in the process and admit complicity in the crimes of the Nazi state.[50]

Soviet leaders took a more comprehensive and directed approach to denazification than did U.S. authorities by implementing in their occupation zone social, political, and economic reforms, such as land reform, nationalization of industry, and direct appointments to leadership positions. In addition to implementing major reform from above, Soviet leaders hoped that antifascist returnee POWs could play a positive role in creating a new Germany. The men who completed antifascist schooling would be given a variety of tasks not only in the Soviet occupation zone but also in the Allied areas. Former POWs were repatriated specifically to fulfill agitation and propaganda tasks or to fill leadership positions in the fledgling East German state, and they went on to work side by side with the German communists who had returned from exile. Starting in May 1945, Soviet officials released reeducated former Wehrmacht officers with the aim of building a new Germany.

The former POWs displayed varying levels of commitment to this mission. At least one admitted to volunteering for the antifascist courses and agreeing with their content out of a desire for self-preservation. Hans Gruber stated that he actively participated in the antifascist program because he feared what might happen if he did not. He wrote, "I had no choice. Either I completely and convincingly played the part of a believer, or I would surely perish on the five-year road project." As for Marx and Engels, "I despised reading them, but I had no choice. It was either conform or die!"[51] While in captivity, he enthusiastically quoted Marx and propaganda slogans to both officials and free Soviet citizens in exchange for being assigned to light work duties in Yalta for six weeks and then early repatriation. However, he immediately stopped supporting the

---

50. Rebecca L. Boehling, *A Question of Priorities: Democratic Reforms and Economic Recovery in Postwar Germany: Frankfurt, Munich, and Stuttgart under U.S. Occupation, 1945–1949* (New York: Berghahn Books, 1996), 15, 52–55, 57, 250–251; Dennis L. Bark and David R. Gress, *From Shadow to Substance: 1945–1963* (Cambridge, MA: Blackwell, 1993), 74–88.

51. Gruber, *Odyssey thru Hell*, 119, 122.

Soviet Union and socialism after being repatriated, bribing an East German ticket processor at the reception camp on the German–Polish border to give him a ticket under a fake name to West Germany.[52]

Gruber likely was not the only POW who did this. POWs probably sensed that participation in these programs could result in better treatment or release. Indeed, participation in antifascist activities often happened right before repatriation in some camps. Many POWs produced albums of camp life officials prior to release. These albums generally followed similar formats that included depictions of everyday life in the camps, ranging from food or medical treatment to leisure activities.[53] Often they included commentary (*otzyvy*) from POWs. All these albums included statements like the one given by Corporal Max Schtrauch: "I live a good life in the POW camp. They take care of everything. There is no blind obedience, everything is voluntary here. You can openly express your opinions."[54] Another POW wrote that he thanked all the camp staff and medical personnel on the day of his repatriation.[55] The positive POW recollections as reported to Soviet officials may have been insincere. These men gave these accounts days or hours before repatriation and may have felt compelled to provide them so they could return home.

Other POWs, however, sincerely believed in the transformation of Germany from a fascist state into a socialist one. Ernst Kehler served as a radio operator on the Eastern Front. The Red Army surrounded and captured his communications unit during the first weeks of the war. In 1943, Kehler excitedly joined the NKFD. Many of his former comrades felt that he was a traitor for doing so, but this did not change his convictions. Kehler worked as a representative of the NKFD on the Leningrad front. By May 4, 1945, Kehler had advanced with the Red Army into Berlin, where he worked with officials of the former German Communist Party, planning for the transition. Having proven himself an ally of the Soviet Union and socialism, Kehler was released from his duties as an NKFD member and captive; he then became the head of Post and Telecommunications in Berlin on June 2, 1945, where he remained until his retirement at sixty years old in 1974.[56] Kehler was not alone. About 300 men

---

52. Gruber, *Odyssey thru Hell*, 122–131.

53. See RGVA, f. 39p, op. 7, d. 1 for an album from a camp in the Moscow province or RGVA, f. 105p, op. 4, d. 15 for an album from Camp No. 27 in Krasnogorsk. Fonds 39p and 105p contain multiple albums of this type.

54. RGVA, f. 39p, op. 7, d. 1, ll. 25–26.

55. RGVA, f, 105p, op. 18, d. 19, l. 29.

56. Ernst Kehler, *Einblicke und Einsichten: Erinnerungen* (Berlin: Dietz, 1989), 75–82, 120–130, 134–142, 229, 241. Kehler remained loyal to the GDR and its values even after its collapse. David Ensikat, "Ernst Kehler," *Der Tagesspiegel*, September 9, 2005, https://www.tagesspiegel.de/wirtschaft/ernst-kehler/640490.html.

returned to the Soviet zone to join the Communist Party of Germany (KPD) or to work with the secret Soviet police apparatus. An additional 100 former Nazi officers returned in September 1948 to join the police force of the Soviet occupation zone. Others later became the commanding officers of the National People's Army (NVA) of the GDR after it was formed in 1956.[57]

Soviet agitprop leaders had numerous tasks to accomplish in preparation for the repatriation of their German POW students. First, they sought to turn them from fascists into antifascists. Second, they wanted to ensure that the POWs would disseminate stories of proper treatment in the USSR and would promote peace and friendship with the Soviet Union. Finally, they relied on the former POWs to support the creation of a democratic, and later socialist, Germany. Soviet leaders hoped to employ the ideologically retrained former POWs as editors and announcers for the All-Union Radio Committee of the Council of Ministers of the USSR. In September 1946, the GUPVI and MVD shortlisted around twenty POWs from Germany, Austria, and Hungary who had finished antifascist schools and courses to do radio broadcasts in both the Soviet Union and their homelands for the Central Committee of the Bolshevik Party.[58] These future radio workers lived either in Camp No. 27 in Krasnogorsk or Camp No. 165 in Iuzha, Ivanovo Oblast. The Minster of Internal Affairs, Sergei Kruglov, personally signed off on the shortlisted candidates. The MVD submitted its recommendations to the Central Committee with a large collection of GUPVI and MVD paperwork. Each screened candidate's paperwork included a character reference form with information on place of birth, ethnicity, and nationality; military rank, location of their military service, and where they were taken captive. Perhaps most importantly, however, these reports chronicled the antifascist training and activities in which these POWs partook and attested that no compromising materials during time in captivity had been discovered. Although archival sources do not include a report confirming the appointment of these POWs to the All-Union Radio, it is likely that they were indeed assigned to these tasks, given that many other reeducated POWs found not only new employment but also early release from captivity because of their value as political agitators.

At the end of 1946, the Central Committee decreed that the MVD and GUPVI establish the Antifascist Department of Education within the Political Department for work with POWs.[59] Along with removing fascist influences and ensuring a conscientious attitude to work in the camps, the new department

57. GARF, f. 9526, op. 6, d. 509, l. 62; Daniel Niemetz, *Das feldgraue Erbe: Die Wehrmachtseinflüsse im Militär der SBZ/DDR (1948/1949–1989)* (Berlin: Ch. Links Verlag, 2012), 34, 37–41.

58. RGVA, f. 4p, op. 6, d. 4, ll. 63–67.

59. RGVA, f. 4p, op. 33, d. 3, ll. 1–11; RGVA, f. 4p op. page 3.

aimed to steadily increase the number of actively antifascist POWs, in the hope that they would partake in the radical transformation of their native countries and uphold a friendly attitude toward the USSR. The Antifascist Department of Education worked hard to realize these tasks.

Antifascist reeducation of POWs gained the attention not only of the political departments of the UPVI and SVAG but also of the highest echelons of the Soviet government. In addition to informing the heads of the Politburo of the POWs' physical conditions and labor contributions, Minister of Internal Affairs Kruglov relayed information on political work among them. On March 13, 1948, he wrote to Stalin, Molotov, Beria, and Zhdanov to report on the political work done in 1947 among MVD camps following the orders and plan from the Central Committee for mass political work among the POWs. Kruglov's report provided statistics for the first and fourth quarters of 1947, highlighting the increase in ideological work over the course of the year. It noted that 3,830,000 POWs participated in 9,206 meetings in the first quarter, increasing to 6,950,000 POWs participating in 16,682 meetings during the fourth quarter. The political organs of the GUPVI also hosted 25,382 lectures and speeches attended by 6,620,000 POWs in the fourth quarter, an almost twofold increase over those in the first quarter. In the first quarter, the MVD had held 4,316 movie screenings compared to 7,295 in the fourth quarter. Film attendance dramatically rose from the first to the fourth quarter: 668,000 POWs had attended screenings in the first quarter, which increased sixfold to 4,120,000 in the fourth quarter. The fourth quarter also saw the performances of 4,698 plays and 16,510 concerts, though attendance figures were not listed. Finally, Kruglov related that in January 1948, POWs had begun to receive newspapers from the Soviet occupation zone, in which they showed great interest. Kruglov credited the newspapers from Germany for improving morale among the POWs.[60]

These statistics illustrate both the great importance of ideological training of the POWs and the ways in which camp structure facilitated mass reeducation. Sources give a population of 1,294,683 German POWs as of April 1, 1947, and 700,447 as of April 1, 1948.[61] Kruglov stated that almost four million POWs had attended antifascist meetings in the first quarter of 1947 and almost seven million had done so in the fourth quarter. Not counting any potential meetings held in the second and third quarters, each POW could have attended at least ten antifascist meetings. Each camp allegedly hosted antifascist training activi-

---

60. GARF, f. 9401, op. 2, d. 199, ll. 403–409, especially ll. 403 and 404. Unfortunately, the document did not list the content or names of the films, lectures, or approved newspapers.

61. GARF, f. 9401, op. 2, d. 169, l. 204 and GARF, f. 9401, op. 2, d. 200, ll. 76–79, in Maksim Matveevich Zagorul'ko, *Voennoplennye v SSSR 1939–1956: Dokumenty i materialy* (Moscow: Logos, 2000), 682.

ties, but if only a select number of the same POWs attended these events, they would have been heavily exposed to antifascist ideologies from meetings alone. Given the large numbers of films, performances, and concerts, it is likely that just as every German POW had to do forced labor in the USSR, so too did every German POW have to experience some form of antifascist programming. The GUPVI camp system then regulated both POW labor and education, with processes borrowed from the Gulag system. Leaders in both systems understood that not every person could be transformed. However, having a captive audience ensured that those targeted for ideological training would receive it. In addition, those deemed worthy of reintegration through their reeducation activities could earn their due release. Gulag prisoners could earn release through labor contributions and by attesting a willingness to partake in the actual construction of the socialist state.[62] GUPVI prisoners too could earn release by showing enthusiasm for a socialist Germany and Soviet–German friendship. Even though GUPVI education programs emphasized the transition from fascism to antifascism above all else, they also stressed the benefits of socialism and how it was superior to capitalism. A GUPVI report from April 1950 emphasized the importance of exposing POWs to the writings of Lenin and Stalin. It also noted that they increasingly received instruction about the benefits of socialism and its superiority to capitalism after the end of the war.[63]

Although the United States had created a program for antifascist reeducation in the hopes of having these men serve the aims of the United States after the war, the American program was far less widespread than the Soviet equivalent. Instead of making each prisoner go through at least some sort of antifascist training, U.S. officials only provided training to those deemed to be the most trustworthy and vocally antifascist—who were those who needed reeducation the least.[64] In this sense, the U.S. reeducation program was much narrower than the Soviet program, which aimed to indoctrinate as many men as possible.

The Soviet training program did have an impact insofar as the majority of repatriated course graduates found some sort of leadership work in their home countries. A later report from Kruglov to the Central Committee summarized the continuing work to reeducate German POWs and send them through antifascist training.[65] Over the course of 1947, 1948, and the first half of 1949, 24,988 Germans completed either the central antifascist schools, three-month antifascist programs, or a month-long antifascist course. The report also stated

62. Barnes, *Death and Redemption*, 57–58.
63. RGVA, f. 4p, op. 33, d. 1, ll. 6–10.
64. Antonio Thompson, *Men in German Uniform: POWs in America during World War II* (Knoxville: University of Tennessee Press, 2010), 117–118.
65. RGVA, f. 4p, op. 33, d. 3, ll. 1–11.

that the returnees had obtained leadership roles in territories not occupied or controlled by Soviet forces. The antifascist reeducation work continued to play an important role in Soviet–German relations through the 1950s.

Antifascist Propaganda Repatriations during the Cold War

As the Cold War intensified, Soviet and East German authorities increasingly turned to antifascist returnee POWs to engage actively in politics in all four occupation zones but especially in the Soviet zone. Political work done by specially trained former POWs increased in each subsequent year after the end of the war. East German leaders used antifascists not only in their own political party, the SED, but also in rival parties to foster denazification among groups that could have been most resistant to the process. Soviet authorities did not limit antifascist POWs to working in denazification efforts in their own territory. When repatriating special groups of antifascist agitprop workers, Soviet authorities released more men combined to the non-Soviet territories than to their own zone. Although the Soviet Union never wanted a divided Germany, Soviet authorities had to grapple with the formation of two German states in 1949. The Soviet response was to increase repatriations of agitprop POWs to support the GDR and oppose the FRG. Here again, reeducation conferred a special status within the camp system.

The intensification of the Cold War in 1948 and 1949 illustrated another major difference in the denazification practices of the American and Soviet occupation forces. U.S. authorities officially ended their denazification process on March 31, 1948, partially due to the logistical difficulties of implementing a process of universal denazification through questionnaires and subsequent vetting of the respondents. The Americans also decided to end their denazification efforts as the Cold War intensified. Their focus shifted from denazification and democratization to anticommunism by means of economic restructuring along capitalist lines to speed up the normalization of German economic and social life.[66] In the Soviet zone, denazification and antifascist reeducation did not end in 1948 or with the creation of two German states. Instead, the division of Germany only increased the importance that Soviet and East German officials placed on denazification and the continued transformation of German society.

---

66. Boehling, *Question of Priorities*, 2–3, 19–20, 55, 60–61; Bark and Gress, *From Shadow to Substance*, 77–78.

In what would become East Germany, political officials anticipated the return of trained antifascists for party work. The National Democratic Party of Germany (NDPD) especially sought to employ reeducated former POWs. Founded in 1948 under the guidance of Stalin and the SVAG, the NDPD aimed to organize former Nazi supporters in the Soviet zone to engage in the political sphere with the SED. SVAG and Soviet officials aimed to provide former military men and the middle class with a direct political outlet so that they would not again support the far right or anticommunist Western allies.[67] The NDPD leadership outlined a series of roles they wanted returnees to fill, including directors of schools, teachers, and speakers.[68] Returning antifascists, NDPD leaders clearly assumed, could also serve a valuable role in the nascent party. Those who had fought on the *Ostfront* and spent time in Soviet captivity could credibly recount the horrors of the war, the bankruptcy of Nazi ideology, and the advantages of an alliance with the Soviet Union. Filling a party meant to attract former Nazi supporters with those who had been reeducated would ensure that a key group in need of denazification would be exposed to a new perspective.

For the Soviet authorities, every moment counted as an opportunity to reeducate the German POWs and prepare them to be allies of the Soviet Union on their return. Those who had been trained to undertake propaganda work at home had their first experiences training their fellow POWs on the train ride home; they hoped this training would increase the number of pro-Soviet Germans who would assist in rebuilding their homeland. For example, in a repatriation of 1,401 POWs in September 1949, 47 POW agitators selected various POWs in the trains to participate in reeducation seminars over the course of the six-day return journey. Before departure, these pro-Soviet German propagandists were encouraged to instill three main ideas in their fellow POWs: it was the duty of every German patriot to support German socialism, Soviet democracy had advantages over Western democracy, and Soviet leaders wanted to promote peace. In addition to these three major propaganda points, the POW agitators were sent back with sixty-two slogans to recite, some of which had been printed on banners and pamphlets in Russian and German; they included "Long Live Soviet–German friendship" and "Long Live the Soviet People and Their Great Leader STALIN."[69] The POW agitators also had their own train car filled with German-language books, pamphlets,

---

67. Vladislav Zubok, *A Failed Empire: The Soviet Union in the Cold War from Stalin to Gorbachev* (Chapel Hill: University of North Carolina Press, 2009), 70–71.

68. "Dringend erfordlicher Mitarbeiter für die National-Demokratische Partei Deutschland," July 21, 1949, SAPMO, DY 16/2568.

69. RGVA, f. 39p, op. 5, d. 72, ll. 19–21.

and newspapers, as well as domino and chess sets. The agitators even had support from a seven-piece band to provide entertainment to the regular repatriates.

During these 1949 mobile lessons, the repatriates participated in a variety of events ranging from lectures and talks about Lenin and Stalin, Anglo–American imperialism, and the importance of Soviet–German friendship; question-and-answer sessions about the domestic and foreign policies of the Soviet Union; concerts of Russian and Soviet classical music; film screenings; and sessions spent writing letters to Soviet authorities about their time in captivity and their plans and intentions for the future. The non-activist POWs actively engaged in these mobile reeducation sessions. During one train ride, about 103 soldiers wrote individual letters, and groups wrote an additional 48 letters to Soviet authorities reflecting on their captivity and future; these letters garnered a total of 1,029 signatures, indicating that almost 75 percent of the returning POWs had participated in and signed off on the antifascist activities. At one general meeting of POWs on the lessons for the German people from the two world wars and the tasks of returnees on their return to their homeland, five POWs called for an active struggle for peace and for the strengthening of Soviet–German friendship.

In addition to being assigned specific reeducation tasks on their train rides home, actively antifascist returning POWs had a variety of assignments on their return. In the fall of 1949, Soviet leaders prepared for the coming official declaration of East German sovereignty by repatriating select groups of actively antifascist POWs. On four days alone in September 1949, 213 men total returned to the four Germany zones specifically to undertake propaganda work.[70] Table 3.1 presents the number of returnees by zone.

The Soviet zone received the largest group of returned men for propaganda work, but only about one-third of the total number of men repatriated for this type of work in September 1949 went to the Soviet zone. Propaganda work, then, remained vital to both the Soviet and non-Soviet zones of a divided Germany and Berlin after the establishment of the FRG and immediately preceding the establishment of the GDR. Most of the 213 men from this group returned to the various parts of Germany to undertake agitation and propaganda work. Table 3.2 shows the breakdowns of their propaganda tasks.

As table 3.2 shows, 163 men, or roughly 76.5 percent, came back to work as agitators or propagandists. In the Soviet Union, propaganda work emphasized targeting the literate members of the population and explaining dogma to them.

---

70. RGVA, f. 39p, op. 5, d. 72, ll. 23–4, ll. 27–27ob, ll. 29–29ob, and ll. 31–31ob. These documents serve as the sources for the following pages and tables 3.1–3.5.

Table 3.1   Political returnees by zone

ZONE	NUMBER	% OF TOTAL
Soviet	71	33.3
British	56	26.3
American	47	22.06
Unknown*	30	14.08
French	9	4.26

* For unknown destinations, archival records left a blank spot in the
ledgers. One man was labeled as being returned to Berlin but did
not specify which sector of the city.

Table 3.2   Job breakdowns for September 1949 propaganda
repatriates

JOB	NUMBER	% OF TOTAL
Agitation	113	53.05
Propaganda	50	23.47
Cultural	28	13.15
Unknown	17	7.98
Leadership of Political Work	2	0.94
Trade union work	2	0.94
Political work	1	0.47

Agitators used materials such as pamphlets, wall newspapers, theater sketches, demonstrations, and meetings to exploit emotions and instill a message without necessarily explaining it.[71] In postwar divided Germany, trained German propagandists and agitators worked within the bounds of the Soviet ideological framework, building support for the Soviet Union in the early Cold War.

These men were assigned to similar tasks in all the zones of occupation, yet only those who returned to the Soviet zone returned to work explicitly in a political sphere. SVAG officials directly appointed Russian and German citizens to work in all spheres of the emerging state.[72] Thus, unsurprisingly, German antifascists returned to the Soviet zone to directly engage in leadership and lower levels of political work, as well as more broadly as agitprop agents; they could have worked for a variety of groups controlled either by the SVAG or its propaganda department, such as the press, social work institutions, the education system, and youth groups. Although two men returning to the American

71. Karel Berkhoff, *Motherland in Danger* (Cambridge, MA: Harvard University Press, 2012), 3.
72. Naimark, *Russians in Germany*, 4, 6, 11–12, and 22.

zone were assigned to work with trade unions, only in the Soviet zone could Soviet authorities ensure the assignment of their antifascist political agents to specific industrial sectors. Working with the trade unions could have allowed the agitprop agents in this sector to reach a broad audience, agitate for better working conditions, and ensure their contact with the working men and women of Germany. The final and smallest group of returnees—only nine men—returned to the French occupation zone in September 1949. The French were awarded a small zone of occupation much later than the other allied powers, and it contained few people or industrial centers.[73] As in the other zones, however, most of the returnees sent to the French zone also had hopes of participation in agitprop work, as well as cultural work. In every occupation zone, GUPVI officials deployed more returnees for agitation and cultural work than in high-level propaganda work.

The Soviet objective for returnee POW agitprop work in Germany was not a secret. The West German press noted in 1949 the arrival of the so-called Antifa-Men at the repatriation transit camp Friedland in Göttingen, West Germany.[74] The transport consisted of 260 men who had completed Soviet political school programs. They had been repatriated for the explicit purpose of going to the industrial regions and largest cities of the British zone and actively agitating for the Soviet Union and its goals. There, these men would be able to reach their largest audiences, targeting groups that historically had been more open to accepting socialism and communism in pre-Nazi Germany.[75] Even before World War I, Germany had a mass socialist movement and a large, well-organized Social Democratic party (SPD). The Communist Party of Germany (KPD) was formed in December 1918. It too grew into a mass party by 1930. Although the Nazis outlawed both the KPD and SPD in 1933, support for left-wing parties did not evaporate but lived on "underground" during the Third Reich and even during total war. Social Democrats, Communists, and trade unionists reemerged to engage in political and trade union work in every zone as soon as the occupying authorities allowed Germans to do so. Soviet authorities were well aware of the history of the German Left and its base of

---

73. Jessica Reinisch, *The Perils of Peace: The Public Health Crisis in Occupied Germany* (Oxford: Oxford University Press, 2013), 261; Richard Bessel, *Germany 1945: From War to Peace* (New York: Simon & Schuster, 2012), 290.

74. "'Antifa-Männer' aus Russland," 1949, in ADCV, 372.15 () Fasz. 2. Unfortunately, the archival folder did not contain the name of the publication or the exact day in 1949. The article, however, gives the location as Kassel.

75. For information on the history of socialism and communism in Germany, see Eric D. Weitz, *Creating German Communism, 1890–1990: From Popular Protests to Socialist State* (Princeton, NJ: Princeton University Press, 1997), esp. 62–64, 132–137.

support among workers. Sending agitprop workers to interact with workers in the industrial sectors of Germany was thus a rational decision.

Although some of the older men sent back for repatriation might have had socialist political backgrounds, other POWs who returned specifically to engage in agitprop work in the fall of 1949 came from Nazi backgrounds. The testimonies of these men attest to their anti-Soviet backgrounds and how they became champions for socialism and advocates for the Soviet Union through their antifascist reeducation programs. One internal report of the Political Division of POW Camps in Moscow and the Moscow Oblast presented interviews with the men awaiting repatriation.[76] Two men self-reported as members of the Nazi Party. Lieutenant Albert Spindler, born in 1907, had a secondary school education, worked as an automotive mechanic, and came from an area that later became the American zone. He stated that he spent his time in captivity learning about the politics of the Soviet Union. He praised the lack of a class system and was impressed that every citizen was able to contribute their knowledge and abilities regardless of their origins.

Another interviewee, First Lieutenant Kurt Peter, born in 1906, had a secondary school education, worked as a teacher, and came from what later became the Soviet zone. He stated:

> When I arrived in the Soviet Union in 1945, I had a very dark impression about socialism and socialist governments. Thanks to the help of the Soviet people and different camps, I had a huge opportunity to study the theories of Marx, Engels, Stalin, and Lenin from books and courses, and then to practice here in Moscow. . . . To my delight, I became a leader of discussion circles, and they were my everything. Returning home, working in my profession, I think it is my first task to instruct the German people to fight for a democratically united Germany, to tell the truth about the Soviet Union.[77]

Peter admitted being hostile to socialism before being taken captive. Through theoretical and practical Marxist-Leninist texts, courses, and discussion circles, however, he became an antifascist and wished to return home to work as a teacher and speak on behalf of the Soviet Union and a united Germany. Peter especially had learned to "speak Bolshevik," using the language of the GUPVI reeducation system; he uttered common phrases of fighting for a democratic and united Germany and promising to tell the truth about the Soviet Union.

---

76. RGVA, f. 39p, op. 5, d. 72, ll. 33–39.
77. RGVA, f. 39p, op. 5, d. 72, ll. 34.

Whether men like Peter were sincere is impossible to know. Given that they had finally been selected for repatriation, they may have said what they thought they were expected to say to ensure their return. Peter's case is also important to highlight because he was not the only antifascist former teacher.

In fact, the Soviet leadership made great use of former POWs in crafting a new school system in their occupation zone. As early as March 1945, Soviet officials planned to return antifascists who had been teachers to help build a new school system.[78] From 1947 to 1949, every POW who had been a professional teacher before the war and who had served as antifascist teachers in the camps returned to Germany.[79] These men returned to shape the educational policies and pedagogies of what would become the GDR. They adopted Soviet pedagogies and proselytized for the USSR, German–Soviet friendship, and a socialist and unified Germany. The antifascist teachers played an enormous role in achieving one of the key Soviet goals for its occupation zone: the eradication of Nazis and Nazi ideology within the apparatus.[80] The school system was a vital target for denazification and for pro-Soviet and socialist indoctrination. The East Germans borrowed from the Soviet educational heritage and developed a school system that emphasized moral education that would develop socialist personalities—ones devoted to the party, to militant atheism, to a collectivist attitude toward labor, to a class-oriented approach to life, and to the international brotherhood of communist nations, especially solidarity with the Soviet Union.[81]

The Soviet government increased the number of repatriations in 1949 with the aim of establishing good relations with the newly formed West and East German governments. From September 1 to November 15, 1949, 4,103 former POWs returned to the German states: 1,202 returned to East Germany and 2,901 to West Germany.[82] Not all the men released in the fall of 1949 were returned so they could engage in agitprop work. However, the mass releases at this time did include a large contingent of actively antifascist returnees. Of the 4,103 men released, 400 were active antifascists, of whom 136 had

78. RGASPI, f. 17, op. 128, d. 723, ll. 23–31 (as RCChIDNI), in *Sowjetische Politik in der SBZ 1945–1949*, 6.

79. Christa Uhlig, *Rückkehr aus der Sowjetunion: politische Erfahrungen und pädagogische Wirkungen: Emigranten und ehemalige Kriegsgefangene in der SBZ und frühen DDR* (Weinheim: Deutscher Studien Verlag, 1998), 63, 74, 83.

80. Charles B. Lansing, *From Nazism to Communism: German Schoolteachers under Two Dictatorships* (Cambridge, MA: Harvard University Press, 2010), 129–131, 161. Lansing notes that even though Soviet occupation forces and the SED strove to remove all teachers associated with Nazism from the school system, they failed to do so, at least in Brandenburg.

81. John Rodden, *Textbook Reds: Schoolbooks, Ideology, and Eastern German Identity* (University Park: Penn State Press, 2010), 14–15.

82. RGVA, f. 39p, op. 5, d. 72, ll. 43–47.

finished antifa school. Thus, nearly one-tenth of those released at the time had some training to engage in antifascist, anti-imperialist, and prosocialist work on their return. And, as with previous transports, all those repatriated regardless of antifascist training status or destination underwent intensive political education: attending meetings and talks, watching educational films, and reading materials from the newspaper *Nachrichten*.[83]

Three additional repatriation transports in November and December 1949 also contained groups of active antifascists. The political department of the Moscow Oblast UPVI only traced the numbers of antifascists in the transports and did not give the total number of men. Nonetheless, certain patterns emerge from the repatriation documents, especially when compared to the earlier, more comprehensive reports from September 1949 and the larger summary report from November 16, 1949. On November 17, November 25, and December 14, 1949, the Moscow Oblast UPVI reported that 364 active antifascists returned to Germany.[84] The information from the reports is summarized in table 3.3.

As table 3.3 shows, most of the antifascists returned to the Soviet zone, but the repatriations in total gave preference to the non-Soviet zones. Although returnees to the Soviet zone comprised 41.59 percent of the November 17 transport, 54.55 percent of the November 25 transport, and 41.45 percent of the December 14 transport, they only amounted to 45.05% of the three transports together. The next largest number of antifascists went to the British zone, representing almost 30 percent of all antifascist returnees in this period. The American and French zone returnees comprised 17.58 percent and 8.24 percent of the total of these transports, respectively. These totals were consistent with the pattern established for political repatriation in September 1949 as represented in table 3.4.

As table 3.4 notes, the largest percentage of individual antifascist returnees were sent to the Soviet zone, although the percentage sent to the other zones together outweighed the Soviet zone. The next largest groups went to the British zone. Over the fall of 1949, Soviet officials increased the number of antifascist returnees to the Soviet zone and the British zone, whereas they decreased those who returned to American, French, and other destinations.

---

83. The origin of this newspaper is unclear. *Nachrichten* was the name of the communist, German-language newspaper of the Volga German Autonomous Soviet Socialist Republic; see Fred C. Koch, *The Volga Germans: In Russia and the Americas, from 1763 to the Present* (University Park: Penn State Press, 2010), 345; and Berkhoff, *Motherland in Danger*, 171 for details. That newspaper ceased to exist by the time of World War II. There were no East German newspapers called *Nachrichten*, but multiple states had newspapers for which their regional name was followed by the word *Nachrichten*.

84. RGVA f. 39p, op. 5, d. 72, ll. 94 and 94ob, 97–98, and 114–114ob.

Table 3.3   Actively antifascist returnees in November and December 1949

DATE	SOVIET	AMERICAN	BRITISH	FRENCH	OTHER*	TOTAL
November 17	47	25	34	6	1	113
November 25	54	13	24	8	0	99
December 14	63	26	47	16	0	152
Total	164	64	105	30	1	364
% of Total	45.05	17.58	28.85	8.24	0.27	100

*One antifascist returned to Saarland on November 17, 1949. After World War II, Saarland was a French protectorate that was only returned to West Germany in 1957.

Table 3.4   Political returnees by zone

ZONE	% OF TOTAL SEPTEMBER 1949	% OF TOTAL NOVEMBER AND DECEMBER 1949
Soviet	33.3	45.0
British	26.3	28.85
American	22.06	17.58
Other	14.08	0.27
French	4.26	8.24

Sources: September 1949 data taken from RGVA, f. 39p, op. 5, d. 72, ll. 23–4, ll. 27–27ob, ll. 29–29ob, and ll. 31–31ob; November and December 1949 data taken from RGVA f. 39p, op. 5, d. 72, ll. 94 and 94ob, 97–98, and 114–114ob.

Although Soviet officials could guarantee employment for active antifascists in key jobs or occupations in the Soviet zone, they could not guarantee that agit-prop men would gain such employment in the other zones. It is unclear whether the POWs released to the four zones for antifascist work actually did that work in the Western zones where they were not guaranteed placement by the SVAG or SED. Although there is no extensive documentation of what these men did after they returned home, a comprehensive MVD report on POW antifascist reeducation from 1946 to 1949 claimed that the vast majority of those who completed antifascist schools found "leadership positions" in their homelands after repatriation.[85] Nonetheless, Soviet officials continued to send allegedly committed antifascists to the other zones of Germany, despite the formalization of divided and opposing states. As with most other instances of repatriation, those who returned went back to their former places of residence in Germany. Soviet authorities still hoped to influence West German citizens either directly or indirectly with the numbers and types of men they sent home. Establishment of two formal Ger-

85. RGVA, f. 4p, op. 33, d. 3, ll. 6–7.

man states meant an initial defeat for Soviet postwar ambitions but did not mean that the fight for refashioning and the spread of socialism was completely lost.

The SED and Activist Returnees

Perhaps even more than Soviet authorities, the SED was deeply interested in the political work and contributions to the building of socialism by activist returnees to the Soviet Occupation Zone. The SED relied heavily on active antifascist returnees for aid in carrying out agitprop tasks. The Institute for Marxism-Leninism of the Central Committee of the SED closely monitored the activities and reactions of returnees to their participation in the propaganda undertaking, creating an employment form to track their training and post-return work.[86] This form asked which antifascist schools the men attended, when they returned, what their abilities were, what types of additional work they could do (organizational, propaganda, agitational, cultural, journalistic, or youth), and what could help them work effectively on their future tasks. The Soviet government had created the framework for former POW agitprop work, and the SED gladly accepted and deployed these men to further its political agenda.[87]

According to the Institute's records, those who returned in the fall of 1949 participated in regional and city-wide conferences and created clubs in 1950. On January 16 and 17, 1950, those who had returned just the month before led four conferences at three East German central schools.[88] Other conferences held at regional levels, such as in Saxony-Anhalt, focused on the topic, "The Party and the Returnee."[89] These conferences stressed the political significance of the returnees, their role in the party, and their mission to end anti-Soviet incitement. An additional fifteen conferences took place between January 15 and 22, 1950; members of the Central Secretariat (the executive committee of the SED) and the regional executive committee of the SED participated in these conferences.[90] In two districts of Saxony, returnees formed clubs as a subset of the Society for German–Soviet Friendship.[91] Returnees formed the leadership

---

86. "Um Ihre Entwicklung nach der Heimkehr," BA-SAPMO DY 30/88578, S. 127.

87. The tracking of active antifascists and their political work continued long after the last POWs returned to the two Germanys. In October 1967, the SED created a list of 104 men who had been through antifascist training in the USSR and joined the party after their return. The document included information on when they joined the party and whether they still engaged in agitprop at their place of employment. "Bürger der DDR," October 16, 1967, BA-SAPMO DY30/88636, S. 1–20.

88. "Abschrift," January 19, 1950, BA-SAPMO DY 30/88578, S. 11–12.

89. "Bericht von Kreiskonferenzen," BA-SAPMO DY 30/88578, S. 22–23.

90. "15 Heimkehrkonferenzen," BA-SAPMO DY 30/88578, S. 26.

91. "Abschrift," February 8, 1950, BA-SAPMO DY 30/88578, S. 31 and Abschrift," February 1, 1950, BA-SAPMO DY 30/88578, S. 32.

of these clubs, which met weekly to discuss issues of life and politics in the Soviet Union. Members of these clubs organized open meetings or groups such as choirs and playgroups to perform programs that they learned during captivity. Between the political discussions and cultural productions, the returnees hoped to change popular opinion of the Soviet Union and curtail any local anti-Soviet sentiments or movements. The returnees even pledged to the president of the GDR, Wilhelm Pieck, that they would continue to expand their circles and promote Soviet–German peace and friendship, as well as German unity.[92] They swore that they now viewed members of the Red Army as friends rather than enemies, and they thanked the Soviet Union and Stalin himself for their friendship and aid in their transition to antifascists.

Although party leaders of the SED understandably appreciated the value of returnees for political work, industrial managers too valued those workers who had undergone training in the Soviet Union. Representatives from the East German Textile Industry appealed to the Soviet Union and Stalin to send actively antifascist returnees in 1949.[93] Just as industrial leaders in the Soviet Union pled with party officials for POWs to accomplish labor tasks, so too did those in East Germany. The leaders of the Textile Industry, themselves members of the party, requested returnees because agitprop workers could fulfill a double burden of industrial output and political work. They were confident that the returnees would be Stakhanovites, who would meet and surpass work quotas and inspire those around them to do the same.

Although the major release of POWs agitators coincided with the formal establishment of the FRG and the GDR in 1949, Soviet officials continued to release antifascist POWs even into 1953. In that year, Stalin's death and a major uprising in the GDR motivated Soviet leaders to release more POWs. Following Stalin's death on March 5, 1953, the first deputy premier and head of the Ministry of Internal Affairs, Lavrentii Beria, launched a series of amnesties of both Gulag and UPVI prisoners.[94] After Stalin's death, both Beria and his rivals quickly enacted changes. Beria aimed to refashion himself as a reformer in the wake of Stalin's death. He attempted to win popular support by promoting liberalization campaigns, such as Gulag amnesties and de-Stalinization.[95] As it turned out, Beria was arrested and executed, but his reforms were taken up by

92. "Abschrift," Annaberg-Bucholz, 1950, BA-SAPMO DY 30/88578, S. 33–35.
93. "Willensbekundung," BA-SAPMO, DY 34/16802.
94. *Istochnik*, 1994. No. 4, pp. 110–112, in Zagorul'ko, *Voennoplennye v SSSR*, 901; Miriam Dobson, *Khrushchev's Cold Summer: Gulag Returnees, Crime, and the Fate of Reform after Stalin* (Ithaca, NY: Cornell University Press, 2009), 16, 25, 33–34, 37–38.
95. Dobson, *Khrushchev's Cold Summer*, 16, 25, 33–34, 37–38; Amy Knight, *Beria: Stalin's First Lieutenant* (Princeton, NJ: Princeton University Press, 1995), 183–185; Barnes, *Death and Redemption*, 204–205.

other reform-minded party leaders, including Khrushchev. As more POWs returned to the GDR and the FRG, those released to East Germany continued to serve as pro-Soviet and antifascist advocates, especially after the great disturbance caused by the June uprising.[96] On June 16 and 17, 1953, riots and demonstrations spread out from East Berlin across the GDR. Initially a workers' protest over economic conditions and work quotas, the uprising grew into a massive political demonstration that argued for overthrowing First Secretary Walter Ulbricht and reunifying Germany.[97] Local SED officials quickly mobilized POWs released in the wake of the uprising to promote socialism and Soviet–German relations. In the small East German town of Rosslau, for example, four former POWs returned on October 22, 1953.[98] The town council planned to have at least one returnee lecture about his impressions of the Soviet Union during November, known as the month of German–Soviet friendship. The SED found itself in a precarious position after the events of June 16 and 17, which ended when Soviet tanks and the *Volkspolizei* crushed the uprising. Soviet officials hoped that additional repatriations would not only bolster popularity for the SED and improve relationships with the USSR but would also provide the SED with additional manpower to spread pro-Soviet propaganda and increase support for the East German government.

One of the repatriates of 1953 played a particularly significant role on his return. After a decade in captivity, the Soviet Union released former field marshal Friedrich Paulus. Paulus had become a strong advocate of the Soviet Union and the GDR. In a letter to Stalin written on May 13, 1950, Paulus discussed his progress toward active antifascism after his capture at the Battle of Stalingrad in 1943.[99] Although he had not initially joined the BDO and NKFD, Paulus explained, he eventually became one of the leading members of these two wartime societies that urged the end of the war and the rejection of Hitler and Nazism. During his years of captivity, Paulus became an ardent antifascist. He participated in the 1946 Nuremberg process and delivered testimony that helped convict his former colleagues and leaders. He also reflected on the development of a divided Germany. He asked Stalin for repatriation not to his homeland of West Germany but to East Germany so that he could place himself at the service of its government. He also noted, "I would not like to leave the Soviet Union with-

---

96. See chapter 4 for more information about the June 1953 uprising in East Germany.

97. Hope M. Harrison, *Driving the Soviets up the Wall: Soviet-East German Relations, 1953–1961* (Princeton, NJ: Princeton University Press, 2011), 22, 35; Christian F. Ostermann, ed., *Uprising in East Germany 1953: The Cold War, the German Question, and the First Major Upheaval Behind the Iron Curtain* (Budapest: Central European University Press, 2001), 1, 163–165.

98. Der Rat des Kreises Rosslau, October 22, 1953, BA-SAPMO, DO 1/8665.

99. RGASPI, f. 82, op. 2, d. 1168, ll. 39–44.

out telling the Soviet people that I came to their country in blind act as an enemy, and now I'll go away as a man who has seen the light, free from Nazi fetters and a friend of this country." Although Paulus remained in Soviet captivity for another three years after writing this letter, he had become a committed supporter of a unified, socialist Germany and Soviet–German friendship and cooperation. Paulus's repatriation in November 1953 was met with a considerable amount of distrust and speculation in the West German media. After his release, Paulus moved to Dresden where he devoted his last years to the regime, remaining a vocal supporter of socialism and the Soviet Union. He worked for the East German Military History Research Unit and gave addresses at conferences and press releases, where he publicly supported both socialist states.[100]

Clearly, Soviet and East German leaders recognized and valued the contribution of antifascist returnee POWs in the creation and shaping of the German Democratic Republic. Both regimes sought after and tracked the agitprop work of the returnees. These men were valued by both states for their pro-Soviet leanings and for their roles in constructing a new state in East Germany. Although all these men had value in the GDR, prominent believers such as Paulus were particularly important. His choice to return to East Germany rather than his native West Germany constituted a major propaganda victory for the Soviet Union and the GDR.

During and after World War II, the Soviet leadership invested considerable time and resources to engage in propaganda work with German POWs. Although their forced labor was the main factor that shaped the POW experience, propaganda and antifascist education also exercised a major influence on life in captivity. The GUPVI borrowed this balance of labor and propaganda from the Gulag. Both systems placed great emphasis on reeducating their captives. Neither system wanted to release anyone who had failed to transform themselves from being enemies of the Soviet system to its supporters. Camp hierarchy and structure provided a stable and effective means to undertake two different phases of POW propaganda and reeducation work during and after World War II.

Although the wartime POW propaganda effort was ineffective in contributing to the end of the war, it did help establish a comprehensive antifascist reeducation program, which would become a defining feature of the POW experience and play an important role in the postwar transition of Germany

100. To Secretary of State Akcermann, October 9, 1953, PA AA, M 1/A15677, S. 348; Correlli Barnett, *Hitler's Generals* (New York: Grove Press, 2003), 372; and Wilhelm Adam and Otto Rühle, *With Paulus at Stalingrad*, trans. Tony Le Tissier (Barnsley, UK: Pen and Sword, 2017), 281–282.

from a fascist state to a socialist one. In both the GUPVI and the Gulag, camp officials created a system of privilege through the reeducation program. Those who had successfully transformed themselves in the Gulag could qualify for reintegration into Soviet society. Those POWs who went above and beyond in the reeducation program could qualify for early repatriation to their homeland and returned in better physical shape than others who were released when debilitated.

After the war, there were three major waves of repatriation tied to the denazification of Germany and the establishment of a socialist German state. These waves of repatriation, which coincided with German capitulation in 1945, the formalization of two German states in 1949, and an uprising in the GDR in 1953, aimed to actively employ reeducated returnee POWs for propaganda work across Germany. Reeducation of POWs, thus, was not only important for shaping the POW experience during the war but also for influencing repatriation after the war, the establishment of the German Democratic Republic, and counteracting the ideological tensions of the Cold War. Indeed, after 1949, the German POWs became more valuable to Soviet officials for their political rather than their economic potential. As the next chapter shows, these men played a pivotal role in Soviet–German relations and the Cold War in Europe.

CHAPTER 4

The Politics of Repatriation

The Soviet Union steadily returned POWs after Germany's capitulation in May 1945. Before 1949, the releases were primarily economic in motivation: prisoners who were too ill or too weak to work were sent home. After 1949, however, other factors, including changes in Soviet domestic and international politics, began to play a role in determining who would be released. This chapter focuses on the role of POWs as political pawns between the two German states and the USSR, as diplomats, citizens, NGOs, and the East and West German press all worked to secure the release of the POWs. This chapter argues that, after 1949, the repatriation of those POWs who were not released because of their poor physical condition or for their use as antifascist propagandists was shaped by political developments within the Soviet Union and by Soviet–German Cold War relations. The POWs who remained after 1949 largely did so at Stalin's insistence. After Stalin's death, the leadership struggle within the USSR strongly affected the fate of the remaining POWs. Those vying for power saw the release of the POWs as a way to further their positions within the Soviet Union and abroad. Changes in Soviet domestic politics after 1953 continued to influence the final instances of repatriation. Although Soviet politicians were influenced by the actions of East and West German officials, as well as by an uprising in the GDR in June 1953, the intensifying Cold War ultimately dictated the course of the last releases. Nikita Khrushchev, reacting to increasing threats to Soviet security in Europe, finally acquiesced to the release of the last POWs to formalize Soviet and West German relations. Khrushchev hoped this gesture would create goodwill within the FRG as well.

The fate of German POWs in the Soviet Union played out publicly in the press of both East and West Germany. The East German press manipulated the POW issue to advance the domestic and international goals of the Soviet Union. Initially, East German journalists used the return of POWs as a tool for pro-Socialist Unity Party (SED) and pro-Soviet propaganda until it became harder to hide their poor physical condition. At the same time, Western powers highlighted the large numbers of detained German POWs and the reasons for their detention to publicly criticize and undermine the Soviet government. Soviet officials and the East German press, in response to heightened Western criticism, modified how they spoke about the POWs. They publicly rebranded them as war criminals to legitimize their continuing detainment.

After the death of Stalin, Soviet leaders used the release of the POWs to build pro-Soviet public sentiment. In April 1953, reform-minded Soviet leaders amnestied Soviet and German prisoners, resulting in a major wave of repatriation for the POWs. A liberalization of domestic policies benefited POWs and Soviet citizens alike. Later, in June 1953, the Soviet government released additional POWs to garner popular support for the SED and Soviet Union in the wake of the crackdown on the uprising in East Berlin that threatened the SED's legitimacy. Finally, the Soviet Union agreed to release the last of the POWs when it formally recognized the government of the Federal Republic of Germany in 1955.

Between 1949 and 1956, various involved parties questioned the official Soviet statistics on the number of POWs in captivity. Indeed, accurate numbers of German POWs and war criminals eluded even the highest members of the Soviet government. Various Soviet organizations and ministries that managed repatriation in the 1940s and 1950s often provided conflicting numbers. Figures cited within internal memos, published press releases, and diplomatic correspondence were rarely consistent. In 1947, the Department for Repatriation Affairs began to oversee the repatriation not only of Soviet citizens from abroad but also of foreign citizens back to their homelands.[1] This department also closely monitored the numbers of repatriated German POWs and produced summary reports for 1947, 1948, and 1949, with some briefer reports for 1950. Yet despite this newly centralized record keeping, Soviet officials still misreported POW totals and contradicted their official press releases by repatriating

---

1. GARF, f. 9526, op. 6, d. 727, l. 22. In Russian, *Upravlenie Upolnomochennogo Soveta Ministrov SSSR po Delam Repatriatsii.*

more POWs than they claimed had been in captivity during 1949 and 1950. Even though press statements suggested that the repatriation process was complete, trains full of POWs continued to travel to Germany. The East and West German governments, families, and nongovernmental organizations (NGOs) were correct to doubt the promises and public statements of the Soviet Union about the release of the remaining captive men.

Lack of information about POW deaths made an accurate assessment of the true number of Germans in Soviet captivity even more difficult. Soviet authorities only released lists of dead POWs on rare occasions, a policy that created problems especially for their allies in the GDR. Often, families had to rely solely on word of mouth from those who had been repatriated to learn the fates of their relatives. One woman wrote to a high-ranking member of the SED to complain about the lack of official news of the death of her son-in-law, after an acquaintance from a camp in the USSR informed the family that he had died while they were in the camp together. The woman wanted to know who was responsible for the POWs' well-being in the USSR and why their family had not been notified of his death.[2] This lack of clarity created additional challenges for the SED, which could not publicly contradict Soviet statements. For the FRG and its allies, it served as the main line of attack on Soviet POW policies.

High Politics and POW Repatriation: 1949–1953

Repatriation of German POWs became a major diplomatic issue in 1949. Soviet officials had earlier promised to return all the German POWs by December 31, 1948; their failure to do so turned the continued detention of the POWs into a huge problem for Soviet authorities. Officials, NGOs, and families in East and West Germany attempted to persuade the leaders of the Soviet Union to release the remaining POWs. The issue did not remain a Soviet–German one: Western allies also recognized the broken promise and used private diplomatic correspondence, UN investigations, and the press to attack the Soviet Union in the intensifying Cold War. In response, Soviet authorities changed their discourse about the POWs. In 1949, they began to claim that the only POWs who remained were war criminals. Indeed, the Soviet Union had conducted a series of war crime trials of Germans between 1945 and 1949. Unintentionally, Soviet press releases, which contained huge discrepancies between the number of men returning and the published totals, only fueled Western attacks.

2. "An Gen. Helmuth Lehmann," December 5, 1946, BA-SAPMO, DY 30/68826, S. 56.

Regardless of the motivation for their release, most prisoners followed a set route for repatriation. Trains from different locations in the Soviet Union went to Brest, where POWs went through customs and transferred to other trains bound for Camp No. 69 at Frankfurt an der Oder in East Germany, a city directly across the border with Poland.[3] One POW noted that the train rides home took weeks. The returnee transports only traveled at night because freight trains took priority during the days.[4] The returnees then spent several days in Camp No. 69 where camp staff assessed their health status and either sent them for treatment in its hospital or transferred them to a representative of the German government serving in the Department of Repatriation of the Soviet Military Administration in Germany (SVAG, or SMAD in German). Information about the number of prisoners, their physical condition, and the transfer to SVAG officials was recorded on standardized forms.[5]

News of repatriations and the ongoing political affairs concerning their release frequently received public attention in the news publications of a divided Germany. As Germany stabilized after the war and the occupiers rebuilt their zones, German newspapers, tabloids, and magazines reported on major issues such as the formation of two German nations and the POWs. Although the publications of East and West Germany had different ideological aims, levels of freedom, and uses as propaganda, all were united in their concern for the fate of the POWs. The newspapers of both states provided frequent coverage of the POWs and their fates, publishing regular updates. They also covered the diplomatic meetings of German and Soviet ministers in which release dates were discussed. Additionally, news media from both German states reprinted announcements from the Telegraph Agency of the Soviet Union (TASS). The most important East German publication was *Neues Deutschland*, the official voice of the SED. The West German press did not have a single national publication but revived the prewar tradition of regional newspapers.[6] A few publications, however, did achieve broad readership, such as the magazine *Der Spiegel* (The Mirror), the newspaper *Frankfurter Allgemeine Zeitung* (Frankfurt General Newspaper), and the tabloid *Bild-Zeitung* (Picture-Newspaper). Each of these

---

3. RGVA, f. 105p, op. 16, d. 3, l. 191–191ob, BA-SAPMO, DO 2/77, S. 1.

4. Dianna M. Popp and Gottfried P. Dulias, *Another Bowl of Kapusta: The True Life Story of a World War II Luftwaffe Fighter Pilot and P.O.W. in Russia* (Bloomington, IN: AuthorHouse, 2004), 203.

5. For information about how all POWs were to be sent to Camp No. 69 for evaluation and treatment, as well as to be handed over to SVAG representatives, see GARF, f. 9526, op. 6, d. 384, l. 49. For examples of the standardized form. see GARF, f. 7317, op. 21, d. 11, l. 13; GARF, f. 7317, op. 21, d. 26, l. 1; or GARF, f. 9526, op. 1, d. 508, l. 38.

6. Albert Düsenberg, *Die Presse in Deutschland* (Bonn: Scholl, 1960), 8, 16, 20; Oron J. Hale, *The Captive Press in the Third Reich* (Princeton, NJ: Princeton University Press, 1973), 1.

major publications had different political leanings, which influenced how they reported on the POWs.

From 1946 to 1949, East and West German press coverage of the returning POWs differed in three major ways. First, the East German press operated under the auspices of the SED and thus only wrote positive things about this party and the USSR. Positive reporting about both the Soviet Union and the East German state with regard to the POWs would help the nascent state, positioning the SED as a tough negotiator and defender of POWs against the occupying authorities. When faced with bad news, such as delayed repatriations or the poor health of the returnees, SED press organs often ignored these issues or buried them within other articles. In contrast, the West German press highlighted these failures to lambast the Soviet regime. The East and West German publications also differed in their coverage of Soviet announcements regarding the numbers of POWs in the USSR and of those released. The East German press reprinted the Soviet statements verbatim, whereas, the West German reporters challenged them, openly disputing the credibility of Soviet authorities. Finally, the press of the two nations diverged in their coverage of the Soviet antifascist reeducation program. The East German press did not mention this topic, whereas the West German press claimed that the USSR offered quicker releases for those who pledged to undertake leadership and propaganda roles on repatriation.

Nearly from its inception, *Neues Deutschland* in East Germany covered the return of POWs in a highly inconsistent fashion. Any update about the POWs was front-page news. Generally, announcements were limited to one or two short paragraphs announcing the numbers of returning POWs or of those expected to return; this information was sometimes accompanied by departure and arrival locations.[7] However, the content of the reports differed greatly from one issue to the next. Its varying content reflected its propaganda role for the SED and the Soviet Union and the restrictions that it faced. It could not publicly fault either the SED or its allies. At times shorter articles hinted at the physical degeneration and debilitation of the POWs, but they were often followed the next day by longer articles and interviews that pictured those who returned as healthy and smiling and praised their Soviet captors.

---

7. *Neues Deutschland* published its first issue on April 23, 1946, one day after the Communist Party of Germany (KPD) and the Social Democratic Party of Germany (SPD) merged to form the Socialist Unity Party of Germany (SED). Licensed and approved by the Soviet Military Administration, *Neues Deutschland* was to serve as the public voice of the SED or according to the masthead, the "Organ of the Central Committee of the Socialist United Party of Germany." The paper, socialist in leaning and sympathetic to the Soviet Union and other socialist countries, was controlled by the SED and overseen by the SVAG. "Über uns," *Neues Deutschland*, accessed May 5, 2015, http://www.neues-deutschland.de/kontakt/9.

In July 1946, for example, *Neues Deutschland* reported on the status of former POWs at arrival camp Gronenfelde in Frankfurt (Oder) in Brandenburg. Some articles described poor conditions in the POW camps in the USSR, and others contained pro-Soviet statements. After an article highlighted the POWs' difficult circumstances, others would follow emphasizing their excellent treatment. In one edition in July, *Neues Deutschland* revealed that East German officials were aware that the returnees would likely be ill or injured, noting that two hospitals had been cleared of patients so they would have room to accept POWs in need of medical treatment. It also noted that reception officials had prepared extra rations for distribution to the returnees.[8] A few days later, however, *Neues Deutschland* downplayed and even tried to hide the poor physical condition of the returnees by featuring interviews that attested to the good care in the Soviet camps and their sizable rations. which equaled those distributed to Red Army soldiers.[9] A few days after that, an article announcing the previous day's repatriation transport arrival again hinted that the USSR released only those could not work. An additional 1,300 POWs arrived after spending about ten days in transport, most of whom were "principally sick and wounded."[10] Journalists again attempted to downplay the information about prisoners' ill health by including a photo of happy POWs in Germany with the caption, "Homecoming in a peaceful Germany," followed by these words: "Finally in the homeland! Released prisoners of war from the Soviet Union left the Silesian Station."[11] Three days later, *Neues Deutschland* again changed its tone in an article titled "What Returnees Report." Twenty-year-old Karl Heinz Fischer from Zittau in Sachsen, for example, reported being assigned to a collective farm with about twenty-five soldiers: "We boarded in a camp, but we could eat as much as we wanted in the kolkhoz. We were treated exactly the same as every other kolkhoz worker: we received plenty of tobacco on time and we had everything that we needed."[12] Other soldiers reported ration increases over the time of their incarceration in the camps. Alfred Niekmann from Reutenham, who was assigned to work in a factory, said that he received 500 grams of bread and three bowls of soup daily through 1944. He did not mention when rations increased, but he said that, once the overall situation in the Soviet Union improved, he and his fellow prisoners received 900 grams of bread in addition to their soup. He also mentioned receiving chocolate and cocoa. The conditions

---

8. "Frankfurt bereit zum Empfang unserer Kriegsgefangenen aus der SU," *Neues Deutschland*, July 19, 1946, 1.

9. "Frankfurt grüßt die Kriegsgefangenen," *Neues Deutschland*, July 23, 1946, 1.

10. "Weitere Kreisgefangene eingetroffen," *Neues Deutschland*, July 24, 1946, 1.

11. "Heimkehr in ein friedliches Deutschland," *Neueus Deutschland*, July 24, 1946, 1.

12. Zentralsekretariat der SED, "Was Heimkehrer berichten," *Neues Deutschland*, July 27, 1946, 1.

were so good, reported Niekmann, that he gained weight over the course of his internment.

At the same time, *Neues Deutschland* worked to portray the SED as a champion for POW rights and repatriation. In July 1946, it published a front-page letter from the Central Secretariat (CS) of the SED about the POWs; it stated that the SED had been instrumental in the Soviet Union's agreement to return 120,000 POWs through October 1946. Additionally, the CS called on citizens of the Soviet Occupation Zone to welcome the returnees and explain the democratic freedoms and differences from the Nazi regime made possible by the Soviet Union and the SED.[13] This publication and subsequent others were part of a conscious effort by the SED to manage the memory of the war and shape East Germany's trajectory. At this time, Wilhelm Pieck asserted that, instead of feeling a collective guilt for their complicity in the war, the German people needed only to blame the ardent fascists for their suffering during the war and in the immediate postwar period. Allegiance to a new political and ideological system would spare them from any future misery. Indeed, returned POWs served as the models for this transformation of Germany. Pieck noted that Hitler's ideology was responsible for causing the war and for the prisoners' subsequent captivity but that these men had benefited from antifascist training and the promise of a socialist future thanks to the Soviet Union.[14] Just as the Soviet Union had been an ally to these men and improved their lives and futures, so too would the Soviet Union engage in this task with East Germany after their return.

By September 1946, a total of 122,215 former prisoners had returned to German soil, over two thousand more than the 120,000 POWs guaranteed by the Soviet government and the SED.[15] Their return, however, did not satisfy the East German public, which appreciated the releases but saw them as still too small and too slow. Both the SED and *Neues Deutschland* were in a precarious position. Both remained subordinate to the USSR and therefore tried to increase popular support for the Soviet Union, a stance that made it difficult for them to appear as effective and tough negotiators on behalf of the POWs. The POW question played an especially important role in the lives of women in East Germany. Because of the large number of war deaths and the continued incarceration of many of their men, there was a huge demographic imbalance in the Soviet Occupation Zone. The detention caused much ran-

---

13. "Hilfe und Gleichberechtigung unseren Heimkehrern," *Neueus Deutschland,* July 31, 1946, 1.

14. "Das 'Neue Deutschland' bei den Heimkehrern in Frankfurt," *Neues Deutschland,* August 8, 1946, 1; Frank Biess, *Homecomings: Returning POWs and the Legacies of Defeat in Postwar Germany* (Princeton, NJ: Princeton University Press, 2006), 53, 56, 58, 60–62, 203.

15. "122,215," *Neues Deutschland,* September 29, 1946, 1.

cor toward both the Soviet Union and the SED. SED officials noticed that the POW issue hurt their ability to gain popular support from women. Publicly, the SED praised the releases but privately feared the negative impact of the slow pace of repatriation and the lack of communication between German citizens and their detained family members. Male and female members of the German Communist Party debated the issue in letters and closed sessions of the Central Secretariat (CS). Female party members argued that the party needed to convince the Soviet government to increase the frequency and number of repatriations.[16]

The dissatisfaction of East German women was not confined to party meetings and internal documents: high-ranking women took the issue to the national press. The headline of *Neues Deutschland* for December 1, 1946, read, "To Our Prisoners of War: Käthe Kern and Elli Schmidt Are Asking for Repatriation."[17] These leaders of the SED's Women's Secretariat launched a direct plea to the SVAG for the return of the remaining husbands, sons, and brothers. Yet the article in its first few paragraphs pointed out that the SED had always taken the issue of the POWs seriously, thereby shifting blame to the SVAG from the Soviet or East German governments. Thus, *Neues Deutschland* carefully tiptoed around the issues. Without accusing the SED or the Soviet government as a whole, the newspaper used the unpopular SVAG occupation regime as a scapegoat.

In March and April 1947, representatives of the Allied Powers met in Moscow for the Foreign Ministers Conference. The conference, like many before it, essentially ended in failure.[18] The Western powers refused to give the Soviet Union reparations payments or resources from the Western sector of Germany, and Soviet officials refused to abandon their effort to establish a socialist Germany. The Soviet representatives also rejected a unified economic policy for all four German occupation zones. The one thing that all the powers could, and did, agree on was the release of all German POWs by December 31, 1948.[19]

The prolonged timeline for the release of German POWs from all the Allied victor nations caused issues for East German leaders. When *Neues Deutschland* had bad news to report concerning the POWs or the SED, it tried to withhold it from the public for as long as possible. Soviet officials announced

16. Donna Harsch, *Revenge of the Domestic: Women, the Family, and Communism in the German Democratic Republic* (Princeton, NJ: Princeton University Press, 2007), 25, 36; Harsch, "Approach/Avoidance: Communists and Women in East Germany, 1945–9," *Social History* 25, no. 2 (May 2000): 163.

17. "Um unsere Kriegsgefangenen: Käthe Kern und Elli Schmidt bitten um Heimsendung," *Neues Deutschland*, December 1, 1946, 1.

18. Roger S. Whitcomb, *The Cold War in Retrospect: The Formative Years* (Westport, CT: Greenwood, 1998), 83–85.

19. Biess, *Homecomings*, 45; Annette Kaminsky, "Vorwort," in *Heimkehr 1948*, ed. Annette Kaminsky (Munich: Beck, 1998), 7.

on May 7, 1947, that they would not return the remaining German POWs until the end of 1948. The newspaper did not report this new development for two weeks, and when it did, it buried the news in the middle of an article about the Moscow Foreign Ministers Conference.[20] The failure to secure an expeditious release of the POWs amounted to a failure for the SED, which it tried to downplay as much as possible. Yet, because the SED still functioned under the guidance of the SVAG, the party could not publicly decry the Soviet decision. The failure of the SED to ensure that the POWs would be released on time and the tension between the Soviet and the future East German government over the broken promise were reflected in the sparse coverage of POWs in *Neues Deutschland* over the course of 1947 and 1948. Although two and a half times as many POWs were repatriated in 1947 as 1946, the topic was not widely discussed in the East German press.[21] Over the course of 1947, there were short announcements whenever soldiers returned, but they merely listed the date of return transports and the numbers of POWs aboard.[22] Another probable reason for the decreased coverage was the Soviet famine, which began in the summer of 1946 and reached its peak from February through August 1947.[23] As Soviet authorities released more and more POWs during the famine, the physical condition of those returning after enduring months of reduced rations was probably worse than before. Given the physical conditions of the returnees, it was harder for the press to extol Soviet kindness and its provision of sufficient rations. The lack of coverage of POWs in the Eastern press continued throughout 1948 as well.

Unsurprisingly, the Western press coverage of the POW question differed greatly from that of *Neues Deutschland*. Where the East German press publicized the victories of the SED, the generosity of the Soviet Union, and the fair treatment of POWs, the West German press highlighted their poor treatment and the Soviet Union's domestic difficulties. When the East German press reduced its reporting at the time of the famine, the West German press emphasized poor conditions in Soviet camps and the difficulties that the men

20. Kaminsky, "Vorwort," 7; "Zu den Ergebnissen von Moskau," *Neues Deutschland*, May 22, 1947, 1.

21. The repatriation total for 1946 is calculated from the monthly camp populations for 1946, as reported in TsKhIDK, f. 1/p, op. 17a, d. 1, l. 24, in Maksim Matveevich Zagorul'ko, *Voennoplennye v SSSR 1939–1956: Dokumenty i materialy* (Moscow: Logos, 2000), 499–500, minus the death total for 1946. The 1947 repatriation figure comes from GARF, f. 9401, op. 2, d. 169, l. 203–212.

22. See, for examplem "Richtung Heimat," *Neues Deutschland*, May 14, 1947; or "Neue Heimkehrertransporte," *Neues Deutschland*, May 30, 1947.

23. Michael Ellman, "The 1947 Soviet Famine and the Entitlement Approach to Famines," *Cambridge Journal of Economics* 24, no. 5 (2000): 607; Donald Filtzer, *The Hazards of Urban Life in Late Stalinist Russia: Health, Hygiene, and Living Standards, 1943–1953* (Cambridge: Cambridge University Press, 2010), 163–164.

experienced on return. In January 1947, the weekly news magazine *Der Spiegel* began publication.[24] In one article, it chronicled the experiences of Walter Holzhausen, a former sergeant of the Wehrmacht, as typical of POW treatment.[25] In contrast to earlier reports from the East German press, Holzhausen reported scarce rations, moldy bread, and illness. Holzhausen contracted malaria and was sent to a camp hospital, where he found many of his fellow inmates suffering from starvation. Eventually, Holzhausen recovered and was sent to antifascist training before his release in 1948.

Unlike their East German counterpart, West German publications scrutinized Soviet press releases and outright accused the Soviet officials of lying. After the March 1947 Council of Foreign Ministers meeting in Moscow, Molotov, the Soviet foreign minister, reported on March 15 that only 890,532 German POWs remained in the Soviet Union and that the Soviet Union had returned 1,003,974 POWs since the German surrender.[26] *Der Spiegel* published the figures cited by Molotov but questioned their authenticity. The paper noted that the British and American delegations had calculated much higher numbers, which had prompted the Soviet officials to do their first public accounting. The paper did not only criticize the Soviet government, however. It also listed the numbers of Germans still in the hands of the Americans (30,976), British (435,295), French (631,483), Belgians (40,000), Poles (30,000), and Yugoslavs (uncertain)—illustrating that captivity concerned the people of Germany regardless of who were the captors.[27]

West German publications also accused Soviet authorities of selectively releasing prisoners to accomplish their political goals. During the war, Soviet officials had created the National Committee for Free Germany (NKFD) and the Union of German Officers to encourage leaders in the German Army to overthrow Hitler. The NKFD worked hard to spread its message to Germans within Soviet POW camps. After the war, former officers who had participated in these two groups returned to Germany. In addition to working for the East German administration, some wrote articles published in *Neues Deutschland*.[28] Although *Neues Deutschland* did not consistently cover propaganda work with POWs and officers, *Der Spiegel* did. *Der Spiegel* charged the Soviet government

24. "Six Decades of Quality Journalism: The History of DER SPIEGEL," *Der Spiegel*, October 5, 2001, accessed May 5, 2015, http://www.spiegel.de/international/six-decades-of-quality-journalism -the-history-of-der-spiegel-a-789853.html.

25. "Kriegsgefangene das war hart genug: 40 Minuten von Frankfurt," *Der Spiegel*, 26/1948, June 26, 1948, 16–17.

26. "890,532 Kriegsgefangene in der UdSSR," *Neues Deutschland*, March 16, 1947, 1.

27. "Millionen im Schatten," *Der Spiegel*, 12/1947, March 22, 1947, 6.

28. Norman M. Naimark, *The Russians in Germany: A History of the Soviet Zone of Occupation, 1945–1949* (Cambridge, MA: Belknap Press, 1995), 10, 18, 120.

with releasing POWs who were NKFD members so they could assume leadership roles in the Soviet Military Administration of Germany or other top government organizations. The article listed, for example, Colonel Steidel, an officer under Field Marshal Paulus, who was appointed the deputy chief of the Central Agricultural Administration in Berlin. *Der Spiegel* called this move by the Soviets an attempt to revert to a Bismarck style of government collaboration with the military. Naturally, *Der Spiegel* asserted, elite officers would accommodate the wishes of the Soviet regime in return for better treatment and early release.[29]

The issue of German POW captivity largely lay dormant over the second half of 1947 and through the course of 1948. Press coverage and attempts at diplomatic intervention stalled with issuance of a formal agreement for all Allies to release their German POWs by December 31, 1948. Although the Western powers largely adhered to this agreement, the Soviet Union did not, which ushered in a new wave of diplomatic tensions and press coverage. TASS issued a press release on January 4, 1949, that caused massive diplomatic headaches for the USSR and served to undermine trust in subsequent reports about Germans still in Soviet captivity. In this release, TASS announced that 17,552 German POWs awaited repatriation and that 1,939,077 had already returned home.[30] Of those still held, 9,717 sentenced war criminals would remain, and 3,815 men still awaited trial. All the other POWs awaiting repatriation, as well as those found innocent, were to be returned by the end of 1949. The announcement suggested that most of the POWs had already returned and that only a small number still awaited repatriation.

After this press release, Soviet authorities redefined "prisoners of war" as "war criminals." The shift in terminology was likely aimed at justifying their decision to detain the remaining POWs after the agreed-on return date. In addition to the change in terminology, subsequent TASS announcements provided inaccurate accountings of the number of German captives. Although Soviet tribunals did not begin to try Germans until after the war, the number of men tried in 1949 alone contradicted the figures publicly released by the Soviet Union. In 1949, Soviet tribunals tried 18,931 Germans, almost five times as many men as Soviet authorities had announced were awaiting trial.[31] Not all these men were

---

29. "Russen fördern Freie Deutsche: Wegbereiter Bismarck," *Der Spiegel*, 9/1947, March 1, 1947, 6.

30. TASS was the central agency for the distribution of international news for all Soviet news media. RGASPI, f. 82, op. 2, d. 488, ll. 10 and repeated 148.

31. Tribunals held during the war, such as the 1943 Krasnodar trial, tried predominantly Soviet citizens for Nazi collaboration. In 1943, when there were numerous highly publicized Soviet military tribunals, only forty-six Germans were tried, twelve of whom were sentenced to death. Only 167 Germans were tried in 1945. Some of the Germans tried were not members of the military. At least 26,000 German civilian internees were tried and sentenced as war criminals. Ilya Bourtman, "'Blood for Blood, Death for

convicted. Some of those who were convicted were charged under the vague Article 58 of the Russian RSFSR Penal Code, "Counterrevolutionary Crimes." Others, who were more likely guilty of committing war crimes, were sentenced under the Presidium of the Supreme Soviet decree from April 19, 1943, which specified Nazi war crimes against the Soviet Union.[32] Unquestionably, many of these men had committed crimes against the Soviet population and as part of the Holocaust. However, some may have been convicted under the presumption of guilt by association. Much of the rationales for the later trials and the guilt of those tried cannot be determined because most of the Politburo documents concerning war crimes and German military tribunals remain classified.[33] The actions of the Russian Military Prosecutor's Office call into question the reliability of the trials, however. In October 1991, the Supreme Soviet of the RSFSR passed the law "On Rehabilitation of Victims of Political Repression." Between its passing and January 2000, the families of German servicemen filed twelve thousand requests for rehabilitation with the Russian Military Prosecutor's office, of which eight thousand were approved.[34]

The West German press wasted no time in attacking the Soviet Union for its failure to fulfill its promise of repatriating all its POWs by December 31, 1948. Four days after the TASS press release of January 4, 1949, *Der Spiegel* praised the Western powers for their continued investigations. Journalists reported that diplomats from the United States, United Kingdom, and France continued to question the Soviet government about the number of POWs who remained, despite the Soviet promise to return them by December 31, 1948. They again noted the discrepancies in Soviet figures. The diplomats challenged Soviet authorities to provide a more accurate and detailed accounting. Once again, the West German press implied that such an accurate account would reveal the number of POWs who had died in Soviet hands. Through surveys of returning POWs, West German officials calculated that 690,000 prisoners died in Soviet captivity through February 1948.[35] Both the press of West Germany

Death': The Soviet Military Tribunal in Krasnodar, 1943," *Holocaust and Genocide Studies* 22, no. 2 (Fall 2008): 247–248; Biess, *Homecomings*, 45.

32. A. L. Kuz'minykh, *Voennyi plen i internirovanie v SSSR (1939–1956 gody)* (Vologda: Drevnosti Severa, 2016), 359–364; A. E. Epifanov, *Organizatsionnye i pravovye osnovy nakazaniya gitlerovskix voennyx prestupnikov i ix posobnikov v SSSR 1941–1956 gg.* (Moscow: Unity, 2017), 234–244; RGVA f. 1p, op. 2t, d. 7; RGVA f. 1p, op. 4t, d. 67; RGVA, f. 1p, op. 7t, d. 4, ll. 103 and 118 and 118ob; Bourtman, "'Blood for Blood,'" 248–249.

33. Bourtman, "'Blood for Blood,'" 259.

34. Cathy Frierson, *Russia's Law 'On Rehabilitation of Victims of Political Repression': 1991–2011, An Enduring Artifact of Transnational Justice*, NCEEER Working Paper, February 28, 2014, 3; Maria Teresa Giusti, *Stalin's Italian Prisoners of War*, trans. Riccardo James Vargiu (Budapest: Central European University Press, 2021), 265.

35. "Jeder Fünfzehnte: Sie leben friedlicher," *Der Spiegel*, 2/1949, January 8, 1949, 8–9.

and diplomats of the Western powers made it clear that the POW question would not be ignored and that they could trust neither the promises nor the reported figures of the Soviet Union.

The East German press could not, and did not, ignore the issue of the Soviet Union's failure to return all prisoners by the end of 1948. However, it adopted a new tactic to deal with the POW question without attacking the East German or Soviet governments: deflecting blame onto the Western powers. The only major article in the East German press about German POWs in December 1948, when there should have been fanfare over the return of a significant portion of the POWs, did not discuss their fate in the hands of the Soviets. Instead, the front-page headline for December 21 was "German POWs Misused for Imperialistic Purposes." The article lambasted the Dutch government for using former Afrika Korps German POWs, who had been held by British and French forces, in their military engagements in Indonesia while trying to retain their overseas colony.[36] Neues Deutschland also blamed General Clay for hiding the truth about the fate of German POWs in Western countries, failing to fulfill France's promise to return the German POWs by the end of 1948, and continuing to employ them in hard labor or the French Foreign Legion. Additionally, Neues Deutschland attacked General Clay and the Western regimes for muddling the truth about the POWs by referring to some as "free workers," a designation that exempted them from agreements concerning their return.[37] Neues Deutschland contrasted the Soviet Union with the West, charging Western governments with creating workarounds to illegitimately detain POWs in their charge as "free workers" or members of their armed forces.[38] Indeed, France had the second-highest number of German POWs after the Soviet Union. Facing pressure to return their POWs as promised by the end of 1948, the French government gave its captives the choice of returning home to a divided Germany or remaining in France as salaried, voluntary workers at their assignments. Most returned, although nearly ten thousand chose to stay.[39] Otto Grotewohl, who would become the first prime

---

36. "Deutsch Kriegsgefangene zu imperialistischen Zwecken mißbraucht," Neues Deutschland, December 21, 1948, 1. It is unclear who these men actually were. It is possible that they had actually been non-German members of the greater German military mechanism. A quick series of searches only revealed that some Dutch citizens who had joined the German Waffen-SS could regain their citizenship by fighting in Indonesia between 1945 and 1949 in support of the Dutch colonial regime's attempt to suppress independence movements. Andrew McGregor, "In the Uniform of the Enemy: The Dutch Waffen-SS," Historynet.com, February 2018, http://www.historynet.com/in-the-uniform-of-the-enemy.htm.

37. "Repatriierungsplan durch General Clay verhindert," Neues Deutschland, January 11, 1949, 1 and 2.

38. "Repatriierungsplan durch General Clay verhindert," 2.

39. Arnold Krammer, Nazi Prisoners of War in America (New York: Stein and Day, 1979), 249–250.

minister of East Germany in October 1949, claimed in *Neues Deutschland* that the issue of POWs was intentionally manipulated by Western governments and media to undermine the Soviet Union. He blamed Western powers for using the former POWs in imperialist campaigns, including Indonesia, as an obstacle to Soviet repatriations: the Soviet government did not want to return the men only for them to be used by Western powers for their own gains. However, Grotewohl stressed that he and the SED would ensure the return of the remaining POWs by the end of 1949.[40] Additionally, *Neues Deutschland* discussed the Soviet antifascist reeducation of POWs but used it to attack the West, claiming that the Allies had confiscated antifascist literature from the POWs who returned from the Soviet Union to the Western Zone.[41] Thus, according to *Neues Deutschland*, not only did Western powers mistreat and misuse their former POWs but they also prevented former Nazis from becoming antifascist citizens who would shape a peaceful Germany.

The January 1949 TASS press release was a diplomatic failure. The Soviet government hoped that it would justify the delayed repatriations but it merely upset its allies in East Germany and fueled early Cold War squabbles with the Western powers. Even though Soviet officials claimed that they only held convicted war criminals after 1949, East and West German citizens and Western government leaders continued to believe that Soviet authorities held onto perhaps millions of German POWs. Many German families clung to hopes that their loved ones remained in Soviet captivity. The wartime and postwar policies of the Nazi regime and the Soviet government allowed these hopes to flourish. During the war, Wehrmacht officials hid the true extent of casualties by telling wives that their husbands were missing rather than dead. Coupled with the Soviet practice of not releasing lists of those in captivity or those who died in captivity, many families hoped that their men were still alive. The absence of accurate accounting for the war dead also allowed families and governments to assume that many more men were alive in Soviet captivity.[42]

In addition to hiding deaths as missing in action, the Wehrmacht also failed to accurately account for deaths during the last year of the war. By the summer of 1944, the Wehrmacht had underreported about a half-million military deaths. In the first third of 1945, the Wehrmacht stated that only 200,000 men had died while in reality 1.2 million lost their lives. Thus, the Wehrmacht stated it had lost 3 million men when it actually lost closer to 4.8 million soldiers. The underrepresentation of these losses led both German families and officials to

---

40. "Otto Grotewohl zur Kriegsgefangenenfrage," *Neues Deutschland*, January 6, 1949, 1.

41. "Kriegsgefangenen wird Literatur beschlagnahmt," *Neues Deutschland*, February 15, 1949, 1.

42. Elizabeth D. Heineman, *What Difference Does a Husband Make? Women and Marital Status in Nazi and Postwar Germany* (Berkeley: University of California Press, 2003), 112.

assume that the Soviet Union held vastly higher numbers of POWs than they reported. This byproduct of anti-Soviet sentiment lingered into the early 1960s.[43]

These popular convictions evoked responses from both the East and West German governments, as well as from the Western allies. The German People's Council (*Deutscher Volksrat*), a political body and essentially a pre-parliament in the Soviet Occupation Zone, passed a resolution on March 3, 1949, stating that the German people were saddened that the Soviet government had not kept its promise to return the last of the POWs by December 31, 1948, but were hopeful that the Soviet Union would keep its promises of January 1949 and return the last of the men over the course of that year.[44] The resolution stated that all the people of Germany needed to work together to bring their citizens home but, careful not to openly antagonize the Soviet Union, also stressed that "all governments" with German POWs needed to release them.

Western officials did not believe the reported numbers and promises of repatriation in the TASS announcement of January 4, 1949: indeed, the published numbers were inaccurate, and the promises of repatriation were empty. A report from the MVD to the first deputy minister of Foreign Affairs of the Soviet Union, Andrei Gromyko, noted that 318,406 German POWs returned home between February 19 and December 1, 1949, and that an additional 73,326 German POWs would be repatriated by the end of the year.[45] At the end of December, the minister of foreign affairs, Andrei Vyshinskii, wrote to Stalin asking for permission to release another TASS article in the wake of West German, Japanese, British, American, and French press campaigns against the Soviet Union over the repatriation of German and Japanese prisoners.[46] Vyshinskii stressed the necessity of stating that the last German and Japanese POWs would be repatriated on January 1, 1950, and that 30,771 Germans would remain in the USSR as sentenced war criminals. Despite Vyshinskii's pleading, it took four months before TASS released any updates on the POW question.

In 1950, the Soviet Union made two announcements via TASS that the repatriation of both German and Japanese prisoners of war had ended earlier in the year, noting that on April 22 and May 5, 1950, 1,939,063 German POWs had been returned.[47] TASS also stated that 9,717 Germans remained as convicted war criminals, 3,815 still awaited trial, and 14 repatriations had been de-

---

43. Nicholas Stargardt, *The German War: A Nation under Arms, 1939–1945* (New York: Basic Books, 2015), 556–558; Rüdiger Overmans, *Deutsche militärische Verluste im Zweiten Weltkrieg* (Munich: Oldenbourg, 2000), 286–289.

44. "Resolution," March 3, 1949, BA-SAPMO DY 34/21185, S. 218–219.

45. RGASPI, f. 82, op. 2, d. 488, ll. 54–55.

46. RGASPI, f. 82, op. 2, d. 488, ll. 56–57.

47. RGASPI, f. 82, op. 2, d. 1089, l. 48.

layed due to ill health of the men, but 11 of them had already recovered and returned. However, records from the Council of Ministers for Repatriation from January 11, 1950, stated that 15,447 German POWs returned home within the first eleven days of the year and that an additional 17,538 Germans returned in April 1950.[48] If repatriations of noncriminal POWs had truly ended as the Soviet government announced through TASS, then roughly 33,000 men should not have returned home in January and April 1950. Furthermore, the TASS announcements stated in both January 1949 and May 1950 that 3,815 POWs awaited trial. In 1949, however, the Soviet Union tried 18,931 German POWs for war crimes. Even if they had all been found innocent, this number is almost half the number of men who returned in two months in 1950. Thus, the Soviet Union released more men than it claimed to hold. The discrepancies between the TASS announcements and the continued mass releases continued to prompt the governments of the United States, Great Britain, and France to demand accurate information about the POW question. These inconsistencies between Soviet press releases and the realities of many more men returning also likely continued to instill false hopes in German families that their relatives were still alive, albeit in what they assumed were secret camps. The mismatch between the Soviet announcements and what actually happened caused many problems for Soviet diplomats.

In the period immediately following the end of the war, U.S. diplomatic correspondence about German prisoners of war revealed little mistrust. Instead, these initial communications attempted to continue the Soviet–American cooperation that had occurred during the war. At times, the United States worked through official diplomatic channels to inquire about Soviet captives who might have committed crimes against U.S. soldiers. In June 1946, for example, the Ministry of Foreign Affairs received a request from the American ambassador to trace or hand over three Germans who participated in shooting down an American airplane over Germany.[49] The deputy minister of foreign affairs wrote to the MVD for assistance in tracking down the Germans named in the letter, but ultimately the MVD responded that it could not locate the men due to a lack of information. Later, in 1948, the Ministry of Foreign Affairs agreed to transfer some German prisoners to the United States to testify in the Nuremburg Trials in exchange for some American-held prisoners.[50] As the Cold War intensified, however, the Western-initiated correspondence switched from pleas for cooperation to attempts to influence the Soviet government.

---

48. GARF, f. 9526, op. 6, d. 727, l. 70 and GARF, f. 9526, op. 6, d. 728, l. 92.
49. AVP RF, f. 0123, op. 30, p. 179, d. 15, ll. 54–55.
50. AVP RF, f. 0123, op. 32, p. 207, d. 18, ll. 23–25.

In July 1950, the Allied ambassadors to the USSR wrote separately to the Soviet Ministry of Foreign Affairs asking for the following: (1) complete information about those sentenced for war crimes and the right for them to correspond with their relatives in Germany; (2) information about the dates of deaths and locations of internment of POWs who died in captivity or transit per the Geneva Convention of July 27, 1929; and (3) a commission comprising representatives of the involved nations or neutral parties to investigate the fate of the POWs in the USSR.[51] In addition, the French ambassador to the Soviet Union asked for information about prisoners of different nationalities who fought for the German Army on the Eastern Front, especially French citizens who had been mobilized into the Wehrmacht. Andrei Gromyko relayed the contents of these letters to Stalin, as well as to other members of the Central Committee including V. M. Molotov, G. M. Malenkov, L. P. Beria, A. I. Mikoyan, L. M. Kaganovich, N. A. Bulganin, and N. S. Khrushchev.[52] He concluded that these letters were aimed at distracting the attention of the German peoples from the imperialistic policies of the Western powers. Gromyko stated that it was necessary to ignore them, but that the Ministry of Foreign Affairs believed it would be acceptable to allow some Germans to write to their families, especially in hopes of maintaining German sympathy for the Soviet Union.

Despite Gromyko's advice, the letters from the Allied ambassadors to the Soviet Union did not go unanswered. The Central Committee ordered the Ministry of Foreign Affairs to respond with an identical statement to each foreign ambassador reaffirming the earlier TASS announcement that all POWs had been released and that the only men remaining were war criminals.[53] The Central Committee also dictated the Ministry of Foreign Affairs' additional response to the French ambassador, stating that the question of the French soldiers had already been answered in a note from the Soviet government on May 15, 1950.[54] The form letter was also to say that these accusations were nothing more than weak attempts to deflect attention from the detrimental policies of the United States, France, and the United Kingdom and to undermine the successes of the GDR. In addition to sending letters to each ambassador, the Central Committee told the Ministry of Foreign Affairs to publish the letter to the American ambassador. Finally, it granted the remaining Germans under the

---

51. RGASPI, f. 82, op. 2, d. 1168, ll. 81–84 for the American letter, RGASPI, f. 82, op. 2, d. 1168, ll. 85–88 for the British letter, and RGASPI, f. 82, op. 2, d. 1168, ll. 89–92 for the French letter.

52. RGASPI, f. 82, op. 2, d. 1168, ll. 75–76.

53. RGASPI, f. 82, op. 2, d. 1168, ll. 77–80; and RGASPI, f. 82, op. 2, d. 1168, ll. 113–118.

54. I have not come across the text of this specific note. Presumably, from the context of RGASPI, f. 82, op. 2, d. 1168, ll. 113–118, it states that the Soviet Union had every right to detain French citizens convicted of war crimes while fighting with the German forces.

control of the Ministry of Internal Affairs permission to correspond with their families in Germany.

The Western allies remained dissatisfied with the Soviet responses to their inquiries and switched from pursuing the issue in private diplomatic correspondence to a more public venue, the United Nations, in 1952. After the large release of POWs in April 1950, very few men were returned during the remainder of 1950 or 1951. The Council of Ministers for Repatriation Affairs noted in 1952 that 17,549 former German POWs were released between March 1, 1950, and March 1, 1951; from March 1, 1951, to February 1, 1952, an additional 4 returned to Germany.[55]

Disbelieving that these men were the last POWs held by the Soviet Union, the Allied powers tried a different tactic in 1952. During a lapse in his tenure as the minister of foreign affairs when he served solely as first deputy premier of the Soviet Union, Vyacheslav Molotov warned Stalin—as well as Malenkov, Beria, Mikoyan, Kaganovich, Bulganin, and Khrushchev—on January 14, 1952, of an impending anti-Soviet campaign to be carried out during an upcoming session of the United Nations.[56] Molotov explained that the UN would host a commission on the Geneva Convention, to which the Soviet Union had been invited; this commission would discuss the question of the German and Japanese POWs still detained in the Soviet Union. He noted that the Ministry of Foreign Affairs recommended sending a note directly to the U.S. government declaring that any further assertion that a large number of German and Japanese POWs remained in Soviet hands would be considered slanderous. Molotov also stated that the UN Commission on Prisoners of War, created by U.S. prompting, was unlawful. Not only had the United States attempted to use a UN commission to criticize the USSR but it had also encouraged representatives of the Australian government to send a similar letter questioning the fate of the remaining POWs. Molotov urged the Soviet government to ignore the chairman of this commission insofar as any response would be acknowledging its legitimacy and would require Soviet representatives to answer its inquiries and demands.

In response to what they deemed to be American provocation, the Central Committee of the All Union Community Party (Bolsheviks) decreed that the Ministry of Foreign Affairs should draft letters to the U.S. Embassy in Moscow and the Australian government and to ignore the letter sent by the UN Commission on Prisoners of War.[57] In these letters, the ministry stated that it

55. GARF, f. 9526, op. 6, d. 1083, l. 25.
56. RGASPI, f. 82, op. 2, d. 1089, ll. 38–39.
57. RGASPI, f. 82, op. 2, d. 1089, ll. 40–41.

had already informed the U.S. Embassy on July 16, 1950, and September 30, 1950, that all the POWs had been repatriated. As such, any continued U.S. assertions that there were hundreds of thousands of POWs still in Soviet hands could only be interpreted as malicious inventions. The ministry saw such actions as a deliberate American plot to diminish the guilt of the war criminals who had attacked the Soviet Union and as part of preparation for a new world war, likely reflecting the escalating tensions between East and West over the formation of the North Atlantic Treaty Organization (NATO) in 1949, the Soviet development of the atomic bomb in 1949, and the start of the Korean War in the summer of 1950.

The United Nations was not the only international body that attempted to broker the release of the POWs. The German Red Cross also tried to intervene on numerous occasions and reached out to other national branches for help. In June 1951, a senior official of the German Red Cross, Dr. Hans Hein, traveled to the United States and met with local and national chapters of the American Red Cross, sharing West Germany's assessment of the true number of German POWs in the Soviet Union and their release.[58] The American Red Cross promised to help the Germans receive accurate information from the Soviet government and to raise the issue with the U.S. secretary of state. The German Red Cross also succeeded in receiving aid from the Swedish Red Cross, which wrote to the Soviet Red Cross and received brief responses stating that the men named on enclosed lists were not known to be in Soviet captivity.[59] The German Red Cross made a major point of pressing the issue of the remaining prisoners in the Soviet Union at the 1952 Red Cross Conference in Toronto.[60] The bevy of press releases and letters between Western and Soviet diplomats, as well as the issue of POWs being brought before the UN between 1949 and 1952, likely were related to the establishment of NATO and the start of the Korean War.

Cold War tensions escalated over the course of 1948. Early in this year, the United States launched the Marshall Plan, which aimed to stop the spread of communism and help Western Europe recover from the economic ravages of the war. A key part of the plan was its promise to create a reindustrialized and capitalist West Germany. Unlike the damaged economy of the Soviet Union, the U.S. economy boomed after World War II. The United States channeled this money into Western Europe to support its vision for a postwar Germany. The Soviet Union could not compete economically, and Stalin feared a

58. "Bericht über meine Verhandlungen mit dem Amerikanischen Roten Kreutz in Washington," June 22, 1951, DRK 2292.
59. "An den DRK-Suchdienst Müchen," July 25, 1951, DRK 2318.
60. "An das Generalsekretariat des Deutschen Roten Kreuzes," June 24, 1952, DRK 2296.

reindustrialized Germany in what he had hoped would become a buffer zone between East and West. In response, Stalin attempted to block the Marshall Plan through a series of maneuvers in Europe.[61] In February 1948, the Soviet government backed a communist coup d'état in Czechoslovakia, firmly placing the state within the Soviet sphere of influence.[62] Unable to agree to the terms of Germany's future and protesting the introduction of the new Deutsche Mark in Western territories, Soviet authorities cut off Allied ground access to West Berlin. Subsequently, the Western allies carried out the Berlin Airlift until May 1949.[63] These events prompted France, the United Kingdom, and the Benelux countries to form the Western Union, a military and economic alliance. In 1949, they asked the United States, Canada, and a few other Western European states to join, forming NATO, an allegedly defensive alliance that the Soviet Union viewed as a threat. No real structure or work on NATO truly took place, however, until the start of the Korean War in June 1950. At this point, the Western allies claimed that they feared an imminent Soviet attack in Europe and began to ramp up defenses there, especially in West Germany.[64]

The Soviet government grew progressively more fearful of NATO and the increase of U.S. weapons in Western Europe. The arms buildup placed the Soviet Union within reach of American bombers. Although the Soviet Union developed the atomic bomb in 1949, Soviet planes did not have the range to bomb the United States and then return home; nor did they have any allied locations where they could land to refuel or from which to depart. U.S. forces, however, benefited from airfields in Norway, Germany, Italy, South Korea, and Japan. U.S. reconnaissance planes frequently entered Soviet airspace, and although many were shot down, these illegal overflights increased the sense of imminent threat.[65] As the Allies kept working to discredit the Soviet Union on the international scene through the plight of the POWs, the Soviet government in turn accused the United States of using the POWs as pawns in their larger objectives to gain military and economic control in Western Europe.

The issue of German POWs remained contentious through the Korean War. During the conflict, captured U.S. soldiers delivered propaganda broadcasts or wrote short articles that blamed capitalism for Jim Crow and denounced the warmongering of Wall Street. As the war transitioned from the

---

61. Benn Steil, *The Marshall Plan: Dawn of the Cold War* (New York: Oxford University Press, 2018), xii.

62. Igor Lukes, *On the Edge of the Cold War: American Diplomats and Spies in Postwar Prague* (New York: Oxford University Press, 2012), 4.

63. Dennis L. Bark, and David R. Gress, *From Shadow to Substance: 1945–1963* (Cambridge, MA: Basil Blackwell, 1993), 213–214, 217.

64. Igor Lukes, *On the Edge of the Cold War*, 4; Bark and Gress, *From Shadow to Substance*, 2–3.

65. William Taubman, *Khrushchev: The Man and His Era* (New York: W. W. Norton, 2004), 243–244.

defense of South Korean to an invasion of North Korea in the fall of 1950, additional U.S. and UN forces soldiers were taken captive by communist forces. The Chinese, however, stopped the invasion, and by summer 1951 the war had turned into a stalemate. Both sides attempted to use their POWs for political statements and propaganda work. Prisoner exchange conditions became vital to the peace negotiations.[66] Although the Soviet Union did not send troops into the conflict, the war became part of their international strategy and relationships with communist allies. In the Cold War, Moscow led one bloc and the United States the other. Events in the European theater of the Cold War were influenced by those in the Asian theater, and vice versa.[67] Western nations continued to interrogate Soviet officials about the status of the German prisoners of war in the USSR to prevent Kremlin officials from publicly decrying the POW politics of the Korean war.

Thus, from 1949 to 1953, the captivity of the German POWs took on an added international political significance as the Cold War heated up. The Soviet government attempted to defend its prolonged incarceration of German POWs by stating that it only held those too ill to repatriate, convicted war criminals, and those awaiting trial. The numbers of men tried and repatriated in 1949 and 1950 led the Germans and the Western allies to continue to question the Soviet government about the true number of remaining men. The formation of Western military alliances, the Soviet development of the atomic bomb, and the start of a new conflict in Korea encouraged the United States, the United Kingdom, France, and the FRG to use the detained POWs as another means to attack the Soviet Union and its ideology.

High Politics and POW Repatriation: 1953–1956

Three major political events in the mid-1950s provided the impetus for the two final waves of repatriation: Stalin's death in March 1953, an East German uprising in June 1953, and Konrad Adenauer's trip to Moscow in September 1955. Each event had direct repercussions for the Soviet Union and the divided German states. Although the latter two events placed external pressure on Soviet leaders, Soviet actions toward the POWs were shaped mainly by the changes in domestic politics and power struggles that emerged after Stalin's death. The

---

66. Charles Steuart Young, *Name, Rank, and Serial Number: Exploiting Korean War POWs at Home and Abroad* (New York: Oxford University Press, 2014), 3, 5–7.

67. For an in-depth discussion of the interrelated nature of European and Asian Cold War events, see, Lorenz M. Lüthi, *Cold Wars: Asia, The Middle East, Europe* (Cambridge: Cambridge University Press, 2020).

final release of the German POWs, then, was the result of post-Stalin Soviet reforms, rather than the successes or failures of Soviet–German Cold War diplomacy.

Stalin's death on March 5, 1953 created a volatile political situation. There was no clear heir apparent, and the leading contenders within the Politburo quickly mobilized to strengthen their power bases. Stalin's potential successors— including Nikita Khrushchev, Lavrentii Beria, Georgy Malenkov, and Vyacheslav Molotov—all sought to distance themselves from Stalin by launching a series of reforms of the structure and staff of the Ministry of Internal Affairs, nationality policies, large-scale economic projects, and agriculture.[68]

One of Stalin's likeliest successors and the head of the MVD, Lavrentii Beria, quickly initiated several reforms that directly affected German POWs. Within less than two weeks of Stalin's death, Beria transformed himself from the feared former head of the NKVD into a champion for change. He supported programs that would promote non-Russian ethnic groups and languages in the USSR, a less heavy-handed approach to East Germany, and a massive overhaul of the Gulag system. Gulag amnesties and reform were some of the most immediate changes. Beria transferred many of the Gulag's industrial enterprises from the control of the MVD to the economic ministries and ended some major construction projects, including a railroad line in northwestern Siberia that was nowhere near completion despite years of labor and billions of rubles of investment. A few days after the Gulag restructuring went into effect on March 27, 1953, the Presidium of the Supreme Soviet enacted the decree "On Amnesty." Soon known as "Beria's Amnesty," it mandated the release of prisoners with sentences shorter than five years and those in special categories such as pregnant women and juveniles. The decree also reduced the sentences of the majority of nonpolitical prisoners. In total, it resulted in the release of 1.2 million prisoners from the Gulag system between April 1 and July 1, 1953.[69] The initial Gulag amnesties extended to the German POWs as well. Molotov and Beria suggested releasing two thousand Germans as part of the wider Gulag amnesty.[70] Soviet authorities soon released many more than those two thousand men, though this was also the result of external factors.

68. Amy Knight, *Beria: Stalin's First Lieutenant*, 183–185; Sergei N. Khrushchev, *Nikita Khrushchev and the Creation of a Superpower*, trans. Shirley Benson (University Park: Penn State Press, 2001), 34–35; Michael Loader, "Beria and Khrushchev: The Power Struggle over Nationality Policy and the Case of Latvia," *Europe-Asia Studies* 68, no. 10 (December 2016): 1759–1761.

69. Knight, 185; Miriam Dobson, *Khrushchev's Cold Summer: Gulag Returnees, Crime, and the Fate of Reform after Stalin* (Ithaca, NY: Cornell University Press, 2009), 7–8; Jeffrey S. Hardy, *The Gulag after Stalin: Redefining Punishment in Khrushchev's Soviet Union, 1953–1964* (Ithaca, NY: Cornell University Press, 2016), 22–23.

70. *Istochnik*, 1994, no. 4, pp. 110–112, in Zagorul'ko, *Voennoplennye v SSSR*, 901.

Soon after Stalin's death and the amnesties, workers in the GDR started a strike in June 1953 that challenged the nation's leadership. The previous year, in July 1952, the SED had rapidly implemented a socialization and collectivization campaign called the "Planned Construction of Socialism," or the *Aufbau* program. Within six months, the East German economy was suffering from elements of the *Aufbau* program, continuing reparations to the Soviet Union, and a lack of raw materials, which were located in Western territories.[71] Soviet leaders were conscious of the tenuous economic situation. At the end of May 1953, the members of the Presidium met to discuss the East German situation. Beria drafted a document titled "Measures to Improve the Political Situation in the GDR" and presented it to the Presidium on June 2, 1953. In the document, Beria called for abandoning the forced construction of socialism and the creation of a united and democratic Germany. The other members of the Presidium, especially Molotov, objected to Beria's plans regarding Germany. Molotov and Khrushchev felt that Beria's position was incorrect and that a socialist East Germany would serve as a model for other Western states to embrace socialism. Nonetheless, Kremlin leaders met with the East German leader Walter Ulbricht from June 2 to 4, 1953, and they went ahead with Beria's suggestions to follow a policy of relaxation and liberalization in East Germany.[72]

Ulbricht and his colleagues grudgingly followed some of the terms of the "Beria Document," but the sudden reversals in government policies led to unrest and civil disobedience across the GDR. On June 10, the East German Politburo announced a "new course" for the state. It promised reduced quotas for peasant farmers and stated that farmers who had fled to the West could have their farms back if they returned. The government also gave amnesty to hundreds of prisoners. However, the Politburo failed to rescind a proposed 10 percent raise in labor quotas. The party and government officials released contradictory statements regarding these quotas, which led to intense dissatisfaction.[73] Unrest grew, turning into riots and demonstrations on June 16 and 17, 1953. Protestors called for a general strike and a halt to the rapid economic and social changes, which they charged had resulted in instability, overwork, food shortages, and poverty. Although most of the protests took place in East

---

71. Hope M. Harrison, *Driving the Soviets up the Wall: Soviet-East German Relations, 1953–1961* (Princeton, NJ: Princeton University Press, 2011), 22, 35; Christian F. Ostermann, ed., *Uprising in East Germany 1953: The Cold War, the German Question, and the First Major Upheaval behind the Iron Curtain* (Budapest: Central European University Press, 2001), 1, 163–165.

72. Knight, *Beria*, 191–193; S. N. Khrushchev, *Nikita Khrushchev*, 36; William Taubman, *Khrushchev*, 247–248.

73. Knight, *Beria*, 192–193.

Berlin, demonstrations took place across all of the GDR, involving more than a half-million people in over 560 cities and communities.

What started as a protest over economic conditions soon turned into a political demonstration calling for Ulbricht's overthrow and German unification.[74] Soviet tanks and troops mobilized with the East German Volkspolizei to crush the uprising, but East German and Soviet leaders understood the precarious nature of the situation.[75] In response to the unrest, the Soviet government decided to release another wave of German POWs in hopes of building public support for the SED and easing tensions between the two countries. In total, the Soviet government released 10,197 German POWs as a goodwill gesture.[76] This release was an emergency measure taken by Soviet leaders to stabilize a situation that had its roots in much wider political and economic concerns.

At the same time, these larger questions concerning the relationship between the USSR and the GDR continued to affect the Soviet leadership struggle. Soon after Stalin's death, Malenkov succeeded him as the chairman of the Council of Ministers. Beria had quickly formed a coalition with Malenkov, which troubled the other political rivals, especially Khrushchev, who formed his own coalition. Beria had collected compromising materials on all his rivals, and they feared his control over the independent and militarized MVD. Khrushchev convinced Malenkov to leave Beria's coalition by asserting that Beria was planning on attacking them. Both Khrushchev and Malenkov felt that Beria would "get them if they did not get him first."[77]

Beria's policies toward East Germany and the June uprising proved to be the final straw that influenced many to join Khrushchev and denounce Beria. Khrushchev interpreted Beria's policy as an abandonment of eighteen million East German citizens to U.S. imperialism and began to mobilize against him. Soviet military leaders also feared Beria's control of the MVD and were increasingly displeased with his handling of the German situation. Beria had undermined Soviet military control of East Germany, replacing an important Soviet general with a civilian and former policeman. Soviet military officials blamed Beria for a policy of appeasement and were angered that they were called to put down the uprising when Beria's reforms backfired and caused unrest. Khrushchev capitalized on the disaster in the GDR, the support of the military, and personal attacks on Beria to lay the groundwork for Beria's removal from power.

---

74. Harrison, *Driving the Soviets up the Wall*, 22, 35; Ostermann, *Uprising in East Germany 1953*, 1, 163–165.

75. "20,000 rebellieren in Ost-Berlin für Freiheit," *Bild-Zeitung*, June 17, 1953, 1; "Russenpanzer walzen Berliner Aufstand nieder: 16 Tote," *Bild-Zeitung*, June 18, 1953, 1.

76. Biess, *Homecomings*, 204.

77. Taubman, *Khrushchev*, 189, 249; Loader, "Beria and Khrushchev," 1779.

On June 26, Khrushchev—with the cooperation of the military and Marshal Zhukov, Bulganin, Malenkov, Molotov, and Brezhnev—had Beria arrested as an enemy of the people and accused him of trying to destroy the party.[78]

Soviet political and military officials recognized the centrality of the East German question to Soviet domestic and international politics. After Beria's arrest, Khrushchev and Molotov denounced Beria's policies regarding Germany at the July 1953 Plenum. They accused him of betraying socialism and collaborating with the West by trying to create a united, neutral, and bourgeois Germany. Ultimately, Beria was executed, and Ulbricht barely managed to remain in power in the GDR.[79] The East German situation deeply shook up Soviet domestic and international politics, and Soviet leaders waited for their domestic political situation to stabilize before they again undertook political measures with either German state.

East German officials made every effort to use the release of the POWs to build popular support and reduce political and economic tension. After the releases, East German officials responded to long-ignored tracing requests from family members. Many families had written to the East German Ministry of the Interior from 1951 to 1953 and not received a response. After the repression of the uprising and throughout 1954, the ministry began responding by sending each family a form letter that stated, "We are pleased that your [husband/son/etc.], following a request by a delegation of the GDR to the government of the Soviet Union, has been released."[80] Although domestic reforms in the Soviet Union and the GDR motivated the repatriations of 1953, this very delayed response letter credited the GDR with having actively worked for their release. Clearly, the SED hoped that the unexpectedly good news would be met with a positive response from those who had made earlier repatriation requests. Family members might believe that their letters had brought their relatives homes and that the GDR government had acted on their behalf by appealing to Soviet authorities for the release of East German citizens.

In fact, the East German government did fight for the return of its citizens.[81] After the release of roughly ten thousand POWs in the late summer

---

78. Taubman, *Khrushchev*, 249; Knight, *Beria*, 196–197; Loader, "Beria and Khrushchev," 1779.

79. Knight, *Beria*, 192, 194; Harrison, *Driving the Soviets up the Wall*, 43; Taubman, *Khrushchev*, 256.

80. For the letters to the Ministry of the Interior and their responses see BA-SAPMO, DO 1/8360.

81. The East Germans were not the only Soviet allies who had troubles obtaining accurate information about the number of their citizens detained in the USSR. During the war, Soviet authorities arrested and deported thousands of Czech citizens. For years, Czech ambassadors attempted to ascertain the true number of their citizens held abroad. As was the case with German POWs, Soviet authorities released conflicting information. Furthermore, Soviet authorities stated that the repatriation of Czech prisoners officially ended in 1948 while continuing to release prisoners into 1949. Czech and German attempts to intervene through the Swedish Red Cross failed. Nonetheless, Czech officials continued to

and fall of 1953, East German and Soviet government officials met to discuss the release of the remaining POWs in the USSR. The men who had returned earlier in 1953 presented a difficult situation for the East German leaders. Publicly, the SED stood by the TASS announcements of 1949 and 1950. They expected no more POWs to return home and dismantled the system for the reception of returning POWs.[82] *Neues Deutschland* also supported the Soviet claims, copied their linguistic shift, and subsequently wrote only of war criminals in Soviet captivity. When these supposed war criminals did return in 1953, the SED grappled with how to present and reintegrate them. Previous returnees, who had been prisoners of war, served as exemplars of antifascist transformation. These men, however, had been defined as war criminals, and their return challenged years of state narratives about the uses and societal roles of returnees. When large numbers of men returned from the USSR in 1946, Wilhelm Pieck solidified his stance against those whom he deemed to be the victimizers of Germany: the unrepentant Nazis and war criminals. However, he also decried those sentenced for crimes in the Soviet Union. He disparaged any notion of a shared collective guilt for the war. Instead, he stated that a small "Hitler clique" had ravaged both the Soviet Union and Germany, forcing millions of Germans to suffer through a war that no one wanted.[83] The returnees up through 1946 did not fall into this category, but those who returned after 1949 did so because of the shift in terminology used by Soviet officials and press releases. East German official documents spoke of "amnestied war criminals" (*amnestierter Kriegsverbrecher*) returning on transports.[84]

The reintegration of the alleged war criminals into East German society also challenged widely promulgated narratives about how to remember and understand World War II. Suddenly, the state graciously accepted and even celebrated the return of those who earlier were blamed for the ravages of the war.[85] Both Soviet and East German authorities had created a state-sanctioned approach to managing the memories of and responsibility for the war, yet only shortly after choosing this course, the release of men who were publicly reported to be convicted war criminals was to be celebrated. Once again in a

---

pursue the case until the remaining small number of Czech prisoners returned home after the amnesty of September 17, 1955, that also brokered the return of the remaining German POWs. Milada Polisenska, *Czechoslovak Diplomacy and the Gulag: Deportation of Czechoslovak Citizens to the USSR and the Negotiation for Their Repatriation, 1945–1953*, trans. Barbara Day (Budapest: Central European University Press, 2015), esp. 127, 139–143, 281, 288, 314.

82. Biess, *Homecomings*, 182–183.

83. Biess, *Homecomings*, 60–61, 182–183, 203.

84. "Staatssekretariat für innere Angelegenheiten Abt. Bevölkerungspolitik Unterkunftsstelle Eisenach," September 29, 1953, BA-SAPMO, DO 1/8666.

85. Biess, *Homecomings*, 60–61, 182–183, 203.

short time frame, East Germans had to reimagine their memory of the war. After the return of the men in 1953, the SED continued to discuss the return of additional captives in private dialogues with Soviet leaders. The East German authorities emphasized that they recognized that these men had followed Nazi ideology and some had been convicted as war criminals. Still, they asked if and when these men would return home.[86] After months of negotiations, the Press Office of the Ministry of the Interior of the GDR announced that the USSR had relented and promised to release 5,374 convicted POWs.[87] Most of the men, 4,057 precisely, would return to West Germany in these 1953 transports.[88]

The renewed SED attempt to broker the return of additional German captives from the USSR intensified after the release of one of the Soviet Union's most famous captives, former field marshal Friedrich Paulus, the commander of the 6th Army at Stalingrad. Since 1948, Paulus had asked to be released to East Germany instead of to his hometown, then in West Germany. He left the Soviet Union in October 1953 and resettled in Dresden.[89] After his return, Paulus did not forget about the soldiers still in Soviet captivity. In a letter to Otto Grotewohl, prime minister of the GDR, Paulus reported that more than one hundred former generals and officers of different branches of the military had met with him to discuss the POW question. The officers, he wrote, had pressed him to convince East Germany to petition the Soviet Union to return the last of the POWs.[90] Grotewohl's representative assured Paulus that the East German government had always been concerned with the so-called

86. "Entwurft zu VSV," September 10, 1953, BA-SAPMO, DO 1/8670.

87. "Entwurft," undated but from 1953, BA-SAPMO, DO 1/8670.

88. The total number of POWs held by Soviet officials in this time period is unclear. Soviet officials held 391,406 German POWs as of December 21, 1949. TsKhIDK, f. 1/p, op. 01e, d. 46, ll. 217–218, in Zagorul'ko, *Voennoplennye v SSSR*, 875. On March 25, 1955, they held only 6,462 according to GARF, f. 9401, op. 2, d. 462, ll. 6–7, in Zagorul'ko, *Voennoplennye v SSSR*, 796. It is unclear how many returned or died between January 1949 and March 1955. In 1950, for example, the Council of Ministers for Repatriation stated that 32,985 Germans returned home on a series of transports in January and April. GARF, f. 9526, op. 6, d. 727, l. 70 and GARF, f. 9526, op. 6, d. 728, l. 92. In 1952, the Department for Repatriation Affairs stated that 17,549 German POWs returned between March 1, 1950, and March 1, 1951; from March 1, 1951, to February 1, 1952, four more German POWs returned. GARF, f. 9526, op. 6, d. 1083, l. 25. Contemporary scholars such as Nicholas Stargardt have tried to ascertain the size of the POW population in this period as well. Stargardt states that most of the POWs had been returned by October 1950 and that only 10,000 remained after 1953. He asserts that the increasing West German agitation over the number of POWs in Soviet hands related purely to the Cold War, in which the Adenauer regime attempted to discredit the Soviet government by raising questions about the captivity and number of missing men caused by mistakes of the Wehrmacht accounting of wartime losses. Stargardt, *The German War*, 556–558.

89. RGASPI, f. 82, op. 2, d. 1163; ll. 101–108, RGASPI, f. 82, op. 2, d. 488, l. 59; "FS Nr. 13 aus Moskau," October 9, 1953, PA AA, M 1/A15677, S. 348.

90. Friedrich Paulus to Otto Grotewohl, February 1, 1955, BA-SAPMO, DC 20/15454, S. 1–3.

POW Question. The representative then noted that the POWs had all been returned and that the only men left in the Soviet Union were convicted war criminals.[91] Paulus's powerful position thus warranted a response from a representative of the prime minister.[92] Paulus and other former Soviet captives clearly believed that some of the remaining men were not in fact war criminals. The SED could not publicly acknowledge this fact, but privately it could use the information provided by returnees to press Soviet leaders for the return of the remaining men.

The German question continued to roil internal struggles for power in the USSR between 1953 and 1955. Because Khrushchev had publicly claimed that Beria had wanted to relinquish control of the GDR and turn it over to the imperialist Western powers, he had to continue to support the GDR and the policies of Ulbricht, even if he disagreed with them. Thus, Khrushchev increasingly positioned himself against German unification.[93] Support for his position, however, was not assured. After Beria's execution, Khrushchev and Malenkov argued over economic and agrarian policies. Both wanted to reform agriculture, and Khrushchev was annoyed that Malenkov first announced the new policies and seemed to get credit for the popular changes that improved life for all citizens. Khrushchev, in turn, expanded on Malenkov's reform in his Virgin Lands Campaign. In early 1955, Khrushchev switched his allegiance, working with Molotov to denounce Malenkov for his associations with Beria. At the Central Committee Plenum in late January, Khrushchev claimed that Malenkov was Beria's right-hand man and that the two were inseparable. Khrushchev and Molotov also derided Malenkov for favoring light manufacturing over heavy industry. They claimed that his preference for consumer goods rather than the growth of heavy industry was the result of capitalist tendencies. Khrushchev and Molotov further denounced Malenkov for his fears of nuclear proliferation leading to war, accusing him of being a coward. Having been discredited before his colleagues and the nation, Malenkov was demoted from prime minister to the minister of electrification.[94] Although Khrushchev ousted Malenkov by deriding his inclinations to make peace with the West, he later adopted many of Malenkov's positions as his own. With his political position secure, Khrushchev turned his attention to the unresolved German question.

---

91. "An den ehemaligen Generalfeldmarschall Herrn Friedreich Paulus," April 15, 1955, BA-SAPMO DC 20/15454, S. 7.

92. "An den Ausserordentlichen und Bevollmächtigten Botschafter der Union der Sozialistischen Sowjetrepubliken," April 18, 1955, BA-SAPMO DC 20/15454, S. 8.

93. Harrison, *Driving the Soviets up the Wall*, 47.

94. Taubman, *Khrushchev*, 260–263, 265–266; Harrison, *Driving the Soviets up the Wall*, 52–53.

In 1955, Khrushchev carried out a series of international diplomatic policy reversals. In April he traveled to Yugoslavia and apologized to Tito for Stalin's harsh treatment of him in 1948. In May, he agreed to remove Soviet forces from Austria and Vienna, resulting in a unified and neutral Austria. Yet despite the liberalization of Soviet international policies, and much to the dismay of Soviet leaders, the FRG joined NATO in May 1955. Although the Western allies steadily increased their military presence in the FRG after 1950, they only began the process to establish a West German army in 1954. In May 1954, the Soviet Union made a bid to join NATO, but it was rejected by the United States and United Kingdom. The FRG joining NATO signaled that the Soviet Union had failed to prevent it from formally allying with the West, a failure that greatly threatened their security and their position in and relations with the GDR. In response, the Soviet Union formed its own military alliance in 1955, the Warsaw Pact, and remilitarized the GDR in 1956 with the creation of the National People's Army (*Nationale Volksarmee*).[95] It also enacted new policies toward both the FRG and the GDR.

After May 1955, Soviet leaders adopted a two-pronged approach to politics with Germany: (1) they increased their control in East Germany by sending more economic aid and by having it join the Warsaw Pact, and (2) Khrushchev reached out to West Germany to improve and formalize relations. He invited the leader of the FRG, Konrad Adenauer, to travel to Moscow. Although his overtures toward the FRG annoyed his East German allies, who felt that the Soviet Union should not formally recognize the FRG when Western powers did not recognize the GDR, Khrushchev acted pragmatically, hoping to directly influence the FRG. He hoped that his overtures would encourage West Germans to move away from a reliance on other Western states.[96]

Khrushchev's new policies for German relations, as well as shrewd negotiations by Adenauer, finally culminated in the return of the last of the POWs. As of March 25, 1955, only 6,462 former German POWs, all deemed war criminals, remained in the Soviet Union.[97] These last men returned to Germany between October 1955 and January 1956 as part of the Soviet Union's agreement to formalize diplomatic relations with the FRG.[98] In September 1955,

95. Harrison, *Driving the Soviets up the Wall*, 53–55; Peter Duignan, *NATO: Its Past, Present, Future* (Stanford: Hoover Press, 2000), 2, 7–8.

96. Harrison, *Driving the Soviets up the Wall*, 55; Robert G. Moeller, *War Stories: The Search for a Usable Past in the Federal Republic of Germany* (Berkeley: University of California Press, 2001), 90–91.

97. GARF, f. 9401, op. 2, d. 462, l. 6–7, in Zagorul'ko, *Voennoplennye v SSSR*, 796. Unfortunately, the document does not give the names of the war criminals. Fond 475p in RGVA has hundreds of files on individual POWs sentenced by military tribunals but Russian privacy law dictates that only relatives or those with explicit written permission of relatives can access the files.

98. Biess, *Homecomings*, 204.

Konrad Adenauer, chancellor of the FRG, traveled to the Soviet Union on an official diplomatic trip. The former mayor of Cologne, Konrad Adenauer had risen to political dominance in West Germany as early as spring 1946. He then led the Christian Democratic Union (CDU) and prioritized economic recovery and political democratization over the judicial investigation of Nazi crimes to avoid the renewal of German nationalism and Nazism.

Adenauer used the question of German POWs in the USSR to gather popular support for his national political career as early as May 1946, speaking of the suffering of POWs in the USSR during his campaign appearances. Reluctant to discuss the crimes of the Nazi past, Adenauer rose to national political dominance, whereas his adversaries, who condemned Germany's previous actions, remained as local officials. After his election as chancellor of the FRG in 1949, Adenauer stated in his inaugural address that it would be important to pass legislation that would help German victims of the war. For Adenauer, POWs constituted an important subset of war victims. They had suffered at the hands not only of the National Socialist regime that had sent them into a senseless war but also of the Soviet socialists by languishing in prison camps for years after the war's end. Indeed, Adenauer carefully avoided using the terms "Nazi" or "Nazism," emphasizing instead the word "socialist" in "national socialist" to discredit the West German Social Democratic Party (SPD), one of his biggest rivals, and the Socialist Unity Party (SED) of East Germany.[99]

Having already capitalized on the POW question, Adenauer again used the POWs to further his political agendas. Adenauer's diplomatic mission to Moscow in 1955 brought one of the FRG's domestic gender issues to the international political scene. Before his trip to Moscow, Adenauer received a flood of personal appeals, mostly from women, that persuaded Adenauer to act not only as the leader of the German state but also as a compassionate father in seeking the return of the nation's missing men. In addition to sounding out the potential for German national reunification, Adenauer's other major goal for his trip to Moscow was to achieve the restoration or reunification of German families by bringing home the last of the POWs.[100] Before the trip, his ministers established stipulations for the formalization of relations between the FRG and the USSR, including the requirement that the USSR release the

99. Jeffrey Herf, *Divided Memory: The Nazi Past in Two Germanys* (Cambridge, MA: Harvard University Press, 1997), 209–210, 219, 222–224, 226; James M. Diehl, *The Thanks of the Fatherland: German Veterans after the Second World War* (Chapel Hill: University of North Carolina Press, 2000), 93–94; Biess, *Homecomings*, 53, 56, 58.

100. Robert Moeller, "'The Last Soldiers of the Great War' and Tales of Family Reunions in the Federal Republic of Germany," *Journal of Women in Culture and Society* 24, no. 1 (1998): 131–133.

remaining German POWs and civilian internees.[101] The Soviet government also agreed to help answer questions regarding the 1.1 million men listed as missing in action on the Eastern Front. Adenauer's trip to Moscow interested not only the leaders and journalists of major Western powers but also the leaders of Japan, who viewed the German negotiations with the USSR as a possible template for their own.[102] After five days of difficult negotiation, both states agreed to resume full diplomatic and trade relations.[103] Khrushchev agreed to release the last of the German POWs, and their repatriation commenced almost immediately after Adenauer's departure.

Adenauer's Moscow trip evoked mixed opinions from the West German population. The formalization of relations between the USSR and the FRG meant that German reunification would not be pursued in the immediate future. Praise for Adenauer's insistence on making the return of the final POWs contingent on the establishment of formal political relations, however, eclipsed other criticisms. Although the state could not be unified, some German families would be, and they would finally receive closure for their losses in World War II. To his contemporaries, Adenauer took on the persona of a compassionate and forceful father who insisted on the release of his nation's sons. His victory in Moscow cemented him as the proper leader of Germany in the eyes of West German citizens. Shortly after Adenauer's death in 1967, 75 percent of West Germans considered his "liberation" of the POWs from the Soviet Union to be his most important political achievement.[104]

In addition to securing the release of the last of the POWs, Adenauer's trip to Moscow created a channel whereby West Germans could ask Soviet officials to trace their relatives, an option that was previously only available to East Germans. In the past, the ambassador of the GDR in the USSR frequently sent tracing requests to the Ministry of Foreign Affairs, which in turn forwarded the letters to the MVD.[105] Often, the letters petitioned for the release of relatives, which the MVD denied, stating that those convicted of war crimes in the USSR could only receive early release with permission from the highest levels of the

101. "Aufzeighnung," June 27, 1055, PA AA, B 2/4, S. 55–56; "Frage, die an die sowjetische Botschaft in Paris zu stellen sind," August 8, 1955, PA AA, B 1/118, S. 81–82; "Zusammensetzung des Sonderzuges," August 8, 1955, PA AA, B 1/118, S. 75.

102. "Telegramm," June 18, 1955, PA AA, B 1/118, S. 39. For more information about the context of Japanese diplomatic affairs with the Soviet Union and the repatriation of Japanese POWs, see Sherzod Muminov, *Eleven Winters of Discontent: The Siberian Internment and the Making of a New Japan* (Cambridge, MA: Harvard University Press, 2022).

103. Biess, *Homecomings*, 204.

104. Moeller, "'Last Soldiers of the Great War,'" 134; Moeller, *War Stories*, 89, 91; Biess, *Homecomings*, 206.

105. RGVA, f. 1p, op. 3t, d. 10, ll. 225–230; RGVA, f. 1p, op. 7t, d. 3, ll. 28–34.

Soviet government.[106] Other times, the MVD responded that the missing family member had died.[107] Transliterating names of Germans into Russian complicated matters of tracking relatives abroad. The Ministry of Foreign Affairs and the Ministry of Internal Affairs shared information about search requests with each other, but at times the MVD could not find the person in question. In one instance, the Ministry of Foreign Affairs wrote back to a German citizen that his son could not be located, whereupon his father responded by providing his son's camp number.[108] Using the number, the MVD later tracked down the man in question, one *ГРЁНСФЕЛЬДЕР* (GRËNSFEL'DER) under the different spelling of *ХРОЕНСФЕЛЬДЕР* (KhROENSFEL'DER). After Adenauer's Moscow trip, however, West Germans gained the same ability as East Germans to find the whereabouts of their relatives. At the end of 1955 and in early 1956, German citizens who visited the Soviet ambassador to the FRG in Bonn succeeded in having their tracing requests passed to the Ministries of Foreign and Internal Affairs.[109] But relatives were told often that either the named person could not be found, had died, or had already returned home.

The final wave of repatriation of German POWs occurred after the Soviet Union again achieved stable leadership under Khrushchev, who emerged as the clear leader of the USSR after his "Secret Speech" to the Twentieth Party Congress in February 1956. But the fate of German POWs remained a major diplomatic issue between the FRG and the Soviet Union even after the last prisoners returned in early 1956. Lack of official reporting of tribunal sentences and death records hurt the ability to build ties. Once the Soviet government began to answer tracing requests, the results were often disappointing. The Ministry of Internal Affairs deemed some information about trials and war crimes too damaging to release. In one instance in April 1956, the wife of a former German colonel wrote to the West German embassy in the USSR, which contacted Premier Bulganin.[110] The wife stated that her husband had surrendered to the Red Army in January 1943 near Stalingrad. One of his fellow soldiers told her that her husband had allegedly been detained in the Lubyanka in 1949. A representative of the Ministry of Foreign Affairs (MID) wrote to the Prison Division of the MVD asking about the man's whereabouts and requesting a death certificate if he had died. The MVD responded in about a week, stating that the man in

106. For a series of requests, the processing of the requests, and the answers to them from the MVD see RGVA f. 1p, op. 3t, d. 6, ll. 37–42 and ll. 79–87
107. RGVA, f. 1p, op. 3t, d. 6, ll. 152–153; RGVA, f. 1p, op. 3t, d. 7, ll. 36–37; RGVA, f. 1p, op. 3t, d. 7, ll. 152–154.
108. RGVA, f. 1p, op. 3t, d. 10, ll. 24–30.
109. RGVA, f. 1p, op. 7t, d. 3, ll. 63–66, ll. 171–173, and ll. 183–184.
110. RGVA, f. 1p, op. 7t, d. 4, ll. 397–399.

question had been tried and sentenced under the order of April 19, 1943, in a war tribunal on January 15, 1947. On March 10, 1947, he had been executed, and his body was cremated. The Prison Division of the MVD suggested that the MID tell his wife that he had been sentenced to twenty-five years of hard labor in a Gulag, where he died of a heart attack. It is unclear whether the MID told the truth or used the MVD's suggested death story. Nonetheless, Soviet officials recognized the potential volatility of the POW question even after Soviet–German relations had improved. It is possible that, in the wake of the post-Stalin reforms and amnesties, members of the Soviet government came to understand that the verdicts of some military tribunals were incorrect; that is, that they had been show trials rather than true trials. Thus, these officials might not have wanted to admit to at least one potentially wrongful execution, which could have resulted in additional international scrutiny and scorn.

Although a major victory for West Germany, the final repatriation of the German POWs caused tensions and questions about reintegration in both East and West Germany. Members of the East German Ministry of the Interior called the men who returned on the December 14, 1955, transport to Camp Fürstenwalde "former war convicts" (*Ehemalige Kriegsverurteilte*).[111] The need to follow the actions of the Soviet Union created a tough situation for the SED when discussing war guilt and reintegration of former POWs. Earlier returnees served as models of antifascist conversion and East German masculinity; they were hard workers and fathers who would instill a strong antifascist socialist worldview in their children.[112] Those who had been allegedly convicted of war crimes, however, would be more difficult to integrate into East German society and certainly could not be considered role models. Thus, the East German officials had to make their own shift in terminology by calling these men "amnestied" or "former" war criminals to reverse their earlier public condemnation of these men.

The Soviet change in terminology was also reflected in different ways by the West German press. Some publications questioned and denounced the change, whereas others accepted the culpability of the men. West German publications' political leanings and the politics of the moment framed their terminological choices between 1949 and 1956. The anti-Nazi *Der Spiegel* did not initially criticize Soviet authorities for detaining war criminals, but as Cold War tensions developed, it began to imply that those sentenced by Soviet military tribunals were improperly convicted in "show trials" or after harsh inter-

---

111. "Ministerium des Innern, Staatssekretariat für Innere Angelegenheiten, Fürstenwalde," December 15, 1955, BA-SAPMO, DO 1/8667.

112. Biess, *Homecomings*, 126–129, 203.

rogations. It charged that some were unfairly charged with criminal offenses and sentenced to as much as twenty-five years of hard labor. It cited the testimony of one former POW, Lieutenant Siegfried Götzl. He stated that his interrogators asked how many Russians he had shot. The interrogators later told him that they would be able to make him say what they wanted him to say. When Götzl refused to answer, he was sentenced to twenty-five years of hard labor based on three charges: giving German youth a fascist education, terrorizing the Soviet population, and stealing from the Soviet people. As a leader in Hitler Youth, he was convicted on the first charge. They convicted him on the second charge as collective punishment for atrocities in the area where his division had served. Finally, they convicted him on the third charge for eating meat stolen from local peasants. Unlike other POWs who had earned extra petty cash through work, Götzl could not afford the 300 rubles for a lawyer. He defended himself in his own trial, which took all of fifteen minutes. Götzl was convicted but later released on February 28, 1950.[113] Using this case to exemplify the system, Der Spiegel accused the Soviet Union of wrongfully extending the stay of those deemed to be war criminals and rigging the legal apparatus against the POWs.

Der Spiegel criticized not only the Soviets but also West German officials for mishandling the return of certain POWs. For example, Soviet authorities released Emil Glasl, who could not receive a permit to enter Germany because he came from a family of Sudeten Germans, who had been expelled from Czechoslovakia at the end of the war. His father died in transit to Germany, and he was unable contact his mother. Glasl was thus stuck in Czech hands from 1947, when he was released from the Soviet Union, until he received an immigration permit in June 1950 after the International Red Cross intervened. He had made contact with his mother earlier in the year but was denied entry into the FRG because housing could not be guaranteed for him. As a result of his experience, Glasl sued the Free State of Bavaria.[114] Der Spiegel stressed that not all return stories ended happily.

Der Spiegel did not soften its critical stance toward the Soviet and West German governments with time. When covering Adenauer's 1955 trip to Moscow, it ignored Soviet designation of the POWs as war criminals and instead called the men "prisoners of war" (Kriegsgefangne). It also criticized Adenauer for only securing a verbal commitment from the Soviet leaders regarding the

113. "Dolmetscherin für pikante Fälle Von weiblichen Posten bewacht Dort drüben hat Hitler gestanden Völlig auf den Hund gekommen Wieder nix, wieder nix . . . ," Der Spiegel, 28/1950, July 13, 1950, 10–11.
114. "Alle taten ihre Pflicht: Kein Wohnraum für Kriegsgefangenen Rückkehr verzögert?" Der Spiegel, 52/1955, December 21, 1955, 16–18.

release of the last 9,626 POWs.[115] The Soviet use of the phrase "war criminals" also colored *Bild-Zeitung*'s coverage of Adenauer's diplomatic negotiations in 1955. The paper explained that two questions were foremost in
Adenauer's mind: the reunification of Germany and the return of prisoners.
Staff for *Bild* felt that many of the remaining men were indeed POWs and not
war criminals. The paper reported that Adenauer felt similarly during his discussions with the premier of the Soviet Union, Nikolai Bulganin, who did not
share Adenauer's opinion and supposedly angrily snapped that there were no
longer any German POWs in the Soviet Union but only 9,626 *Kriegsverbrecher*
(war criminals).[116] Throughout the coverage of Adenauer's trip to Moscow
and subsequent updates about the returnees, *Bild* always referred to the Germans in Soviet hands as *Gefangene* (prisoners). It never used the terms "*Kriegsgefangene*" (prisoner of war) or "*Kriegsverbrecher*" (war criminal). In the eyes of
one conservative German publication, *Bild*, these men had ceased to be prisoners of war, nor were they proven to be war criminals. Instead, they were
merely prisoners of the Soviet Union, unfairly held until Adenauer's persever-
ance resulted in the negotiation of their release.

From October 1955 through January 17, 1956, *Bild* published front-page announcements of the numbers of returnees on trains, using neutral language
with no mention of their Nazi pasts or experiences in the Soviet Union: the articles referred to them only as "returnees" (*Rückkehrer* or *Heimkehrer*).[117] *Bild*
thus participated in the mass reshaping of war memory in the FRG, removing
references to the war entirely from its language. Instead, it discussed these men
not in the context of World War II but in that of the new Cold War, emphasizing their Germanness and status as Soviet prisoners. Although generally com-
plementary of the Soviet government for upholding its agreement, *Bild* did
question whether the 472 returnees on the last transport that arrived on January 16 really were the last of the captive Germans. According to the article written after the final train of returnees, only 9,499 "prisoners of war" of the
promised 9,626 had returned. Where were the remaining 127 men? Were they
still in the Soviet Union or had they died?[118] Although *Bild* did not publicly take
a stand on the issue, it noted that one hundred of those who returned on the
last transport were seriously ill and that the missing men might have died.

115. "Lesen Sie Karl Marx: Der Eisenhower-Stil Ein Botschafter tobt Seht, da ist China Bulganin
tippt an die Stirn Molows Aktenschräncke ‚Mündlich ist nichts vereinbart," *Der Spiegel*, 39/1955, 9–15.

116. "Moskau-Konferenz in der Sackgasse," *Bild-Zeitung*, September 12, 1955, 1 and 2.

117. "Moskau-Konferenz in der Sackgasse"; "Dramatisches Ende der Moskau-Konferenz: Chance
für Gefangene," *Bild-Zeitung*, September 14, 1955, 1, 2; "Sie Kommen! Die esrsten Gefangenen am
Wochenende," *Bild-Zeitung*, October 4, 1955, 1; "Friedland überfüllt: Bisher 3,700 heimgekehrt," *Bild-
Zeitung*, October 17, 1955, 1.

118. "Waren es wirklich die Letzten aus der Sowjetunion?" *Bild-Zeitung*, January 17, 1955, 1.

The conservative but staunchly anti-Nazi West German newspaper *Frankfurter Allgemeine Zeitung* (F.A.Z.) also took a critical stance toward West German officials and the last men remaining in Soviet captivity. Initially, F.A.Z. was supportive of Adenauer's trip to Moscow. It excitedly announced the Soviet agreement to return the remaining 9,626 men, but it used very different language than did either *Bild* or *Der Spiegel*. F.A.Z. referred to the men by another Soviet designation—*Kriegsverurteilte* (war convicts)—and continued to use strong language when writing about return transports, referring to them as prisoners of war or war criminals. Only in reports of their homecoming on the front page did F.A.Z. call the men "returnees."[119] Unlike *Bild*, in which arrivals were always front-page news, F.A.Z. relegated reports of the returnees to either the fourth or eighth page. Moreover, the subsequent announcements all followed the same format and used the same language:

The Names of the Returnees

We continue today the list of names of returned prisoners of war. At the same time we publish the list with all due reservations and without any guarantee.

On [day of the week] the following [number] of returnees have arrived in Friedland.[120]

Another common variation was simply, "We continue today the list of names of the returned POWs," followed with the ending, "The list will be continued."[121] In between the formulaic opening and closing lines, the articles would list the names, birth years, and home cities of the returning prisoners. Unlike *Bild*, which questioned whether all the POWs had returned, F.A.Z. did not make a special announcement about the last transport or amend its format between December 1955 and early January 1956. F.A.Z. also took a much different approach than *Bild* to the question of war memory. It strongly criticized the last captives for their complicity in war crimes, and it also minimized coverage of their return. Whereas *Bild* considered men Soviet ideological captives, F.A.Z. buried the news of their arrival so as not to celebrate the return of men of questionable moral standing.

From 1949 to 1956, both the East and West German press used the question of German POWs (and not only those in Soviet hands) to attack each other's

---

119. "Botschafterausctausch und Rückkehr der Gefangenen," *Frankfurter Allgemeine Zeitung*, September 15, 1955, 1; "Willkommen für die Heimkehrer in Friedland," *Frankfurter Allgemeine Zeitung*, October 10, 1955, 1.

120. "Die Namen der Heimkehrer," *Frankfurter Allgemeine Zeitung*, October 10, 1955.

121. "Die Namen der Heimkehrer."

respective governments. Despite the differing ideological approaches to the POWs, the presses of a divided Germany were united in their efforts to release the captives and publishing information about their return. The commitment to the return of the last POWs constituted the only commonality between the presses of East and West Germany and indeed among the publications within the FRG. As it did when covering POW questions from 1946 to 1949, *Neues Deutschland* followed the party line when reporting on the issue up to 1956. It wrote in ways that complimented both the SED and the CPSU while also grappling with the issue of how to reintegrate men convicted of war crimes abroad. The West German press, however, was divided on what to call the last POWs, how to interpret Adenauer's trip to Moscow, and who to blame for problems concerning the returnees' reintegration.

As was the case with the motives for initial postwar detention, Soviet domestic concerns shaped the repatriation of German POWs. Although economic needs initially motivated Soviet authorities to mobilize and keep as many German POWs as possible for reconstruction, after 1949 the repatriation of German POWs occurred largely for political rather than economic reasons. When the Soviet Union failed to comply with its promise to release all the German POWs by December 31, 1948, the remaining men on Soviet soil became bargaining chips in Cold War diplomacy. In January 1949, the Soviet Union announced that the majority of POWs had been repatriated. According to Soviet officials, the men who remained, with the exception of a few, were not prisoners but war criminals. Yet this shift in terminology was largely ineffective in shielding Soviet leaders from international scrutiny and pressure. Western governments and various international organizations joined German families and the press in attempting to determine the number of captives and broker their return.

Ultimately, Stalin proved to be the greatest barrier to complete repatriation. After his death on March 3, 1953, Soviet leaders immediately enacted a series of domestic and international reforms that allowed the last men to return. The first reforms sent German POWs home as part of nationwide amnesties and prison reform. Three months after Stalin's death, the uprising in the GDR in June 1953 influenced Soviet leaders to again release more German POWs to improve Soviet–German relations and to garner support for the East German regime. The uprising continued to shape Khrushchev's policies toward the GDR. Khrushchev's strategies for Soviet–German relations were influenced by his desire to portray himself as a reformer without abandoning a commitment to socialism and a socialist Germany. His German policies also leaned toward pragmatism. Hoping to draw the West Germans away from their Western allies by establishing formal diplomatic relations when the Western powers did not recognize the GDR, Khrushchev welcomed Adenauer and ultimately acceded to his demands to release the final POWs as a condition for normalizing relations. Although the Western allies, both German governments, NGOs and relief organizations, German citizens, and news publications of both German states put pressure on the Soviet government for many years to repatriate the POWs, none of these elements together or alone could persuade Soviet leaders to release the last men. Only the complexities of Soviet domestic politics, and their relationship to Soviet international politics, resulted in the final phases of repatriation.

The political significance of the German POWs did not end with their final repatriation in 1956. Their long-lasting captivity continued to condition German and Soviet domestic and international politics well until the collapse of the USSR. It was not only the returnees who shaped politics and memory but also those who died on Soviet soil. Anywhere from 363,000 to as many as 700,000 Germans died in Soviet hands.[122] Indeed, the legacy of living and dead German POWs continued and continues to shape relations between a reunified Germany and the Russian Federation.

---

122. Rüdiger Overmans believes that it is possible to confirm 363,000 German deaths in Soviet captivity from Wehrmachtsauskunftstelle records. These records also list almost 700,000 soldiers missing in action on the Eastern Front, many of whom could have been captured and died in Soviet camps. At the moment, it is impossible to verify these claims even with access to Soviet archival sources. Many records relating to POW deaths and burials remained classified well into 2017. Overmans, *Deutsche militärische Verluste*, 286–289; Rüdiger Overmans and Ulrike Goeken-Haidl, *Soldaten hinter Stacheldraht: Deutsche Kriegsgefangene des Zweiten Weltkriege* (Munich: Ullstein, 2000), 246.

CHAPTER 5

Commemoration of German POWs in the USSR and Russia

In both the USSR and the Russian Federation, memory of World War II, or the Great Patriotic War as it is known there, has been used to further political aims. Stalin and Khrushchev strongly controlled public memory of the war, including which aspects could be openly discussed. Under their leadership, the war remained important, but its memory did not dominate the state-imposed memory regimes like the cults of Lenin or Stalin. By the twentieth anniversary of victory in World War II, however, public memory of the war and its political uses had evolved into a full-blown cult. Most early research focused on how the political elites of the Brezhnev era (1964–1982) shaped the cult.[1] More recent histories on Soviet war memory have explored the nuances of the cult's control of history and its weakening during the collapse of the Soviet Union.[2]

---

1. The first and still most influential work on Soviet war memory is Nina Tumarkin, *The Living & the Dead: The Rise and Fall of the Cult of World War II in Russia* (New York: Basic Books, 1994).

2. See, for example, Steven Maddox, *Saving Stalin's Imperial City: Historic Preservation in Leningrad, 1930–1950* (Bloomington: Indiana University Press, 2015); James V. Wertsch, *Voices of Collective Remembering* (Cambridge: Cambridge University Press, 2002); Lisa Kirschenbaum, *The Legacy of the Siege of Leningrad, 1941–1995: Myth, Memory, and Monuments* (Cambridge: Cambridge University Press, 2006); Polly Jones, *Myth, Memory, Trauma: Rethinking the Stalinist Past in the Soviet Union, 1953–70* (New Haven: Yale University Press, 2013); Jonathan Brunstedt, *The Soviet Myth of World War II: Patriotic Memory and the Russian Question in the USSR* (Cambridge: Cambridge University Press, 2021); and David L. Hoffmann, ed., *The Memory of the Second World War in Soviet and Post-Soviet Russia* (New York: Routledge, 2022).

However, none of these studies explores in detail the portrayal of the enemy in Soviet and Russian sites of commemoration. Yet both German soldiers and German prisoners of war have been memorialized in Russia, appearing in grandiose state-built monuments and museums, as well as in smaller, local cemetery memorials. In fact, the portrayal of German POWs in Soviet and Russian monuments is an important part of the rise, fall, and resurrection of the cult of World War II. It provides a unique case study of four memory regimes and states: the Soviet Union, the Russian Federation, the German Democratic Republic, and a reunified Germany. In three distinct eras—the 1960s, the 1980s, and the 1990s and beyond—German POWs were commemorated as enemies, potential allies, and fallen soldiers on Soviet and Russian soil. POW commemoration reveals the changing memory regimes of the Soviet Union and the Russian Federation. Domestic reforms and international relations shaped the evolution of memory in these two states.

German POWs were first included in Soviet memorials during the boom of World War II commemoration, which reached new heights with the twentieth anniversary of the Soviet victory over fascist Germany in 1965. In this era, the Soviet state portrayed the German POWs as "fascist war dogs" or as living trophies and symbols of Red Army success. This was in keeping with the main state-supported interpretations of the war at the time. After the war, Nina Tumarkin, preeminent scholar of Soviet World War II memory and commemoration, argues that Stalin initially tried both to control and diminish the memory of the war. By 1947, Victory Day (May 9) had been demoted from a state holiday to a workday. The ravages of the war left little time for celebrations, and Stalin sought to downplay the role of wartime heroes, particularly military leaders. From 1947 to 1965—the twentieth anniversary of the war—Victory Day celebrations remained informal affairs of veterans' gatherings and meetings in cemeteries. After Stalin's death in 1953, his successor Nikita Khrushchev began to de-Stalinize the nation, its memories, and its celebrations. A new approach to the war began to emerge with organized symbols that eventually formed the basis for the cult of the Great Patriotic War. The Khrushchev era laid the foundations for the cult, which above all emphasized that Soviet socialism was a cause worth supporting because it had defeated Nazi Germany. But the cult, in all its features, did not fully emerge until Leonid Brezhnev came to power in 1964.[3]

In the mid-1980s, the state's official interpretations and discourse of World War II began to shift, resulting in a different portrayal of German POWs.[4] By

3. Nina Tumarkin, "The Great Patriotic War as Myth and Memory," *European Review* 11, no. 4 (2003): 597–598; Tumarkin, *Living & the Dead*, 133–134; Maddox, *Saving Stalin's Imperial City*, 12, 192.
4. Tumarkin, *Living & the Dead*, 175, 181, 190.

the fortieth anniversary of victory, the Soviet government had broadened its understanding of Germans during the war. In 1985, the Central Committee of the Communist Party of the Soviet Union ordered the establishment of a museum commemorating the German antifascists who worked in both Germany and the Soviet Union to defeat Nazi Germany. Over only five months, the Central Committees of the USSR and of the Socialist Unity Party of Germany (SED) worked together to construct the Memorial Museum of German Antifascists at a former Moscow POW camp.[5] With the passage of many years, Soviet authorities deemed it more acceptable to commemorate those German antifascists and communist exiles who worked in the POW camps to reeducate the prisoners and spread antifascist propaganda. This shift in the portrayal of Germans also served to improve relations between the USSR and East Germany, which had been strained throughout the 1940s and 1950s because of the long-lasting Soviet incarceration of German POWs.

A more open discussion of the past began under Gorbachev as part of the new policy of *glasnost*, but full freedom of speech on the topic and archival access were not granted until the early 1990s with the collapse of the Soviet Union. After the dissolution of the USSR, Russians began to openly discuss both the Soviet successes and failures in World War II.[6] The freedom to explore all aspects of the war also provided room for Germans to commemorate their war dead, including the POWs who died on Russian soil. In the post-Soviet era, Russians and foreigners alike could gain access to formerly classified holdings and discuss long-standing questions about the war, including the Katyn Massacre and a full accounting of Soviet war deaths.[7] Archival access also allowed individuals, governments, and NGOs to answer enduring questions about the fate of German POWs. Germans could travel to Russia and visit the gravesites of their countrymen. Additionally, the Russian Federation gave Germans permission to put up memorials around grave sites, which still happens to this day.[8] In a span of roughly thirty years, memorial depictions of German POWs on Soviet and Russian soil evolved from "fascist war dogs" to fallen men.

---

5. RGALI, f. 3175, op. 1, d. 35, l. 18.

6. Tumarkin, *Living & the Dead*, 210–211; Wertsch, *Voices of Collective Remembering*, 111–112.

7. See, for example, Tumarkin, *Living & the Dead*, 176–177, on the Katyn Massacres and how access to the archives allowed at least one researcher to learn the full extent of the orders and cover-up operation.

8. Full text of the agreement and its subsequent bill, as well as its history, can be found at "Deutscher Bundestag: 12. Wahlperiode. Druchsache 12/5837," http://dipbt.bundestag.de/dip21/btd/12/058/120 5837.pdf.

"Fascist War Dogs"

During World War II, Soviet officials and writers waged a brutal anti-German hate propaganda campaign in their speeches and published works. In the early months of the war, Stalin gave an address to the Moscow Soviet on the twenty-fourth anniversary of the October Revolution: he referred to the Germans as "oppressors" and "wild beasts" and stated that the goal of the Soviet Union was to "exterminate to the last man all the German occupiers."[9] A year later, for the twenty-fifth anniversary, Stalin uttered these words: "Execration and death to the German-fascist invaders, to their state, their army, their 'new order in Europe!'"[10] For the twenty-sixth anniversary, Stalin began to discuss Red Army success in the war in his address. He mentioned victory at Stalingrad numerous times, referring to defeating the "Germans" and the "German-fascist army," and he concluded with the phrase, "Death to the German invaders!"[11] In addition to leading Soviet officials, Soviet writers, many of whom served as war correspondents, published works calling for hatred, violence, and vengeance against Germans broadly speaking, and not just German fascists. Ilya Ehrenburg, for example, wrote on November 7, 1941: "The Russian people have a big heart. They know well how to love. They also know how to hate. . . . We shall repay the Germans for all the abuses, for all the grief. . . . We shall make [German] females cry their eyes out. . . . Russian widows will sit in judgement over Hitler."[12] Another important Soviet writer and war correspondent, Konstantin Simonov, wrote the poem titled "Kill Him," with these verses: "Kill a German, kill him soon / And every time you see one—kill him."[13] During the war years, then, writers and officials described all Germans, not just fascists, as beasts and called for their deaths. These vilifications of the German nation and peoples continued until April 1945, when the leader of the agitprop department of the

---

9. Joseph Stalin, "24th Anniversary of the Great October Socialist Revolution," in *Soviet War Documents: June, 1941—November, 1943: Addresses, Notes, Orders of the Day, Statements*, Embassy of the Union of Soviet Socialist Republics (Honolulu: University Press of the Pacific), 9, 15, and 17.

10. Joseph Stalin, "25th Anniversary of the Great October Socialist Revolution," in *Soviet War Documents: June, 1941—November, 1943*, 41.

11. Joseph Stalin, "26th Anniversary of the Great October Socialist Revolution," in *Soviet War Documents: June, 1941—November, 1943*, 59, 61, 62, 69.

12. Ilya Ehrenburg, quoted by Louise McReynolds, "Dateline Stalingrad: Newspaper Correspondents at the Front," in *Culture and Entertainment in Wartime Russia*, ed. Richard Stites (Bloomington: Indiana University Press, 1995), 35. McReynolds cites Alexander Kaun's 1944 translation of Ehrenburg's *The Tempering of Russia*, pages 82 and 83, as the source of this quote.

13. Konstantin Simonov, "Kill Him," as quoted in Richard Stites, "Soviet Russian Wartime Culture: Freedom and Control, Spontaneity and Consciousness," in *The People's War: Responses to World War II in the Soviet Union*, ed. Robert Thurston and Bernd Bonwetsch (Champaign-Urbana: University of Illinois Press, 2000), 180.

Central Committee of the VKP(b), Georgii Aleksandrov, published a long article in *Pravda* denouncing Ehrenburg for oversimplification and incorrectly conflating the German people with Hitlerite fascist ideology.[14]

With the defeat of Nazi Germany in sight, the need for anti-German hate propaganda ceased to exist. If anything, a reversal needed to take place. Soviet officials wanted to create a socialist Germany in the postwar era, one that would ally itself with the Soviet Union and would not wage a third war against its territories. As the Cold War began to intensify, official state representations of the war emphasized the enemy not as ethnic Germans themselves but as the ideologies of fascism and imperialism.[15] The shifting narratives of the war and recharacterization of the USSR's wartime enemies resulted in an alteration in the understanding of German POWs. The same political changes that resulted in their final release from the USSR also resulted in changes in how they were initially immortalized on Soviet war memorials.

Perhaps no Russian World War II monument is as well known as that on the hill, Mamaev Kurgan, in Stalingrad (present-day Volgograd). Overlooking the city, Mamaev Kurgan was the site of some of the fiercest fighting of the Battle of Stalingrad (August 23, 1942–February 2, 1943). German forces managed to capture parts of the hill and used the position to their advantage, launching devastating sniper attacks from it. Red Army tacticians recognized the strategic importance of retaking and controlling the hill. They also recognized its propagandistic importance. During the Russian Civil War, Stalin had led the defense of the city, then named Tsaritsyn, from the base of Mamaev Kurgan. Soviet officers used this fact to motivate their soldiers, speaking of it as a "sacred place, the place where Stalin had been" and emphasizing the need to defend it to the death. After many casualties on both sides, the Red Army managed to retake the hill.[16]

Known extensively for the *Rodina Mat' Zovët* (The Motherland Calls) statue, Mamaev Kurgan also features a wide array of other monuments (figure 5.1). It is an interactive memorial complex, called a "memorial-ensemble" by its designer.[17] Indeed, the official title is the "Memorial-Ensemble 'to the Heroes

14. See "'Our Cause is Just': Loyalty, Propaganda, and Popular Moods," in *Fortress Dark and Stern: Life, Labor, and Loyalty on the Soviet Home Front during World War II*, ed. Wendy Goldman and Donald Filtzer (Oxford University Press, 2021), chap. 10; Karel C. Berkhoff, *Motherland in Danger: Soviet Propaganda during World War II* (Cambridge, MA: Harvard University Press, 2012), 176–201; Alexander Werth, *Russia at War: 1941–1945* (New York: E. P. Dutton, 1964), 411–417.

15. Tumarkin, "Great Patriotic War as Myth and Memory," 597.

16. Jochen Hellbeck, *Stalingrad: The City That Defeated the Third Reich* (New York: Public Affairs, 2015), 11, 304–305, 332–336, 341, 344–346.

17. All the names for the components of the Mamaev Kurgan Memorial Complex are taken from E. V. Vuchetich et al., *Geroiam Stalingradskoi Bitvyi: Pamiatnik-ansambl' Mamaev Kurgan* (Leningrad: Khudozhnik RSFSR, 1969).

FIGURE 5.1.   *Rodina Mat'* on the hilltop with "Stand to the Death" at the base. Photo by author.

of the Stalingrad Battle.'" The visitor walks up to the hill to an initial complex of statues, "Stand to the Death," and passes the "Wall Ruins" to proceed to "Heroes' Square." Passing under the watchful eyes of Lenin, visitors enter the "Hall of Military Glory," and then walk up past the eternal flame before exiting at the "Square of Sorrow," featuring a mother cradling her dead soldier son in the style of Michelangelo's *Pieta*. From there, visitors follow a path that winds up the hill face, which covers a mass grave, before arriving at the base of *Rodina Mat'*, placed on what was known during the war as Height 102. A visit to the complex is an extremely sobering and contemplative experience, one that instills within the viewer the gravity of the battle's tremendous suffering and military triumph.

Tumarkin describes the Mamaev Kurgan complex as "the most celebrated of the flamboyant memorial ensembles constructed during Brezhnev's tenure as general secretary of the Central Committee"; it bears "all the hallmarks of totalitarian kitsch," including bas-reliefs, sound recordings of radio broadcasts from the battle, a "snarling motherland figure," and "an eternal flame blazing up from a hand clasping a stone torch, like a submerged Statue of Liberty." Tumarkin asserts that the ensemble aims to make the visitor feel "sympathy

for the harrowing ordeal that was Stalingrad, admiration for the valor of Soviet lives lost, and gratitude for the victory to its organizer and inspirer, the
Communist Part of the Soviet Union."[18] Although Tumarkin correctly as-
sesses the goals of the monument and the reaction that it produces, she incorrectly attributes its form to the Brezhnev war cult. In fact, Soviet creative
unions and artists created plans for the content and form of the ensemble well
before Brezhnev's rise to power in 1964.

In fact, the evolution of the monument speaks more to the politics of
Khrushchev and changes in war memory during his tenure as first secretary
of the Central Committee of the CPSU than to those of the Brezhnev period.
Khrushchev had a well-established memory project tied to de-Stalinization,
which was later co-opted into Brezhnev's program to develop patriotism, especially relating to World War II.[19] For nearly three years after Stalin's death
on March 5, 1953, high officials of the nation engaged in a power struggle.
Each of Stalin's potential political successors expressed or implied a desire to
break from his policies ranging from Gulag amnesties, relations with the Eastern bloc and the West, and the economy immediately following his death.[20]
Ultimately, Nikita Khrushchev emerged as the leader of the Soviet Union after
he delivered his "Secret Speech" at the Twentieth Party Congress in February 1956. In his speech, Khrushchev denounced Stalin and articulated a formal campaign of de-Stalinization across the Soviet Union, which included
removing statues of him and renaming streets, villages, and cities. The process
of de-Stalinization played out in the planning and creation of the Mamaev Kurgan monument. In his "Secret Speech," Khrushchev called for the resurrection of the importance of the Communist Party: it had to replace the personal
figure of Stalin in the people's minds.[21] Thus, over time, the Union of Architects and individual artists grappled with how to remove Stalin from a monument that initially aimed to prominently honor him and his namesake city.

The planning for a Stalingrad monument began early, one year after Stalin's
death. Yet the political uncertainty that followed his death resulted in a schizo-
phrenic design that would simultaneously promote Stalin's cult of personality
while also emphasizing the role of the party. Members of the Ministry of Culture of the Russian Soviet Federative Socialist Republic (RSFSR), the Directory
of Affairs under the Council of Ministers of the RSFSR, the Executive Commit-

---

18. Tumarkin, *Living & the Dead*, 47–48.

19. Tyler C. Kirk, "From Enemy to Hero: Andrei Krems and the Legacy of Stalinist Repression in
Russia's Far North, 1964–1982," *Russian Review* 82, no. 2 (April 2023): 292–306, https://doi.org/10.1111
/russ.12440.

20. Jones, *Myth, Memory, and Trauma*, 17.

21. Jones, *Myth, Memory, and Trauma*, 18–19, 22–24, 28–33.

tee of the Stalingrad City Council, and the Union of Architects of the USSR came together to announce a competition for the project of building a State Museum of Defense of Tsaritsyn-Stalingrad.[22] The museum was to show the efforts of the Soviet people during both the Russian Civil War and the Great Patriotic War, which would doubly immortalize two of Stalin's military victories. Stalin had received credit for victory at the Battle of Tsaritsyn, a key battle of the Russian Civil War. His victory there led to the renaming of the city in his honor in 1925. The Ministry of Culture also wanted to emphasize the tactical and propagandistic victories of the Red Army's defeat of the Wehrmacht at Stalin's namesake city during World War II. The museum would not only emphasize Stalin's personality cult but also would "clearly show the superiority of the Soviet socialist system over the capitalist, the great organizing role of the Communist Party, as the inspirer of all the victories of the Soviet people."[23]

Mere months after the death of Stalin, however, party leaders moved to minimalize Stalin's role and emphasize that of the Communist Party in the war narrative. The Soviet cultural ministries, then, worked with Soviet leaders to reinterpret the war. In fact, Stalin would be removed from the monument altogether after Khrushchev delivered his "Secret Speech" in February 1956. Khrushchev stated, "Not Stalin, but the Party as a whole, the Soviet government, our heroic Army, its talented leaders and brave soldiers, the whole Soviet nation— they are the ones who assured victory in the Great Patriotic War."[24] Stalin's name was removed from the war narrative over the course of the 1950s and early 1960s, and the war became a legitimizing myth for the Soviet state as a whole. Rather than emphasizing Stalin's personal leadership, the new narrative highlighted the role of the party, which not only had organized and supplied its citizens during the war but also dealt a crushing defeat to a capitalist power. The state firmly anchored the victory in the socialist system.

The state-sponsored narratives of socialist success went hand in hand with depicting the German soldiers as casualties or symbols of Red Army victory. In the initial plans for the museum competition in 1954, the Ministry of Culture gave detailed instructions regarding the number of rooms in the museum and what they were to depict. For example, the twenty-third room had to show the "liquidation of the German-fascist forces, surrounded at Stalingrad." According to the organizing committee, "The defeat of the German troops near Stalingrad is the crown of military art, the most outstanding victory in the history of the great war." To illustrate this, the artists were to design an entire

22. RGALI, f. 674, op. 3, d. 1954, l. 1.
23. RGALI, f. 674, op. 3, d. 1954, l. 2.
24. Tumarkin, *Living & the Dead*, 108–109.

panorama for the twenty-fourth room that would illustrate the destruction of the German forces at Stalingrad.[25]

State planners had decided how they wanted to depict the war and the main themes of the narrative, but it was up to the artists to design the mandated content. Sculptor Yevgeny Viktorovich Vuchetich won the contract for the Stalingrad museum. On January 23, 1958, the Council of Soviet Ministers of the RSFSR ordered Vuchetich to work with the architect Yakov Borisovich Belopol'skii and the artist Anatolii Andreevich Gorpenko to create a monument to the battle of Stalingrad on Mamaev Kurgan, including a panorama, by May 9, 1961.[26] For numerous reasons, the project was repeatedly delayed; in 1961, the war consultants, artists, and the Ministry of Culture of the RSFSR were still arguing about what to portray in the panorama and how many scenes it should include. A recurring theme in the multitude of memoranda was the portrayal of German POWs. In May 1961, a group of war consultants led by Marshal of the Soviet Union Andrei Ivanovich Yeryomenko, one of the leaders in the Battle of Stalingrad, urged inclusion of a scene depicting "against the background of the destroyed Stalingrad . . . the massive surrender of German-fascist troops. Columns of prisoners with exhausted faces, many wounded and frost-bitten; Soviet medical personnel are helping them; from field kitchens they are being fed. Around them is a large number of abandoned weapons and tanks. In the distance, crosses of German field cemeteries are visible."[27]

To those who had fought in this battle, the capture of German prisoners constituted a major moment that needed to be displayed in any large-scale depiction. This was the first mass capture of German soldiers, and it was an important symbol of the changing tide of the war. However, even though these prisoners were enemies and their capture a symbol of victory, Soviet officials still wanted to ensure the portrayal of the proper treatment of the prisoners, providing a sharp contrast with the policies of the Wehrmacht toward Red Army prisoners. This would be another symbolic representation of the superiority of socialism over fascism. Even on a ravaged home front, where the civilian population had struggled to receive food and medical supplies, scarce resources had still been made available to the captured Germans. A later

25. RGALI, f. 674, op. 3, d. 1954, l. 14–15.

26. GARF, f. A-501, op. 1, d. 2429, l. 2.

27. Scott Palmer chronicled the evolution of Vuchetich's designs for the Mamaev Kurgan memorial complex, as well as the delays in its construction in his article, "How Memory Was Made: The Construction of the Memorial to the Heroes of the Battle of Stalingrad," *Russian Review* 68 (July 2009): 373–407; GARF, f. A-501, op. 1, d. 4313, ll. 70, 76–66.

memo also suggested adding a panorama scene featuring the capture of Field Marshal Paulus.[28]

However, Vuchetich ultimately decided to place the panorama elsewhere in the city and replace it with the "Hall of Military Glory," which would house a sculpture with an eternal flame and mosaics of the names of 7,200 Red Army soldiers who died during the battle.[29] Without a panorama, Vuchetich needed to create another way to depict scenes from the battle within the complex, which he did by fashioning a wall relief leading to the entrance of the "Hall of Military Glory."[30] The focal point of the relief is a portrait of Lenin flanked by jubilant Red Army soldiers with the inscription, "Long live the party of Lenin—the in-spirer and organizer of all of our victories." In this relief, the Communist Party receives the credit for Red Army victory in the battle and the war, and Lenin sup-plants Stalin as the face of Soviet leadership and war victory as part of Khrush-chev's de-Stalinization campaign. However, Lenin and the Red Army are not the only figures carved into the face of the building. Indeed, another very important group of people appear on the complex. Just to the right of the entrance of the "Hall of Military Glory" is a smaller scene that shows cold and forlorn German soldiers. The caption above the soldiers reads, "The fascist war dogs wanted to see the Volga; the Red Army gave them this 'opportunity'" (figure 5.2).[31]

For the designers of the complex, the scene of the Communist Party lead-ing the Red Army, workers, and soldiers to victory was incomplete without a depiction of the capture of the Germans. These men, however, were not called "Germans" or "German soldiers" in the caption. They are described only as "fascist *voiaki*," a pejorative term for soldiers that is best translated as "war dogs" in this case.[32] Yet, this branding of the German foes as fascist war dogs

---

28. GARF, f. A-501, op. 1, d. 4313, ll. 79.

29. Palmer, "How Memory was Made," 389, 400; GARF, f. A-501, op. 1, d. 4313, l. 211. The panorama eventually opened at the Volgograd State Defense Museum, the city's major war museum, on May 31, 1982. "Iz istorii muzeya-zapovedknika," Muzei-Zapovednik Stalingradskaya Bitva, accessed April 27, 2018, http://www.stalingrad-battle.ru/index.php?option=com_content&view=article&id=14&Itemid=8.

30. The commemoration and importance of the capture of the POWs in Volgograd did not end with the collapse of the Soviet Union. In 2003, the museum, "Memory," opened in the basement of the former Central Department Store (ЦУМ, TsUM), the location of the bunker of Field Marshal Paulus, perhaps the most famous German POW, and where he surrendered to the Red Army on January 31, 1943. "Iz istorii muzeya-zapovedknika," Muzei-Zapovednik Stalingradskaya Bitva, accessed April 27, 2018, http://www.stalingrad-battle.ru/index.php?option=com_content&view=article&id=14&Itemid=8 and "Muzei 'Pamyat,'" Muzei-Zapovednik Stalingradskaya Bitva, accessed April 27, 2018, http://www.stalingrad-battle.ru/index.php?Itemid=38&id=1278&option=com_content&view=article.

31. In Russian, "Фашистские бояки хотели увидеть Волгу; Красная Армия дала им эту 'возможность'…."

32. Multitran, for example, gives the possible translation of *бояки* (*voiaki*) as "war dogs" in addition to "the military" or "warriors." While writing this book, I discussed the monument with Russians, who

FIGURE 5.2. "Fascist War Dogs" next to the entrance of the "Hall of Military Glory." Photo by author.

in the relief already constituted softening of the wartime propaganda portrayal of Germans dominated by hate.

The word "Germany" is found nowhere at Mamaev Kurgan. The inscription on the relief, placed under the German foes who are identified by their uniforms, refers to them solely as "fascist war dogs" without naming their nationality. The Soviet Union, firmly allied with the GDR, had no reason to denounce Germany. These Cold War allegiances would become increasingly important to war commemoration and the memory of German POWs in the USSR during the 1980s.

The commemoration of the Great Patriotic War in the Soviet Union in the 1950s and 1960s highlighted the role of the Communist Party in leading the USSR to victory. It was not simply a victory of one state over another but rather of one way of life over another—that of socialism over fascism.[33] Planning

---

agreed that "war dogs" serves as the best translation. The use in the case is pejorative and has a connotation of cockiness, which the second half of the inscription elucidates. https://www.multitran.ru/c/m.exe?l1=1&l2=2&s=вояки.

33. Jonathan Brunstedt, "Building a Pan-Soviet Past: The Soviet War Cult and the Turn away from Ethnic Particularism," *Soviet and Post-Soviet Review* 38 (2011): 157. See also Brunstedt, *The Soviet Myth of World War II.*

commissions urged artists to create content that would illustrate the triumph of the socialist Red Army over the fascist Wehrmacht. Produced in the style of socialist realism, these monuments featured workers, peasants, and soldiers coming together under the leadership of Lenin's party to defeat the foes, who had marched onto Soviet soil and threatened the socialist state. Iconic human elements—Red Army and Wehrmacht soldiers—figured prominently in these monuments. In the case of the Battle of Stalingrad, taking German prisoners was a major symbol of the changing tide of the war. Yet despite changes in the representation of the role of Stalin and the party, depictions of German soldiers did not change much between 1945 and 1965. They were still seen as fascist enemies, not even worthy of the title of soldiers but rather of war dogs.

German Antifascist Allies

For the fortieth anniversary of the Great Patriotic War in 1985, Soviet leaders, in cooperation with those of East Germany (GDR), decided to undertake a new era of war commemoration, envisioning a museum that would foster good relations between the two states during an important anniversary of Soviet triumph. Both states sought to commemorate the German socialists who had escaped Nazi Germany to live in the Soviet Union and aid the war effort. To do this, the USSR and the GDR worked together to create the Memorial Museum of German Antifascists at the former POW Camp No. 27 in Krasnogorsk, a suburb that later became part of Moscow. The museum founders aimed to show that "the Soviet people never, even during the hardest times during the first stages of the war, confused Hitler's Germany with the German people."[34] The museum had to portray the Soviet leaders' humane attitude toward German POWs and solidarity with German antifascists. It broadened the understanding of Germans soldiers to include the socialists and communists among them.

During the Adenauer era, from 1949 to 1966, the West German government pursued policies of integration into the West or *Westpolitik*. The Federal Republic of Germany (FRG) joined NATO, reconciled with France, and initially refused to conduct diplomatic relations with any nation that recognized the German Democratic Republic (GDR). Under the next chancellor, Willy Brandt, the FRG sharply reversed its international policies and attempted to develop relations with the GDR and other socialist states with the policy of *Ostpolitik*. Relations between the FRG and the Soviet allied nations worsened, however, under the successive chancellors Helmut Schmidt and Helmut Kohl. Détente

---

34. RGALI, f. 3175, op. 1 d. 35, l. 20.

between East and West collapsed, and the USSR and the United States under-took new waves of arms buildup.[35] In the 1980s, the Soviet Union faced renewed tensions with the FRG. Because of their worsening relations with the West, the Soviet Union made attempts not only to improve relations with the GDR for the fortieth anniversary of the Great Patriotic War but also with the FRG. Soviet leaders felt that reshaping the representation of Germans during the war years would improve relations with both nations.

As part of the renewed effort to strengthen relations with both East and West Germany, members of the Central Committees of the Communist Party of the Soviet Union and the SED worked together over a span of five months to create a museum that would commemorate not only the fortieth anniversary of the victory of the Soviet people in the Great Patriotic War but also antifascist movements in Germany and the "Free Germany" movement, based in the Soviet Union, during the war.[36] The museum would stress that not every German was an enemy and demonstrate that there were German anti-fascists and socialists who had sacrificed their lives or worked alongside So-viet forces to bring about the end of the war. In fact, many of the members of the "Free Germany" movement were German communists, who later be-came members of the SED; they included Wilhelm Pieck and Walter Ulbricht. POW Camp No. 27 was chosen as the location for the museum because it was the site for the July 12–13, 1943, conference of the national antifascist com-mittee "Free Germany," which united the German communists and the POWs. Camp No. 27 was also the location of the central school for antifascist reedu-cation, which prepared POWs to produce radio or printed propaganda to be distributed along the frontlines or within POW camps.[37] More than five thou-sand Germans went through antifascist schooling at Krasnogorsk, and Camp No. 27 oversaw the training of more than fifty thousand men of over twenty nationalities throughout the entire Soviet POW camp system.[38]

The commemoration of German antifascists proved to be a radical break from previous depictions of Germans during the war and in earlier forms of commemoration. Soviet officials and writers often used the words "German" and "fascist" interchangeably from mid-1942 to April 1945; however, in the

---

35. Lily Gardner Feldman, *Germany's Foreign Policy of Reconciliation: From Enmity to Amity* (Lan-ham, MD: Rowman & Littlefield, 2012), 25–26, 31, 36.

36. RGALI, f. 3175, op. 1, d. 35, l. 18.

37. RGALI, f. 3175, op. 1, d. 35, ll. 18–19.

38. S. I. Pobezhimov et al., *Memorial'nyi Muzei Nemetskikh Antifashistov: filial Tsentral'nogo muzeya Velikoi Otechestvennoi voiny. g. Krasnogorsk* (Krasnogorsk: Filial Fonda Rozy Lyuksemburg v Rossiiskoi Federatsii, 2015), 6–7.

1960s official Soviet commemoration reflected the new policies adopted at the end of the war. By the 1980s, political currents had changed, and memory of the Germans had softened, allowing for the use of the national identifier of "German" in official commemorations with more positive connotations. Although it was clear that Germans had been enemies during the conflict, not *all* Germans were seen as enemies. As the Memorial Museum of German Antifascists explicitly aimed to promote, German communists and many POWs had sided with the Red Army and the Soviet Union.

The Memorial Museum of German Antifascists was a true collaborative effort between the USSR and the GDR. One of the former POW camp buildings was chosen to house the museum. The façade of the building was unchanged, but the interior was redesigned to house exhibits. The assistant minister of culture of the USSR, T. V. Golubtsovoi, and the Department of Agitation and Propaganda of the Ministry of Culture of the Central Committee of the Communist Party of the Soviet Union controlled the Soviet contributions to the project. The East Germans provided representatives from the Institute of Marxism-Leninism, the Institute of War History, the Museum of German History, the Central Museum of the National Peoples' Army of the GDR, and veterans from the German Antifascists to provide materials for the exhibitions. The East Germans also supplied equipment such as lighting, slides, and information written in both German and Russian.[39]

In addition to the message that German communists helped the Soviet war effort, the Soviet Ministry of Culture emphasized the humane treatment of German POWs. Although much of the museum focused on antifascist movements and individuals, large sections illustrated what life had been like in Soviet captivity. A series of exhibits chronicled the "humanity of Soviet laws in relation to prisoners of war, on their concrete implementation, documents and facts about the norms of allowance for them, about medical assistance to them, [and] about everyday life and the life of prisoners of war in the Soviet Union."[40] Because it was important to Soviet officials that East German citizens have a positive attitude toward the Soviet Union, they emphasized that they had treated the German POWs with care. Museum designers illustrated that, despite their country's losses, Soviet authorities and citizens did not act vindictively toward the German POWs. The exhibits presented a stark contrast between the Soviet and Nazi approaches to the treatment of POWs. The Germans used their Soviet prisoners for slave labor, starved them to death, withheld medical care and

39. RGALI, f. 3175, op. 1, d. 35, l. 20.
40. RGALI, f. 3175, op. 1, d. 35, l. 22.

shelter, experimented on them with poison gas, and forced them to dig their own graves before shooting them. In contrast, Soviet officials provided their German POWs with food, shelter, and medical care, as well as a reeducation program to help them divest themselves of their fascist ideology.

Within five months of its conception, the Museum of German Antifascists opened. On May 5, 1985, just before the fortieth anniversary of Soviet victory, a delegation from the GDR traveled to Moscow for the museum's official opening. It was indeed a momentous occasion: the delegation included the general secretary of the Central Committee of the SED, Erich Honecker, as well as other leaders of the German Communist Party (DKP) and the SED. At the museum opening, they met with members of the Politburo of the Central Committee of the CPSU, the Ministry of Culture of the CPSU, and the Society of Friendship with the GDR.[41] Although not front-page news, the opening of the monument received an entire page of coverage in *Pravda*. Articles recounted the history of the museum and the role of the German antifascists in aiding the Soviet Union's war effort against Hitlerism, as well as the importance of Soviet–German friendship and cooperation.[42] Honecker gave a speech at the opening in which he said, "The museum is an exciting symbol of internationalism, humanism, and German-Soviet friendship."[43] The hope, expressed by both countries, was that the museum would serve to foster close relations between the Soviet Union and the GDR. If the two groups of people could cooperate during the war, then they could cooperate years after the war in friendship.

The opening of the museum drew the attention not only of the allies of the USSR and German Democratic Republic but also of the Federal Republic of Germany. The West German newspaper *Frankfurter Allgemeine Zeitung* reported on Honecker's trip to the Soviet Union in early May 1985. Although the article focused on Honecker's travels and discussions with Gorbachev on the "unresolved German question," it noted that he attended the inauguration of the museum "commemorating the 'German antifascist' fight against Hitler."[44] Its mention of Honecker's activities in Moscow illustrated West German interest in a Soviet museum that honored the activities of German antifascists.

Honecker's travels and appearance at the opening ceremony coincided with President Ronald Reagan's visit to both the Bergen-Belsen concentration camp and the Bitburg soldiers' cemetery in honor of the fortieth anniversary of the war. Unlike Honecker's trip, which commemorated German antifascists, Rea-

---

41. RGALI, f. 3175, op. 1, d. 35, l. 30.
42. "V pamyat' nemetskikh antifashistov," *Pravda*, May 6, 1985, 4–5.
43. RGALI, f. 3175, op. 1, d. 35, l. 31.
44. "'Die deutsche Frage ist nicht ungelöst,'" *Frankfurter Allgemeine Zeitung*, May 6, 1985, 6.

gan's trip to Bitburg became a public relations disaster. Reagan planned to visit German war graves to symbolize how former enemies, the United States and Germany, had become allies. Bitburg, however, contained not only the graves of regular German soldiers but also those of about fifty soldiers in the Waffen-SS, the armed wing of the SS—the most intensely ideological Nazi organization that carried out a genocide of Jews and Roma. Germans and Americans alike disapproved of Reagan's trip. He considered canceling the entire trip but instead stuck to his plan to visit the graves. Although he added the trip to Bergen-Belsen (which he had originally planned to avoid), Reagan found himself the center of an international controversy related to the memory of the war.[45] Honecker's trip, however, avoided controversy.

By 1985, the fortieth anniversary of Soviet victory, it was possible to reimagine and reshape the narrative of the war and of the role of Germans and German POWs. Both the passage of time and the need to improve Soviet–German relations meant that it was permissible to give more attention to that small group of Germans who had resisted Hitler and aided the antifascist cause. Even though most Germans were not antifascists, a few did serve alongside Soviet forces, contributing to the eventual Soviet victory. This change in the narrative was meant to help strengthen relations between the USSR and the GDR.

Even after the collapse of the Soviet Union and the reunification of Germany, the Memorial Museum of German Antifascists continued to house exhibits that praised the work of German socialists who tried to undermine the Nazi regime.[46] It also continued to illustrate the humane treatment of German POWs, especially in comparison to the German treatment of Soviet POWs.[47] In recent years, the focus of the museum has shifted from the antifascist movement to a balance of exhibits on antifascism and the phenomenon of prisoners of war. In 2003, the Memorial Museum of German Antifascists became a branch of the Central Museum of the Great Patriotic War. As such, the museum has increased its exhibits on POW life in the USSR, especially because it is now possible to discuss the topic openly, including the forced labor of the POWs, with access to declassified archive sources after the Soviet collapse.[48]

45. On Reagan's visit to the Bitburg Cemetery see John P. Diggins, *Ronald Reagan: Fate, Freedom, and the Making of History* (New York: W. W. Norton, 2007), 366–371; Tumarkin, *Living & the Dead*, 30; "'Wir waren Feinde, wir sind jetzt Freunde' Kohl und Reagan in Bergen-Belsen und Bitburg," *Frankfurter Allgemeine Zeitung*, May 6, 1985.

46. Pobezhimov et al., *Memorial'nyi Muzei*, 51–68.

47. Pobezhimov et al., *Memorial'nyi Muzei*, 44–50, 69–86.

48. Pobezhimov et al., *Memorial'nyi Muzei*, 8, 112.

Mourned Men and Reconciliation

The current phase of POW commemoration could only have happened after the collapse of the Soviet Union. In the early 1990s, Russian archives opened to native-born and foreign scholars. In a wave of declassification, it was finally possible to uncover far more information about the Great Patriotic War and the fate of the German POWs. Both scholars and German organizations had access to new materials. The German Red Cross and several German veterans' associations worked with the Russian government and archives to track down the burial sites of German POWs who did not return home. Many German families finally discovered the fate of their loved ones. Additionally, the Russian federal government allowed the German Red Cross, veterans associations, and private individuals to mourn their lost loved ones by making the locations of POW graves public and permitting Germans to construct monuments and hold commemorative ceremonies there. With the passage of time, the Russian government moved toward reconciliation with Germany. Living POW veterans could return to Russia to see where they had spent time in captivity, and those who died in Russia could be openly mourned by families and friends.

Even after Gorbachev came to power and instituted reforms in the Soviet Union, however, officials from the German Red Cross could not obtain information about German war graves.[49] Only on December 16, 1992, when representatives of the newly unified Federal Republic of Germany and the Russian Federation met in Moscow to sign an agreement between the two nations for the care of war graves, did Germans gain access to the information they had sought for decades. According to the agreement, each nation could maintain graves on the territory of the other nation. The Russian government would pay for the upkeep of its war graves in Germany, and the German government would do the same for its graves in Russia. The agreement served as a revision to a treaty from November 9, 1990, between the newly reunified Germany and the Soviet Union, which allowed Soviet officials continued access to Soviet war graves in Germany. After the Soviet Union collapsed, the German and Russian governments worked together to continue access to each other's burial sites and to protect the graves. On October 4, 1993, Helmut Kohl, chancellor of the Federal Republic of Germany, finalized the decision to uphold the terms of the agreement with Russia after the Bundesrat, the legislative body that represents the sixteen Länder (federal states) at a national level, approved the bill on September 24, 1993.[50]

---

49. "Gemeinsames Protokoll," July 7, 1987, DRK 3549, S. 4.

50. Full text of the agreement and its subsequent bill, as well as its history, can be found at "Deutscher Bundestag: 12. Wahlperiode. Druchsache 12/5837," http://dipbt.bundestag.de/dip21/btd/12/058/120 5837.pdf.

The agreement and subsequent law included thirteen articles that guaranteed the rights of Germany on Russian soil for its war graves in German-built graveyards, as well as for sections of Russian cemeteries where German war dead were interred. Whereas the Soviet Union was a victor nation in World War II and its officials had knowledge of the locations of many of the sites of its war dead, neither East nor West Germany officials had access to such information. Cemetery information, at least with respect to deceased POWs, was classified as top secret in the Soviet Union. After German reunification and the collapse of the USSR, however, the Russian government allowed Germans to obtain all possible access to documentation about war graves. In addition to knowledge of their locations, the agreement noted that the Russian Federation was required to give the Germans "suitable space" for the "establishment of simple and dignified memorial sites" at grave sites on German requests. It also gave Germans the right to disinter graves for the purposes of repatriation or identification, but only with prior consent of the Russian Federation. Moreover, all actions of Germany on Russian soil would be paid for by the Federal Republic of Germany. To streamline the process of gravesite maintenance, the German War Graves Commission would represent the German government for these matters, and the Association of International Military-Memorial Cooperation "Military Memorials" would act as the Russian representative.[51]

For Russians living in smaller cities, the presence of the German POWs was never a secret. In Ulyanovsk, for example, Soviet citizens frequently interacted with German POWs around the city and at job sites.[52] What was not openly known, however, was the burial locations of the deceased POWs. The GUPVI and the NKVD had a set system for recording POW deaths and burials for each camp: secret ledgers recorded the information of the deceased, including name, date of birth, nationality, rank, date of death, date of burial, and location of burial within the plot.[53] Most camps had their own ledger, if not multiple ledgers, covering the years of their operations. One of the ledgers for Ulyanovsk, for example, detailed the location of the cemetery on Barataevka

---

51. On the notion of permissions for German gravesite memorials, see especially Article 5.4 or page 8 of the bill. For information about German access to Russian documents about gravesites see Article 9.1 or page 9. For information about representation of the two governments being through the German War Graves Commission and "Military Memorials," see Article 8 or page 9.

52. Anecdotal evidence in the city points to a great deal of interaction between free Soviet citizens and the German POWs. For a written account, see the recollections of Lyalya Bykova, in G. A. Demochkin, *Devochki i mal'chishki: semero iz detei voiny* (Ulyanovsk: Ulyanovsk State Technical University, 2016), 56–61. She describes having seen the former POWs in town and having interacted with them on occasion.

53. See for example RGVA, f. 511p, op. 1, d. 1, ll. 1–81, especially page 17 for Camp No. 215 in Ulyanovsk; RGVA. F. 105p, op. 2, d. 19, 20, 23 for Camp No. 27 in Krasnogorsk.

Street, which is near the central airport today.[54] The cemetery, however, was not marked as an official site. Ulyanovsk Camp No. 215 closed in 1948, and by the 1970s, the location of the cemetery had been forgotten. There were no gravestones, so construction workers only discovered the bones and evidence of the cemetery while building a streetcar depot. The remains were then transferred to the Isheevskoe Cemetery to the north of the city, where they were placed in a mass grave. In the early 1990s, members of the German Embassy in Russia contacted officials in Ulyanovsk in hopes of creating a memorial at the mass grave site.[55]

The local Russians did not widely support creation of the memorial, and the local press did not report on the competition for its design.[56] Given the huge damage that Germany had wrought on the Soviet Union during the war, many citizens had strong negative feelings about marking enemy graves. Unlike the war memorials commemorating the Soviet defeats and victory, the POW memorial was not openly discussed in the local news media until the later stages of the process. Initial commemoration efforts at the grave site in 1994 were not reported in either of Ulyanovsk's major local newspapers, *Ul'ianovskaia Pravda* and *Simbirskii Kur'er*. However, both local papers had numerous articles that year on the contributions of local Soviet battalions to the war.

Eventually, the commemoration of the fallen German POWs attracted the attention of the local press, which covered the opening ceremony in the cemetery. On May 15, 1998, the Ulyanovsk State Committee of the Red Cross started the process of erecting a memorial in the cemetery to commemorate the 1,532 POWs who died between 1944 and 1949 in the Ulyanovsk region. Soon after, youth from the Hannover section of the German Red Cross traveled to Ulyanovsk for the unveiling of the memorial plaque that reads, "In memory of the German POWs who died in Ulyanovsk" in both Russian and German (figure 5.3).[57] Commemoration of the fallen German POWs in the Ulyanovsk cemetery has continued into the twenty-first century. By the summer of 2014, staff had marked the location of the communal German POW grave on the main map of the cemetery (figure 5.4).

The plot for the German POWs is located in the main area of the cemetery. Although it is marked off by a fence, it is surrounded by the graves of ordinary Russian citizens. The German War Graves Commission maintains the POW

---

54. RGVA, f. 511p, op. 1, d. 11, ll. 6–7.

55. *Simbirskie Gubernskie Vedomosti*, July 22, 1995, 2–3.

56. For images of the different monuments from the competition, see the folder "Monument to German Prisoners" in the G. A. Demochkin collection in the Research Institute of History and Culture of the Ulyanovsk Region in the name of N. M. Karamzin.

57. *Simbirskii Kur'er*, June 6, 1998, 3.

FIGURE 5.3. "In Memory of the German POWs who Died in Ulyanovsk." Photo by author.

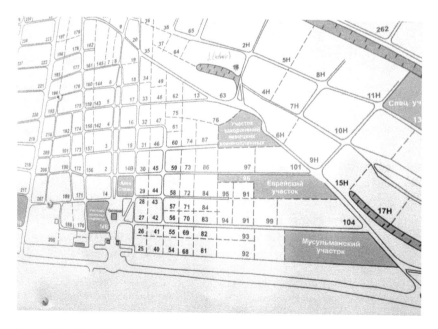

FIGURE 5.4. Map of the Isheevskoe Cemetery in Ulyanovsk. To the right of plots 76 and 87 is the burial plot for German POWs. Photo by author.

FIGURE 5.5.   The cross and plaque at its base in the center of the POW plot in July 2014. Photo by author.

plot.[58] The grave site has expanded from the initial memorial stone of 1998. At the main entrance of the German POW section, a large cross was erected with an additional plaque at its base, reading "Here lie POWs, victims of the Second World War"[59] (figure 5.5). The use of the word "victims" on the plaque is indicative of a great change in thinking about the war. In the Russian caption it appears as *"zhertvy"* and in German as *"opfer,"* words that signal a sharp shift in discourse. For Russians, the word "victim" is heavily charged and is usually

58. Founded in 1919, the German War Graves Commission was tasked with finding and maintaining gravesites from both world wars around the globe. After 1991, the commission received the right to tend to the graves in former Soviet territories. "Volksbund," the German War Graves Commission, accessed October 9, 2020, https://www.volksbund.de/volksbund.html.

59. In German, "Hier ruhen Kriegsgefangene Opfer des Zweites Weltkrieges." In Russian, "Здесь покоятся военнопленные жертвы второй мировой войны."

used only when discussing Soviet citizens who died during the war or those who died during the repressions of the Terror. Indeed, during the final months of the Soviet Union, the Supreme Soviet of the RSFSR enacted a law titled "On Rehabilitation of Victims of Political Repression" on October 18, 1991. Even in the context of political repression, the term was highly contested.[60]

For the Germans, however, "victims" has a different connotation. In the years after World War II, both East and West Germany envisioned themselves as victims of Nazism. For the East Germans, victimhood meant learning from the mistakes of the past. Reeducation in socialism and antifascism would reshape the new German Democratic Republic and allow it to reinvent itself and its people. In the Federal Republic of Germany, however, victimhood did not emphasize transformation. During the leadership of Konrad Adenauer, the POWs in Soviet captivity became symbols of German suffering, though now at the hands of Soviet socialism, in addition to National Socialism. West German citizens could move on from the war, but these men continued to endure needless punishment at the hands of Soviet leaders. In January 1954, the West German government passed a law that had been promoted by the Association of Returnees (Verband der Heimkehrer, VdH). The act compensated POWs one German mark a day for each day spent in captivity after January 1, 1946, and two German marks a day after January 1, 1949. Though the date range meant that Germans could receive compensation for being held captive by any of the Allied victors, the overwhelming majority of those eligible had spent time in Soviet captivity. In essence, these men were compensated for prolonged military service; they were not to be compensated as victims, although the notion of German victimhood at the hands of both Nazism and Soviet socialism existed.[61]

After the early Cold War years, West Germans began to accept accountability for the war. Nonetheless, contemporary Germans, drawing on the legacy of the West German government, still view the deceased POWs as victims. The recent monument in the cemetery in Ulyanovsk does not clarify whether the POWs are victims of Nazism, Stalinism, or both. Yet, despite the ambiguous meaning

---

60. Cathy Frierson, *Russia's Law "On Rehabilitation of Victims of Political Repression": 1991–2011, An Enduring Artifact of Transnational Justice*, NCEEER Working Paper, February 28, 2014, 3; Tyler C. Kirk, *After the Gulag: A History of Memory in Russia's Far North* (Bloomington: Indiana University Press, 2023), esp. chapter 5.

61. On the notion of German suffering during and after the war, see Robert G. Moeller, *War Stories: The Search for a Usable Past in the Federal Republic of Germany* (Berkeley: University of California Press, 2001), esp. 3–4, 6, 8, 19, 39, 79. Frank Biess also discusses the different East and West German interpretation of suffering in his book, *Homecomings: Returning POWs and the Legacies of Defeat in Postwar Germany* (Princeton, NJ: Princeton University Press, 2006), 6, 37, 42, 68–69. Jeffrey Herf likewise notes the two notions of suffering in the postwar era, as well as the notion of suffering from whom, in his monograph *Divided Memory* (Cambridge, MA: Harvard University Press, 2013), 1–2, 8, 39, 222, 394. For information on the POW compensation championed by the VdH, see Biess, *Homecomings*, 111–112.

FIGURE 5.6.   The central POW memorial in the Isheevskoe Cemetery in June 2017. Photo by author.

of the marker, many Germans did feel that their brethren had suffered because of the war. Although neither the Russian government nor Russian citizens funded or erected the monument, they did permit this interpretation of the war to be publicly displayed on their soil.

By 2016, individual Germans had done more work to develop the POW plot in the Ulyanovsk cemetery. Unlike in the 1990s when state institutions or NGOs provided the funding to design and erect these structures, individuals now began to take an active role in commemoration. In 2016, the German businessman Wolfgang Vogel provided the funds to greatly expand the central monument. He paid for the installation of a brick area around the central cross and two large granite slabs that commemorate the "German POWs and internees as well as POWs of other nations who died in the following communities: the Samara Oblast, the Ulyanovsk Oblast, the Penza Oblast, and the Republic of Mordovia" (figures 5.6 and 5.7). In some sense, then, commemoration of German dead also served as a way to preserve the legacy of the younger generations. Vogel, a man who was not a POW, is allied with them by having his name inscribed on a brick among memorials to the fallen men.

The Ulyanovsk cemetery illustrates two major shifts in commemoration of the German POWs on Russian soil. First, the Soviet government initially

DIE MITTEL FÜR DIE
ERRICHTUNG DES GEDENKPLATZES

WURDEN GESTIFTET VON

DIPL.-KFM

WOLFGANG VOGEL

BAD SASSENDORF, DEUTSCHLAND, 2016

СРЕДСТВА НА СТРОИТЕЛЬСТВО
ПОМИНАЛЬНОГО МЕСТА

ПОЖЕРТВОВАЛ

ДИПЛОМИРОВАННЫЙ ЭКОНОМИСТ

ВОЛЬФГАНГ ФОГЕЛЬ

БАД ЗАССЕНДОРФ, ГЕРМАНИЯ, 2016

FIGURE 5.7. "The Means for the Construction of the Commemorative Space Was Donated by Wolfgang Vogel." Photo by author.

commissioned memorials that included the German POWs as part of the commemoration of its victory and its losses. The monuments served Soviet
political goals and promoted Soviet narratives about the war. They were never
designed to mark German losses or grief—and they certainly did not portray
captured German soldiers, responsible for so much killing on Soviet soil, as
"victims" of World War II. Once NGOs and private citizens gained access
to cemetery records and obtained permission from the Russian government to
produce monuments on Russian territory, Germans could commemorate the
POWs in their own way and finally grieve their dead family members.

When German organizers began creating their own monuments, their forms
changed as well. As in the case of Western European war monuments, which
included classical, romantic, or religious themes that signified bereavement,

the various stages of POW commemoration in the Ulyanovsk cemetery contained a religious component.[62] The original stone monument from 1998 featured an engraving of a cross. The stone added before 2014 featured many engraved crosses at the base of a large metal cross. Finally, the businessman's additions to the plot in 2016 included more crosses and stones that accentuated the earlier metal cross. With each addition to the cemetery, Christian religious symbols proliferated. Although Soviet war memorials to the Soviet dead also borrowed from classical Christian religious art, such as the grieving mother statue at Mamaev Kurgan based on Michelangelo's *Pieta*, Soviet state-sanctioned art did not contain the religious symbol of the crucifix. Thus, in addition to allowing Germans to grieve their losses, the Russian government enabled Germans to include religious symbols in their commemorative mourning structures.

The opening of monuments like those in Ulyanovsk speaks to a movement toward reconciliation between Russians and Germans. As many scholars of Soviet war memory and of memory more generally have noted, there is always a tension between official and individual memory. Collective memory, or better termed "collected memory," is based on the recollections of individuals, but the political conventions of a given era shape the construction of physical monuments.[63] Before official memorials for the German dead were built on Russian soil, there were small-scale acts of reconciliation and commemoration. In the early 1990s, a woman from Ulyanovsk began to travel to Germany to visit her relatives. While in an unnamed location there, she became acquainted with a man named Wigfried Hofman, who had been a POW in Ulyanovsk. Hofman noted that there were about fifty living former POWs from Ulyanovsk who used to gather annually.[64] Eventually, this story made its way back to Ulyanovsk and the Ulyanovsk Automobile Factory (UAZ), where he had worked. The leadership of the factory then decided to include the former POWs in its celebration of the fiftieth anniversary of victory in World War II. The director of the factory's museum reached out to older

---

62. On the connection between war memory and the grieving process, see Jay Winter, *Sites of Memory, Sites of Mourning: The Great War in European Cultural History* (Cambridge: Cambridge University Press, 2014), esp. 5. At least one similar monument exists in Poliske, Ukraine, at the burial site for the POWs who died there. Like in Ulyanovsk, Russia, the gravesite features a large cross and a plaque memorializing the POWs who died in the camp. German families who had visited the final resting places of their relatives have gone to the site with local Ukrainian priests, who have said blessings at the site. Information for this gravesite comes from the personal family album of Klaus H Kaak, "Spurensuche in der Ukraine 2002, Poliske 2002."

63. James Young, *The Texture of Memory: Holocaust Memorials and Meaning* (New Haven: Yale University Press, 1993), esp. viii, xi; J. M. Winter, *Remembering War: The Great War between Memory and History in the Twentieth Century* (New Haven: Yale University Press, 2006), esp. 1–3, 9, 11.

64. *Narodnaia Gazeta*, May 17, 1995, 5.

people in the community to gather the stories of those who had worked along-side the POWs. She also began to organize a meeting between the former POWs and their Soviet acquaintances. Unfortunately, due to various bureau-cratic obstacles, the trip did not happen in time for the anniversary; however, a group of former POWs did travel later to Ulyanovsk where they toured the factory and its museum and met with those they had known in the commu-nity.[65] The former enemies who had worked alongside Soviet citizens after the war had been deemed worthy of inclusion in a war commemoration cere-mony in at least one city.

Since Vladimir Putin's ascendancy to the presidency of the Russian Feder-ation in 2000, he has resurrected the cult of the Great Patriotic War. There are massive Victory Day parades across all of Russia, with a central parade on Red Square. Building on earlier Victory Day parades, modern Russia's Victory Day parade has become the equivalent of the Soviet Union's Revolution Day parade—displaying thousands of marching troops and hundreds of pieces of military technology, including tanks, nuclear missile launchers, and airplanes. Just as Brezhnev's government returned repeatedly to the memory of the war to reinforce its own legitimacy and instill national pride in its citizens, so too does Putin's government. Yet Putin's war cult, Soviet in its emphasis on pride for the achievements of the war years, has also discarded many features of the earlier Soviet cult, including its emphasis on multinationalism, the role of the Communist Party, and even antifascist ideology. The new narrative emphasizes Russian nationalism, legitimizing the history of the Soviet Union and its "finest achievement," and encouraging national unity and support for the military.[66]

The return of the cult of World War II has ushered in new waves of re-membrance. Older citizens have shared their memories of the war with new generations of scholars hoping to produce works that glorify Russia and its contribution to the war. In recent years, residents of Ulyanovsk have also be-gun to give interviews about their experiences with the German POWs. Lia-lia Bykova, for example, recounted meeting German POWs in her youth. Her story illustrates the differences between official portrayals of Germans at the time and the feelings of ordinary people. Lialia believed that the Germans were human beings just like her and that they were not to be feared. Instead, she even mentioned offering some of her food to the German POWs.[67] An-other resident of Ulyanovsk, Natal'ia Khramstovaia, also recounted giving a

65. *Panorama UAZ*, December 1, 1994, 1, 3, *Narodnaia Gazeta*, May 17, 1995, 5.
66. Tumarkin, "Great Patriotic War as Myth and Memory," 609–610; Nikolay Koposov, *Memory Laws, Memory Wars: The Politics of the Past in Europe and Russia* (Cambridge: Cambridge University Press, 2017).
67. Recollections of Lialia Bykova in Demochkin, *Devochki i mal'chishki voiny*, 56–61.

portion of her scarce bread during the 1946 famine to a German POW. She stated that at the time everyone suffered from a lack of food, yet her family gave a portion of their meager bread supply to a German who had helped construct the building in which they lived.[68] Although the Soviet propaganda department portrayed the Germans as beasts until the spring of 1945 for the sake of the war effort, propaganda could not change the feelings that were created by personal interactions in a safe, home-front situation. As various memory scholars have shown, stories such as these allow for the rewriting of the official narrative once the political climate permits or supports it.[69]

The presence of graveside commemorations and more open discussion of the German POWs in the USSR should not be seen as exemplifying full reconciliation between combatant nations or a shift in thinking about the war. The war was deeply destructive to the Soviet Union, and the topic of the war dead is still heavily charged, as the recent case of high school student Nikolai Desyatnichenko demonstrates. The Russian Prosecutor General's Office investigated Desyatnichenko for the crime of rehabilitation of Nazism after his November 2017 speech before the German Bundestag, in which he stated that prisoners of war who died in the Soviet Union were also victims of World War II.[70] The event marked a reversal of the progress made toward broadening the understanding of German antifascists initiated in 1985 with the Memorial Museum of German Antifascists. During that time, the Soviet state began to propagate the notion that not all Germans were believers in the Nazi system. Indeed, as the museum shows, there were many soldiers who were forced to fight against their will, and some actively attempted to undermine the Nazi war effort or switched their allegiances when given the opportunity. Under Putin, however, there has been a return to an earlier and narrower representation of the war. Although Putin does not use the war to promote socialism, he does use the victory to emphasize Russian glory and strength and to counter anti-Russian commemorations of former Soviet Republics, such as that of the Ukrainian Insurgent Army (UPA), which sided with the Nazi occupiers, murdered thousands of Poles and Jews, and fought a guerilla war against the Soviet

---

68. G.A. Demochkin, *Dvadtsatyi vek Natal'i Khramtsovoi*, (Ulyanovsk: Ulyanovsk State Technical University, 2015), 111.

69. In the Soviet and Russian context, see Wertsch, *Voices of Collective Remembering*, and Kirschenbaum, *Legacy of the Siege of Leningrad*. For other instances of this happening see Peter Novick's discussion of memory of World War I, the Holocaust, and the Vietnam War in *The Holocaust and Collective Memory: The American Experience* (New York: Bloomsbury, 2001).

70. "Rossiiskii skol'nik pokayalsya za nevinno pogibshikh soldat vermakhta," *Lenta.ru*, November 20, 2017, https://lenta.ru/news/2017/11/20/nazi_shkolnik/; and "Genprokuratura proverit uchitelei rasskazavshego o nemetskikh soldatakh shkol'nika," *Lenta.ru*, November 21, 2017, https://lenta.ru/news/2017/11/21/zaverte/?utm_medium=more&utm_source=rnews.

state. The topic of the German POWs, then, remains relevant to contemporary Russian politics.

With the passage of time, the Russian government granted Germans the ability to commemorate their war dead in Russia in ways that they see fit, portraying their loved ones as "victims" of a war sought by Hitler and not the German people. This marks a major break from earlier Soviet policy and the state-sanctioned depictions of the German POWs. Commemoration of German POWs in the Soviet Union and Russia has long been linked to domestic and international politics. From the end of the war until 1985, German POWs were portrayed as symbols of the Red Army victory and the humanity of the Soviet state. In 1985, however, Cold War relations between the Soviet Union and the GDR necessitated a shift in the portrayal of the POWs. The Central Committees of the CPSU and the SED celebrated a select few Germans as antifascist allies who had helped the war effort. The massive shift from "war dogs" to recognition of German antifascist allies marked a differentiation between the German people and their Nazi leadership. After the collapse of the USSR, another monumental shift in commemoration occurred. It became possible to represent the German POWs, especially those who died while in captivity in the years after the war, in a different way. Relations between Germany and Russia had improved enough over the past quarter-century to allow Germans to commemorate and mourn their war dead on Russian soil. Whether this shift will continue, however, remains unclear, given the renewed fractures between Russia and Western Europe following Russia's 2022 invasion of Ukraine.

Conclusion

From the end of World War II through January 1956, the Soviet Union held onto captives from the German Army. The long-lasting incarceration of the Germans POWs initially stemmed not from a wish for vengeance but rather from a need to rebuild the Soviet Union, at least until 1949. The postwar agendas of rebuilding the Soviet Union and establishing a socialist Germany meant that retribution could not and would not be the main motivating factor behind captivity. Initially, Soviet officials chose to deploy the POWs in the state's well-defined forced-labor system. Soviet leaders drew on experience from World War I, international standards for captivity, and the infamous Gulag system to mobilize German prisoners in three ways: to work in economic sectors disrupted by the loss of the occupied territories, to staff new industries in the East, and replace Soviet workers killed over the course of war. The Council of People's Commissars gave the People's Commissariat for Internal Affairs (NKVD) the responsibility to establish and run the Main Administration for Affairs of Prisoners of War and Internees (GUPVI). The NKVD used its years of experience in administering the Gulag to run the POW camps, including the systems of provisioning, evaluating, reeducating, and mobilizing prisoners. The goal of the POW camps was to get the most economic output from the lowest resource input. Soviet officials, however, expended greater resources on the foreign captives than on their Soviet charges because of the politics of international relations. Soviet officials dared not risk creating any grounds for foreign officials to publicly criticize the Soviet Union. The NKVD also heavily invested in turning the German captives into antifascists who would support the Soviet Union on their return home. Again, this aspect of the GUPVI system speaks more to its corrective than punitive functions. Eventually, the political considerations underlying POW incarceration and repatriation surpassed economic needs.

Between 1945 and 1956, five major waves of POW repatriations occurred. Repatriation was never just the end of captivity but rather was an economic and political process. The first waves were motivated by economic concerns and the later ones by political considerations. The first large wave occurred between May and December 1945. Just prior to German surrender, on May 8, 1945, the Red Army held 3,180,000 German POWs.[1] Roughly six months later, on December 14, 1945, 1,666,391 German POWs remained in the Soviet Union, suggesting that almost half the German POWs had either returned to Germany or died.[2] Repatriation of German POWs commenced immediately after German capitulation. Soviet officials wasted little time in returning POWs who were incapable of contributing to postwar reconstruction. Ill or weak prisoners who could not be put to work rapidly and cheaply were sent home to Germany. Victory in the war came at an extremely high price for the Soviet Union: the losses due to occupations, bombings, and battles were great. The country faced a severe labor shortage, as well as shortages in housing, food, and shelter for its free citizens. Soviet leaders had little interest in keeping prisoners who required food and care but could not work.

The second major wave of economically driven repatriations occurred in 1946 and 1947, coinciding with a famine. Soviet leaders released German prisoners in larger numbers in this period so it could allocate precious resources to its own citizens. Many men were sent home before they could develop or die from starvation-related diseases. Yet, despite the poor conditions caused by the famine, Soviet leaders were still committed to having POWs contribute to the national economy. In May 1947, camp officials told the remaining POWs that they would likely not be repatriated until December 31, 1948, at the earliest. Camp directors closely monitored how this announcement was perceived by the POWs and sent reports detailing their reactions to Stalin, Molotov, Beria, and Zhdanov. The normally pro-USSR and prosocialist German statements about the POWs turned into ones of outrage or depression. POWs were shocked by this announcement, with many feeling they would die in the Soviet Union.[3]

1. Michael Borchard, *Die deutschen Kriegsgefangenen in der Sowjetunion: Zur politischen Bedeutung der Kriegsgefangenenfrage 1949–1955* (Düsseldorf: Droste Verlag, 2000), 43.
2. GARF, f. 9401, op. 1, d. 2227, l. 152–153.
3. GARF, f. 9401, op. 2. d. 169, l. 367–376.

The state's reluctance to release POWs before 1949 coincided with a major economic goal: the fulfillment of the Fourth Five-Year Plan, which ran from 1946 to 1950. The goal of this plan was the reconstruction of the national economy.[4] By 1950, the Soviet economy was well on its way to recovery and did not need to rely on POW labor to the same extent that it did in the immediate aftermath of the war. Moreover, POWs had been central to the recovery. However, it was not completely achieved by 1950. Only by the time of Stalin's death in March 1953 did the Soviet Union reach its prewar level of production; in several sectors, the economy even grew beyond its prewar level.[5] Their importance also decreased around 1946 and 1947, when the Gulag received a massive influx of prisoners related to postwar crackdowns. The POWs had initially served to replace a shortage of forced labor caused by wartime amnesties and deaths in the Gulag. When the Gulag population again increased, the POW population's importance lessened.

By 1949, the motives for repatriation became more political, and the third large wave of repatriation occurred in this year. Since Germany's capitulation, actively antifascist German POWs had steadily returned to each occupation zone to engage in pro-Soviet propaganda work. This mission increased in relevance in 1949, when in May and October, West Germany and East Germany officially became two separate states. After 1949, many of those who received antifascist training took leadership positions in institutions in the GDR. The emphasis on rehabilitation that played a central role in the Gulag also played a central role in the GUPVI. Those POWs who successfully transformed themselves from Nazis into antifascists were more likely to secure release. In this sense, Soviet forced labor shaped not only Soviet society but also the formation of two new societies in East and West Germany.

With the intensification of the Cold War, the POWs remaining on Soviet soil became bargaining chips. Their long-lasting incarceration prompted intervention not only from the East and West German governments but also from officials from the other Allied powers, the United Nations, the Red Cross, and German Catholic and Protestant relief organizations. The diplomatic maneuvering over the men played out both publicly and privately. The news publications of both German states closely tracked the status of returnees and clamored for the return of the remaining men. Indeed, the issue of captivity shaped the politics and media in the two emerging and diametrically opposed German states. As the Cold War intensified, the issue of repatriation remained

---

4. Eugène Zaleski, Marie-Christine MacAndrew, and John Hampton Moore, *Stalinist Planning for Economic Growth, 1933–1952* (Chapel Hill: University of North Carolina Press, 1980), 347.

5. Donald A. Filtzer, *Soviet Workers and Late Stalinism: Labour and the Restoration of the Stalinist System after World War II* (Cambridge: Cambridge University Press, 2002), 247.

important. Neither German state abandoned the men in Soviet captivity, though the East German officials only privately voiced their concerns to Soviet leaders.

The fourth wave of repatriations occurred in 1953 as a result of Stalin's death. Rival Soviet political leaders enacted a series of reforms hoping to distance themselves from Stalin and to garner support. L. P. Beria, the head of the NKVD, proclaimed amnesties not only for the Gulag but also for German POW prisoners. The uncertainty of the future of Soviet political leadership, combined with an uprising in the GDR in June 1953, meant that more POWs would be released to serve the needs of Soviet officials back home, as well as to build support for the unpopular SED government.

The fifth and final wave of repatriation occurred between October 1955 and January 1956 as a result of Konrad Adenauer's September 1955 trip to Moscow to formalize diplomatic relations between the FRG and the USSR. Although Adenauer and many West Germans claimed this repatriation wave as his diplomatic victory, it really came about because of domestic Soviet politics. Fearing NATO and its threatening buildup of arms in Western Europe, Nikita Khrushchev acted to improve relations with the West via the FRG. Although East German leaders were not pleased, Khrushchev aimed to formalize diplomatic relations with the FRG even though Western powers refused to recognize the East German government. He hoped that the West Germans might pull away from the influence of other Western powers. Adenauer, who partially won his election to chancellor of the Federal Republic of Germany on the memory and suffering of the POWs, refused to concede on the question of the last German captives. Khrushchev grudgingly relented and promised to return the remaining Germans to accomplish his own domestic and international political goals.

The legacies of these men continued to be of importance to Soviet leaders and ordinary people even after their return. In the 1960s and the 1980s, Soviet leaders used the representation of the POWs in grandiose commemorations of World War II. Initially, these men symbolized military victory and the superiority of socialism. Later, in the mid-1980s, they served to illustrate long-lasting Soviet–German cooperation and the German commitment to socialism. The antifascist German POWs served as a link between the Soviet Union, the German Democratic Republic, and the German nation as a whole. Finally, after the collapse of the Soviet Union, negotiations between the Russian Federation and the unified Federal Republic of Germany at last gave Germans the right to learn about the deaths of the POW relatives and openly mourn their losses at newly created cemetery monuments. More recently, discussion of the deaths of German POWs in Soviet captivity launched investigations by the Russian government. German POWs, then, have shaped the politics of the Soviet Union and will continue to shape those of Russia for many years to come.

Appendix 1

Calculation of Daily Calories

The calculation for daily calories is approximate. To calculate the energy values for the foods, I put the grams into the Russian calorie website, http://www.calorizator.ru/. I used the Russian from the source documents to try to get approximate calorie values for the foods listed in the ration norms. I had initially used an English-language calorie counter, http://www.acaloriecounter.com/, but the foods on that website do not always capture ones found in Russian and Soviet cuisine. I made selections for food types, which are explained in full detail later, based on my contemporary knowledge of Russian and Soviet cooking and products. Many of the foods listed in the ration norm tables are vague; for example, "meat." In those cases, which I note I detail, I tried a variety of different products and chose the one that had the highest caloric content to approximate an upper bound for daily POW calories.

For grits/different cereals, I tried oatmeal, buckwheat, and semolina. Oatmeal had the highest caloric content, so I used it. For rice I used white rice. For meat, I looked up the calorie ranges for chicken, beef, and pork. I also looked up canned beef and pork, the ubiquitous Russian тушёнка (tushёnka). Of all of these, tinned pork had the highest caloric content, so I used it. For fish, I tried the two major types of salmon—*сёмга (sёmga)* and *лосось (losos')*— and herring, *сельдь (sel'd')*. I used fresh, not cured, fish in all instances. It is likely that the fish fed to POWs varied greatly by region. Different Russian waterways are known for their specific fish, but I chose the ones that are the most common for Russian/Soviet cuisine. Herring had the highest caloric content, so I used it. There was no option to differentiate the butter via fat content, so I used the one cream-based butter option in the calorie calculator. I used the common Russian Cheese (*сыр Российский, syr Rossiiskii*) for cheese. For bacon/mixed fats, I used *сало* (*salo*). For vegetable oil, I used sunflower oil. I used granulated sugar for sugar. For vinegar I used table vinegar, 9%. I chose to use boiled potatoes to represent potatoes because this was likely the easiest way to cook mass quantities of potatoes. For dried fruit, I looked at dried pears, apples, apricots, and raisins. Raisins had the highest caloric content. For milk, I used 3.2%, which is whole milk in America. For fresh vegetables, I used the broad vegetables (*овощи, ovoshchi*) option in the calorie counter. I also tried looking at the popular combination of tomatoes and cucumbers (with 100 grams for each to make the 200-gram serving) and found that it had fewer calories than general vegetables, so I used the calculation for vegetables. The Russian calorie counter did not have an option for potato flour, so I used the American counter. The Russian calorie counter did not have a specific option for baker's yeast but only for yeast (*дрожжи, drozhzhi*) or beer yeast (*дрожжи пивные, drozhzhi pivnye*). Both had the same caloric content and beer yeast was listed in the Russian documents as a substitute for baker's yeast, so I used that calorie value. For cabbage, I looked at the values for fresh and preserved. Fresh cabbage (*капуста белокочанная, kapusta belokochannaya*) had more calories than preserved (*капуста квашеная, kapusta kvashenaya*). The Russian documents stated that the onion for enlisted men was *лук репчатый* (*luk repshatyi*), which was in the Russian calorie converter. It is a common onion, bulb onion. For the ration of root vegetable, greens, cucumber, I chose to use cucumber, which is a staple food in the Russian/Soviet diet.

APPENDIX 2

Supplemental Maps and Map Creation

Color Maps and Time Sequence Maps of German Prisoner of War Camps in the USSR, Yearly, December 1941– December 1955

https://hdl.handle.net/1813/113398

Notes on the Map Creation Process

The first step in creating the maps for the POW camps was to scan the book *Orte des Gewahrsams von deutschen Kriegsgefangenen in der Sowjetunion 1941–1956: Findbuch* (Places of Detention of German Prisoners of War in the Soviet Union 1941–1956: Encyclopedia) by Chvatova et al.[1] This book, produced by a team of Russian and German scholars, provides information on 4,360 German POW camps that operated on the territory of the Soviet Union from 1941 to 1956. The book gives the number of each camp or subcamp and the Soviet republic,

---

1. Veronika Chvatova et al., *Orte des Gewahrsams von deutschen Kriegsgefangenen in der Sowjetunion (1941–1956): Findbuch; [Standorte von Kriegsgefangenenlagern, Arbeitsbataillonen, Friedhöfen sowie Einrichtungen des Frontlagernetzes; auf der Grundlage von Dokumenten der Kriegsgefangenenverwaltung aus dem Staatlichen Russischen Militärarchiv]* (Dresden: Stiftung Sächsische Gedenkstätten zur Erinnerung an die Opfer politischer Gewaltherrschaft, 2010).

state, city, and village that it is nearest. After the book was scanned, the images were converted to text using the program ABBYY FineReader.[2] This process is known as optical character recognition (OCR). The text was exported from AB-BYY FineReader into a Microsoft Excel Spreadsheet. From there, the errors caused by the OCR process were cleaned by hand. Some of the tabular data from the book were corrupted during the OCR process. I also ran OCR using Tabula, a web-based service that reads tabular data from PDFs.[3] I looked at the spreadsheet output from ABBYY FineReader and copied and pasted chunks from the Tabula output file when possible. At other times, I input information manually.

The maps presented in the book represent their fourth iteration. The first iteration was to look up the coordinates for Ukraine individually. I then used R-Studio and ggmaps and ggplot to find the locations of the camps for the entire Soviet Union, but that resulted in many erroneous automatic location results. I then worked with a programmer, Casidhe Hutchison, who wrote a Python-based script for me to request latitude and longitude coordinates from GoogleMaps. Her script is available online.[4] The Python script made these requests to Google.de, the German Google, because the source material had been transliterated into German. The script also was set to only return locations within the boundaries of the Soviet Union, and these returned locations had to match a list of counties in the USSR. The script was set to search for the most precise location and then return a location for the next broadest location if the smallest location could not be found. That is, if the location was listed as Nowobelizkaja, Gomel, Belarus, the script would look for Nowobelizkaja. If it could not find that, the script would then look for Gomel and give its address, and so on. When no result was found at all, a note was placed in the output file indicating such. When the script had to use the secondary location, such as Gomel in the earlier example, it also noted that it had returned the fallback location. The script had a few hundred erroneous locations, many of which were caused by the German transliteration.

I checked the first 1,200 locations by hand with Google maps and filled in locations with no result. Generally, to find those locations, I needed to sound out the German location and then type it in Cyrillic. With that method, I quickly found most of the locations that were missing. To speed up the process, I opened the CSV file of location names and changed some of the common German transliterations into more accepted English ones and reran the script.

---

2. https://www.abbyy.com/en-us/finereader/.
3. https://tabula.technology/.
4. https://github.com/cas-gray/csv_geolocator.

For example, I changed w to v, ch to sh, ja to ya, je to ye, and sh to zh. In some cases, I used the find and replace function to fully change the major city from the German transliteration to the English one, such as in the case of Chelyabinsk. This resulted in more accurate returns. I then took these coordinates and mapped them.

With the mapping program open, I opened the attribute tables and highlighted camps via republic, selected any camps that appeared within a given republic's selection that should not have been there, and wrote down the ID numbers to clean in the spreadsheet. I also wrote down the ID numbers for any camps appearing outside their correct republic to again correct the automated location process. This is how I wound up with a total of 4,314 camps that operated in the USSR. I had to remove some camps from Chvatova et al.'s collection because they were in Poland, Romania, or listed as operating on various battlefronts, for which I could not find locations with GoogleMaps. Of the 4,314 camps that I selected as being ones that operated for POWs in the USSR, I was able to find 4,266, or almost 99 percent.

Bibliography

Archival Sources

Russia

State Archive of the Russian Federation (*Gosudarstvennyi arkhiv Rossiiskoi Federatsii*) (GARF)

Russian State Economic Archive (*Rossiiskii gosudarstvennyi arkhiv ekonomiki*) (RGAE)

Russian State Military Archive (*Rossiiskii gosudarstvennyi voennyi arkhiv*) (RGVA)

Archive of Foreign Policy of the Russian Federation (*Arkhiv vneshnei politiki Rossiiskoi Federatsii*) (AVP RF)

Russian State Archive of Socio-Political History (*Rossiiskii gosudarstvennyi arkhiv sotsial'no-politicheskoi istorii*) (RGASPI)

Russian State Archive of Literature and Art (*Rossiiskii gosudarstvennyi arkhiv literatury i iskusstva*) (RGALI)

State Archive of Contemporary History of the Ulyanovsk Region (*Gosudarstvennyi arkhiv noveishei istorii Ul'ianovskoi oblasti*) (GANI UO)

Research Institute of History and Culture of the Ulyanovsk Region in the name of N.M. Karamzin (*Nauchno-issledovatel'skii institut istorii i kul'tury Ul'ianovskoi oblasti im. N.M. Karamzina*)

Germany

Federal Military Archive (*Bundesarchiv-Militärarchiv*) (BA-M)

Federal Archive—Foundation Parties and Mass Organizations of the GDR (*Bundesarchiv -Stiftung Archiv der Parteien und Massenorganisationen der DDR*) (BA-SAPMO)

Political Archive of the Federal Foreign Office (*Politisches Archiv des Auswärtigen Amts*) (PA AA)

Archive of the German Caritas Association (*Archiv des Deutschen Caritasverbandes*) (ADCV)

Evangelical Central Archives in Berlin (*Evangelisches Zentralarchiv Berlin*) (EZA)

German Red Cross Archive (*Archiv des Deutschen Roten Kreuzes*) (DRK)

United States

National Archives and Records Administration (NARA)

Hoover Institution Library and Archives

Newspapers

Bild (Zeitung)
Der Spiegel
Der Tagespiegel
Frankfurter Allgemeine Zeitung
Narodnaia Gazeta
Neues Deutschland
The New York Times
Panorama UAZ
Pravda
Simbirskii Kur'er

Published Sources

"A byli li Kolya iz Urengoya. Skandal-to druzhno zatushili." *Dzen.ru*. Accessed
    January 24, 2021, https://dzen.ru/a/YArQTLfJOU0wijA7.
"A Calorie Counter—FREE Food Journal & Diet Tracker." *A Calorie Counter*.
    Accessed March 12, 2019. http://www.acaloriecounter.com/.
"About the Project—Mapping the Gulag—Russia's Prison System from the 1930s to
    the Present." *Gulagmaps*. Accessed March 7, 2019. http://www.gulagmaps.org/.
Adam, Wilhelm, and Tony Le Tissier. *With Paulus at Stalingrad*. Barnsley, UK: Pen
    and Sword, 2017.
Adler, Nanci. *The Gulag Survivor: Beyond the Soviet System*. Piscataway, NJ: Transac-
    tion, 2004.
Agafonow, Alexander. *Erinnerungen eines notorischen Deserteurs*. 1. Aufl., aufgrund des
    russ. Orig.-Ms. gekürzt . . . Sevastopol': Rowohlt, 1993.
Alexievich, Svetlana. *Secondhand Time: The Last of the Soviets*. Translated by Bela
    Shayevich. New York: Random House, 2016.
Alexopoulos, Golfo. "Amnesty 1945: The Revolving Door of Stalin's Gulag." *Slavic
    Review* 64, no. 2 (2005): 274–306. https://doi.org/10.2307/3649985.
Alexopoulos, Golfo. *Illness and Inhumanity in Stalin's Gulag*. New Haven: Yale
    University Press, 2017.
Applebaum, Anne. *Gulag: A History*. New Haven: Yale University Press, 2011.
Bacon, Edwin. *The Gulag at War: Stalin's Forced Labour System in the Light of the
    Archives*. New York: New York University Press, 1994.
Bacque, James. *Other Losses: An Investigation into the Mass Deaths of German Prisoners
    at the Hands of the French and Americans after World War II*. Vancouver:
    Talonbooks, 2011.
Barenberg, Alan. *Gulag Town, Company Town: Forced Labor and Its Legacy in Vorkuta*.
    New Haven: Yale University Press, 2014.
Bark, Dennis L., and David R. Gress. *From Shadow to Substance: 1945–1963*. Cam-
    bridge, MA: Basil Blackwell, 1989.
Barnes, Steven A. *Death and Redemption: The Gulag and the Shaping of Soviet Society*.
    Princeton, NJ: Princeton University Press, 2011.
Barnett, Correlli. *Hitler's Generals*. New York: Grove, 2003.

Bartov, Omer. *Hitler's Army: Soldiers, Nazis, and War in the Third Reich.* Oxford: Oxford University Press, 1992.

Beevor, Antony. *Stalingrad: The Fateful Siege, 1942–1943.* New York: Penguin, 1999.

Behrends, Jan C. *Die erfundene Freundschaft: Propaganda für die Sowjetunion in Polen und in der DDR.* Böhlau: Verlag Köln Weimar, 2006.

Bell, Wilson T. *The Gulag and Soviet Society in Western Siberia, 1929–1953.* Toronto: University of Toronto Press, 2011.

Bell, Wilson T. *Stalin's Gulag at War: Forced Labour, Mass Death, and Soviet Victory in the Second World War.* Toronto: University of Toronto Press, 2018.

Bell, Wilson T. "Was the Gulag an Archipelago? De-Convoyed Prisoners and Porous Borders in the Camps of Western Siberia." *Russian Review* 72, no. 1 (2013): 116–141.

Bellamy, Chris. *Absolute War: Soviet Russia in the Second World War.* New York: Knopf Doubleday, 2008.

Belz, Willi. *Soldat gegen Hitler: Ein Antikriegsbuch.* Röderberg, 1987.

Berkhoff, Karel C. *Motherland in Danger: Soviet Propaganda during World War II.* Cambridge, MA: Harvard University Press, 2012.

Bessel, Richard. *Germany 1945: From War to Peace.* New York: Simon & Schuster, 2012.

Biess, Frank. *Homecomings: Returning POWs and the Legacies of Defeat in Postwar Germany.* Princeton, NJ: Princeton University Press, 2006.

Bischof, Günter, and Stephen E. Ambrose. *Eisenhower and the German POWs: Facts against Falsehood.* Baton Rouge: Louisiana State University Press, 1992.

Bischof, Günter, Stefan Karner, and Barbara Stelzl-Marx. *Kriegsgefangene des Zweiten Weltkrieges: Gefangennahme, Lagerleben, Rückkehr.* Vienna: Oldenbourg, 2005.

Blackwell, Martin. *Kyiv as Regime City: The Return of Soviet Power after Nazi Occupation.* Rochester, NY: University of Rochester Press, 2016.

Bodnar, John E. *Remaking America: Public Memory, Commemoration, and Patriotism in the Twentieth Century.* Princeton, NJ: Princeton University Press, 1992.

Boehling, Rebecca L. *A Question of Priorities: Democratic Reforms and Economic Recovery in Postwar Germany: Frankfurt, Munich, and Stuttgart under U.S. Occupation, 1945–1949.* New York: Berghahn Books, 1996.

Böhme, Kurt W. *Aufzeichnungen über die Kriegsgefangenschaft im Westen.* Bielefeld: Gieseking, 1973.

Böhme, Kurt W. *Zur Geschichte der deutschen Kriegsgefangenen des Zweiten Weltkrieges.* Bielefeld: Gieseking, 1974.

Bonwetsch, Bernd, Gennadij Bordjugov, and Norman Naimark. *Sowjetische Politik in der SBZ 1945–1949: Dokumente zur Tatigkeit der Propagandaverwaltung (Informationsverwaltung) der SMAD unter Sergej Tjul'panov.* Bonn: Dietz, 1998.

Borchard, Michael. *Die deutschen Kriegsgefangenen in der Sowjetunion: Zur politischen Bedeutung der Kriegsgefangenenfrage 1949–1955.* Düsseldorf: Droste Verlag, 2000.

Bourtman, Ilya. "'Blood for Blood, Death for Death': The Soviet Military Tribunal in Krasnodar, 1943." *Holocaust and Genocide Studies* 22, no. 2 (Fall 2008): 246–265.

Brandenberger, David. *Propaganda State in Crisis: Soviet Ideology, Indoctrination, and Terror under Stalin, 1927–1941.* New Haven: Yale University Press, 2014.

Brezhnev, Leonid Il'ich. *How It Was: The War and Postwar Reconstruction in the Soviet Union.* Oxford: Pergamon, 1979.

Brochhagen, Ulrich. *Nach Nürnberg: Vergangenheitsbewältigung und Westintegration in der Ära Adenauer.* Hamburg: Junius, 1994.

Brooks, Jeffrey. *Thank You, Comrade Stalin! Soviet Public Culture from Revolution to Cold War.* Princeton, NJ: Princeton University Press, 2000.

Brown, Kate. *Plutopia: Nuclear Families, Atomic Cities, and the Great Soviet and American Plutonium Disasters.* Oxford: Oxford University Press, 2013.

Browning, Christopher R. *Ordinary Men: Reserve Police Battalion 101 and the Final Solution in Poland.* New York: HarperCollins, 2017.

Brudny, Yitzhak M. *Reinventing Russia: Russian Nationalism and the Soviet State, 1953–1991.* Cambridge, MA: Harvard University Press, 2009.

Brunstedt, Jonathan. "Building a Pan-Soviet Past: The Soviet War Cult and the Turn away from Ethnic Particularism." *Soviet and Post-Soviet Review,* no. 38 (2011): 149–171.

Brunstedt, Jonathan. *The Soviet Myth of World War II: Patriotic Memory and the Russian Question in the USSR.* Cambridge: Cambridge University Press, 2021.

"Calorizator.Ru—Pravil'noe Pitanie." *Calorizator.ru.* Accessed March 12, 2019. http://www.calorizator.ru/.Cartellieri, Diether. *Zur Geschichte der deutschen Kriegsgefangenen des Zweiten Weltkrieges: Die deutschen Kriegsgefangenen in der Sowjetunion: Die Lagergesellschaft. Eine Untersuchung d. zwischenmenschl. Beziehungen in d. Kriegsgefangenenlagern / Diether Cartellieri. [Ktn.: Johann Anton].* Bielefeld: Gieseking, 1967.

Cas-gray. *A Handy Little Tool for Geolocating Things. Contribute to Cas-Gray/Csv_geolocator Development by Creating an Account on GitHub.* Python, 2018. https://github .com/cas-gray/csv_geolocator.

Chvatova, Veronika, Ulrich Austermühle, and Rossija Archivnoe Agentstvo. *Orte des Gewahrsams von deutschen Kriegsgefangenen in der Sowjetunion (1941–1956): Findbuch; [Standorte von Kriegsgefangenenlagern, Arbeitsbataillonen, Friedhöfen sowie Einrichtungen des Frontlagernetzes; auf der Grundlage von Dokumenten der Kriegsgefangenenverwaltung aus dem Staatlichen Russischen Militärarchiv].* Dresden: Stiftung Sächsische Gedenkstätten zur Erinnerung an die Opfer politischer Gewaltherrschaft, 2010.

Clarke, Roger A. *Soviet Economic Facts 1917–1970.* London: Macmillan, 1972.

"Coal Quality and Resources of the Former Soviet Union—USGS OFR00–104." *US Geological Survey.* Accessed March 14, 2019. https://pubs.usgs.gov/of/2001 /ofr-01-104/readme.htm.

Conquest, Robert. *Kolyma: The Arctic Death Camps.* New York: Viking, 1978.

Cook, Ruth Beaumont. *Guests behind Barbed Wire: German POWs in America: A True Story of Hope and Friendship.* Birmingham, AL: Crane Hill, 2007.

Dähler, Richard. *Die japanischen und die deutschen Kriegsgefangenen in der Sowjetunion 1945–1956: Vergleich von Erlebnisberichten.* Vienna: Lit, 2007.

Demochkin, G. A. *Devochki i Mal'chishki: Semero Iz Detei Voiny.* Ulyanovsk: Ulyanovsk State Technical University, 2016.

Demochkin, G. A. *Dvadtsatyi Vek Natal'i Khramtsovoi.* Ulyanovsk: Ulyanovsk State Technical University, 2015.

Dengler, Gerhard. *Zwei Leben in einem.* Berlin: Militärverlag der Deutschen Demokratischen Republik, 1989.

"Deutscher Bundestag: 12. Wahlperiode. Druchsache 12/5837." n.d. http://dipbt .bundestag.de/dip21/btd/12/058/1205837.pdf.

Diamond, Hanna. "'Prisoners of the Peace': German Prisoners-of-War in Rural France 1944–48." *European History Quarterly* 43, no. 3 (2013): 442–463.

Dieckmann, Johannes. *50 Jahre Oktoberrevolution—50 Jahre deutsch-sowjetische Beziehungen*. Berlin: Staatsverlag der Deutschen Demokratischen Republik, 1967.

Diehl, James M. *The Thanks of the Fatherland: German Veterans after the Second World War*. Chapel Hill: University of North Carolina Press, 2000.

Diggins, John P. *Ronald Reagan: Fate, Freedom, and the Making of History*. New York: W. W. Norton, 2007.

Dobson, Miriam. *Khrushchev's Cold Summer: Gulag Returnees, Crime, and the Fate of Reform after Stalin*. Ithaca, NY: Cornell University Press, 2009.

Dolgun, Alexander, and Patrick Watson. *Alexander Dolgun's Story: An American in the Gulag*. New York: Knopf, 1975.

Doyle, Peter. *World War II in Numbers: An Infographic Guide to the Conflict, Its Conduct, and Its Casualties*. Richmond Hill, Ontario: Firefly Books, 2013.

Draskoczy, Julie S. *Belomor: Criminality and Creativity in Stalin's Gulag*. Boston: Academic Studies Press, 2013.

Duignan, Peter. *NATO: Its Past, Present, Future*. Stanford: Hoover Press, 2000.

Düsenberg, Albert. *Die Presse in Deutschland*. Bonn: Scholl, 1960.

Edele, Mark. *Soviet Veterans of the Second World War: A Popular Movement in an Authoritarian Society, 1941–1991*. Oxford: Oxford University Press. 2008.

Edele, Mark. "Take (No) Prisoners! The Red Army and German POWs, 1941–1943." *Journal of Modern History* 88 (June 2016): 342–379.

Ellman, Michael. "The 1947 Soviet Famine and the Entitlement Approach to Famines." *Cambridge Journal of Economics* 24, no. 5 (2000): 603–630.

Epifanov, Aleksandr E. *Organizatsionnye i Pravovye Osnovy Nakazaniya Gitlerovskix Voennyx Prestupnikov i Ix Posobnikov v SSSR 1941–1956 gg*. Moscow: Unity, 2017.

Epstein, Catherine. *The Last Revolutionaries: German Communists and Their Century*. Cambridge, MA: Harvard University Press, 2009.

Ermolaeva, Oxana. "Health Care, the Circulation of Medical Knowledge, and Research in the Soviet Gulag in the 1930s." *East Central Europe* 40, no. 3 (2013): 341–365. https://doi.org/10.1163/18763308-04003008.

Evseeva, Svetlana Dmitrievna, and Svetlana Vladimirovna Troshina. "Vzaimootnosheniya Sovetskix Grazhdan s Nemetskoi Voennoplennymi v Ul'yanovskoi Oblasti: Izmeneniye Vzgyadov." *Natsional;Naya Slava: Vzglyad Cherez Proshloe Rodnogo Kraya. IV Malye Syinskie Chteniya*, 35–43, April 28, 2015.

Feldman, Lily Gardner. *Germany's Foreign Policy of Reconciliation: From Enmity to Amity*. Lanham, MD: Rowman & Littlefield, 2012.

Felman, Shoshana, and Dori Laub. *Testimony: Crises of Witnessing in Literature, Psychoanalysis and History*. New York: Routledge, 2013.

Filtzer, Donald. *The Hazards of Urban Life in Late Stalinist Russia: Health, Hygiene, and Living Standards, 1943–1953*. Cambridge: Cambridge University Press, 2010.

Filtzer, Donald. *Soviet Workers and Late Stalinism: Labour and the Restoration of the Stalinist System after World War II*. Cambridge: Cambridge University Press, 2002.

Frierson, Cathy. *Russia's Law 'On Rehabilitation of Victims of Political Repression':
1991–2011, An Enduring Artifact of Transnational Justice.* NCEEER Working
Paper. Washington, DC: National Council for Eurasian and East European
Research, February 28, 2014.

Frieser, Karl-Heinz. *Krieg hinter Stacheldraht: Die deutschen Kriegsgefangenen in der
Sowjetunion und das Nationalkomitee "Freies Deutschland".* Mainz: v. Hase &
Koehler, 1981.

Fuchs, Helmut. *Wer spricht von Siegen: der Bericht uber unfreiwillige Jahre in Russland.*
Munich: A. Knaus, 1987.

Ganson, Nicholas. *The Soviet Famine of 1946–47 in Global and Historical Perspective.*
New York: Palgrave Macmillan, 2009.

Garner, Ian. *Stalingrad Lives: Stories of Combat and Survival.* Montreal: McGill-Queen's
University Press, 2022.

German War Graves Commission. "Über Uns." Accessed March 14, 2019. https://
www.volksbund.de/en/presse/volksbund.html.

Geyer, Michael, and Sheila Fitzpatrick. *Beyond Totalitarianism: Stalinism and Nazism
Compared.* Cambridge: Cambridge University Press, 2009.

Gheith, Jehanne M., and Katherine R. Jolluck. *Gulag Voices: Oral Histories of Soviet
Detention and Exile.* London: Palgrave Macmillan, 2011.

Giusti, Maria Teresa. *Stalin's Italian Prisoners of War.* Translated by Riccardo James
Vargiu. Budapest: Central European University Press, 2021.

Goebeler, Hans, and John Vanzo. *Steel Boat, Iron Hearts.* Philadelphia: Casemate,
2008.

Goldman, Wendy Z., and Donald A. Filtzer. *Fortress Dark and Stern: The Soviet Home
Front during World War II.* New York: Oxford University Press, 2021.

Goldman, Wendy Z. *Hunger and War: Food Provisioning in the Soviet Union during
World War II.* Bloomington: Indiana University Press, 2015.

Gregory, Paul R., and Valery Lazarev. *The Economics of Forced Labor: The Soviet Gulag.*
Stanford: Hoover Press, 2003.

Grieder, Peter. *The East German Leadership, 1946–73: Conflict and Crisis.* Manchester:
Manchester University Press, 1999.

Gruber, Hans. *My Odyssey thru Hell.* Bloomington, IN: Authorhouse, 2013.

Grunewald, Susan. "Applying Digital Methods to Forced Labor History: German
POWs during and after the Second World War." In *Rethinking the Gulag:
Identities, Sources, Legacies,* edited by Alan Barenberg and Emily D. Johnson,
129–154. Bloomington: Indiana University Press, 2022.

Grunewald, Susan. "'Victory or Siberia': Imaginings of Siberia and the Memory of
German POWs in the USSR." *German History* 40, no. 1 (March 2022): 88–106.
https://doi.org/10.1093/gerhis/ghab088.

Gunderson, Brian S. "Leaflet Dropping Operations in World War II." *Air Power
History,* 1998.

Halbe, August. *5 Jahre kriegsgefangener Priester im Ural: Ein Erlebnisbericht von Vikar
August Halbe.* Bochum-Weitmar: Pfarramt Heilige Familie Heimkehrer-
Dankeskirche, 1959.

Halbwachs, Maurice. *On Collective Memory.* Chicago: University of Chicago Press,
1992.

Hale, Oron J. *The Captive Press in the Third Reich*. Princeton, NJ: Princeton University Press, 1973.

Hall, Kevin T. "The Befriended Enemy: German Prisoners of War in Michigan." *Michigan Historical Review* 41, no. 1 (Spring 2015): 57–79.

Hardy, Jeffrey S. *The Gulag after Stalin: Redefining Punishment in Khrushchev's Soviet Union, 1953–1964*. Ithaca, NY: Cornell University Press, 2016.

Harris, Wesley L. *Fish out of Water: Nazi Submariners as Prisoners in North Louisiana during World War II*. Ruston, LA: RoughEdge, 2004.

Harrison, Hope M. *Driving the Soviets up the Wall: Soviet-East German Relations, 1953–1961*. Princeton, NJ: Princeton University Press, 2011.

Harsch, Donna. "Approach/Avoidance: Communists and Women in East Germany, 1945–1949." *Social History* 25, no. 2 (May 2000): 156–182.

Harsch, Donna. *Revenge of the Domestic: Women, the Family, and Communism in the German Democratic Republic*. Princeton, NJ: Princeton University Press, 2007.

Healey, Dan. "Lives in the Balance: Weak and Disabled Prisoners and the Biopolitics of the Gulag." *Kritika: Explorations in Russian and Eurasian History* 16, no. 3 (August 29, 2015): 527–556. https://doi.org/10.1353/kri.2015.0047.

Heineman, Elizabeth D. *What Difference Does a Husband Make? Women and Marital Status in Nazi and Postwar Germany*. Berkeley: University of California Press, 2003.

Hellbeck, Jochen. "Breakthrough at Stalingrad: The Repressed Soviet Origins of a Bestselling West German War Tale." *Contemporary European History* 22, no. 1 (February 2013): 1–32. https://doi.org/10.1017/S096077731200046X.

Hellbeck, Jochen. *Stalingrad: The City That Defeated the Third Reich*. New York: PublicAffairs, 2015.

Herf, Jeffrey. *Divided Memory: The Nazi Past in Two Germanys*. Cambridge, MA: Harvard University Press, 1997.

Hilger, Andreas. *Deutsche Kriegsgefangene in der Sowjetunion, 1941–1956: Kriegsgefangenenpolitik, Lageralltag und Erinnerung*. Schriften der Bibliothek für Zeitgeschichte =; n.F., Bd. 11; Variation: Schriften der Bibliothek für Zeitgeschichte; n.F., Bd. 11. Essen: Klartext, 2000.

Hilger, Andreas, Mike Schmeitzner, and Clemens Vollnhals. *Sowjetisierung Oder Neutralität? Optionen Sowjetischer Besatzungspolitik in Deutschland und Österreich 1945–1955*. Göttingen: Vandenhoeck & Ruprecht, 2006.

Hoffmann, David L. ed. *The Memory of the Second World War in Soviet and Post-Soviet Russia*. New York: Routledge, 2022.

Holl, Adelbert. *After Stalingrad: Seven Years as a Soviet Prisoner of War*. Translated by Tony Le Tissier. South Yorkshire, UK: Pen and Sword Military, 2016.

Hull, Isabel V. *Absolute Destruction: Military Culture and the Practices of War in Imperial Germany*. Ithaca, NY: Cornell University Press, 2006.

"In the Uniform of the Enemy: The Dutch Waffen-SS." *HistoryNet*, December 21, 2017. https://www.historynet.com/in-the-uniform-of-the-enemy.htm.

Ivanova, G. M. *Istoriia GULAGa, 1918–1958: Sotsial'no-ekonomicheskii i politico-pravovoi aspekty*. Moscow: Nauka, 2006.

Jaehn, Thomas. "Unlikely Harvesters: German Prisoners of War as Agricultural Workers in the Northwest." *Montana: The Magazine of Western History* 50, no. 3 (Autumn 2000): 46–57.

Jarausch, Konrad Hugo. *Die Umkehr: deutsche Wandlungen 1945–1995*. Munich: Deutsche Verlags-Anstalt, 2004.

Jones, Heather. "A Missing Paradigm? Military Captivity and the Prisoner of War, 1914–18." *Immigrants and Minorities* 26, nos. 1 & 2 (July 2008): 19–48.

Jones, Heather. *Violence against Prisoners of War in the First World War: Britain, France and Germany, 1914–1920*. Cambridge: Cambridge University Press, 2011.

Jones, Jeffrey W. *Everyday Life and the Reconstruction of Soviet Russia during and after the Great Patriotic War, 1943–1948*. Bloomington, IN: Slavica Publishers, 2008.

Jones, Polly. *Myth, Memory, Trauma: Rethinking the Stalinist Past in the Soviet Union, 1953–70*. New Haven: Yale University Press, 2013.

Kaak, Klaus. *Spurensuche in Der Ukraine 2002, Poliske 2002*. Self-published, n.d.

Kaminsky, Annette. *Heimkehr 1948*. Munich: Beck, 1998.

Karner, Stefan. *Im Archipel GUPVI: Kriegsgefangenschaft und Internierung in der Sowjetunion 1941–1956*. Vienna: R. Oldenbourg, 1995.

Kehler, Ernst. *Einblicke und Einsichten: Erinnerungen*. Berlin: Dietz, 1989.

Kenez, Peter. *The Birth of the Propaganda State: Soviet Methods of Mass Mobilization, 1917–1929*. Cambridge: Cambridge University Press, 1985.

Khlevniuk, Oleg V. *The History of the Gulag: From Collectivization to the Great Terror*. New Haven: Yale University Press, 2004.

Khrushchev, Sergei N., and Shirley Benson. *Nikita Khrushchev and the Creation of a Superpower*. University Park, PA: Penn State Press, 2001.

Kirk, Tyler C. *After the Gulag: A History of Memory in Russia's Far North*. Bloomington: Indiana University Press, 2023.

Kirk, Tyler C. "From Enemy to Hero: Andrei Krems and the Legacy of Stalinist Repression in Russia's Far North, 1964–1982." *Russian Review* 82, no. 2 (April 2023): 292–306. https://doi.org/10.1111/russ.12440.

Kirschenbaum, Lisa A. *The Legacy of the Siege of Leningrad, 1941–1995: Myth, Memories, and Monuments*. Cambridge: Cambridge University Press, 2006.

Knight, Amy. *Beria: Stalin's First Lieutenant*. Princeton, NJ: Princeton University Press, 1995.

Knowles, Anne Kelly, Tim Cole, and Alberto Giordano. *Geographies of the Holocaust*. Bloomington, IN: Indiana University Press, 2014.

Koch, Fred C. *The Volga Germans: In Russia and the Americas, from 1763 to the Present*. University Park, PA: Penn State Press, 2010.

Kochavi, Arieh J. *Confronting Captivity: Britain and the United States and Their POWs in Nazi Germany*. Chapel Hill: University of North Carolina Press, 2005.

Kokebaeva, G. K. *Germaniia- Rossiia—SSSR: Politika, Voĭna i Plen*. Almaty: Kazak Universiteti, 2009.

Kolwes, Ann-Kristin. *Die Frauen und Kinder Deutscher Kriegsgefangener: Integriert, ignoriert, und instrumentalisiert, 1941–1956*. Bielefeld: transcript Verlag, 2021.

Konasov, V. B., and A. L. Kuz'minykh. *Nemetskie voennoplennye v SSSR: Istoriografiia, bibliografiia, spravochno-poniatiinyi apparat*. Vologda: Vologodskii in-t razvitiia obrazovaniia, 2002.

Konasov, V. B. (Viktor Borisovich). "The Exchange of POWs between the USSR and Her Allies on the Territory of Occupied Germany." *Journal of Slavic Military Studies* 21 (2008): 472–474.

Koposov, Nikolay. *Memory Laws, Memory Wars: The Politics of the Past in Europe and Russia*. Cambridge: Cambridge University Press, 2017.

Koschorrek, Günter K. *Blood Red Snow: The Memoirs of a German Soldier on the Eastern Front*. London: Greenhill, 2005.

Kotkin, Stephen. *Magnetic Mountain: Stalinism as a Civilization*. Berkeley: University of California Press, 1997.

Krammer, Arnold. *Nazi Prisoners of War in America*. New York: Stein and Day, 1979.

Krammer, Arnold. *Prisoners of War: A Reference Handbook*. Westport, CT: Greenwood, 2008.

Krivosheev, G. F. *Soviet Casualties and Combat Losses in the Twentieth Century*. London: Greenhill, 1997.

"Kuda podevalsya chelovekolyubivyi mal;chik Kolya iz Novogo Urengoya?" *Dzen.ru*, March 24, 2021. https://dzen.ru/media/motivators_demotivators/kuda -podevalsia-chelovekoliubivyi-malchik-kolia-iz-novogo-urengoia-605b017f372 97b3abd6b17a8.

Kuz'micheva, I. P. *70 Let Natsional'nomu Komitetu "Svobodnaya Germaniya" Sbornik Materialov*. Moscow: Sabashnikovykh, 2014.

Kuz'micheva, I. P. *Skvoz' Plen: Nemetskiye Voennoplennye v Sovetskom Soyuze*. Moscow: Sabashnikovykh, 2007.

Kuz'minykh, A. L. *Inostrannye voennoplennye Vtoroi mirovoi voiny na Evropeiskom Severe SSSR (1939–1949 gg.)*. Vologda: Knizhnoe nasledie, 2005.

Kuz'minykh, A. L. *Voennyi plen i internirovanie v SSSR (1939–1956 gody): Monografiia*. Vologda: Drevnosti Severa, 2016.

"Land Resources of Russia." *Web Archive*. Accessed March 14, 2019. http://webarchive.iiasa.ac.at/Research/FOR/russia_cd/trans.htm.

Langer, Lawrence L. *Holocaust Testimonies: The Ruins of Memory*. New Haven: Yale University Press, 1991.

Lansing, Charles B. *From Nazism to Communism: German Schoolteachers under Two Dictatorships*. Cambridge, MA: Harvard University Press, 2010.

Laurie, Clayton David. *The Propaganda Warriors: America's Crusade against Nazi Germany*. Lawrence: University Press of Kansas, 1996.

Lehmann, Albrecht. *Gefangenschaft und Heimkehr: Deutsche Kriegsgefangene in der Sowjetunion*. C. H. Beck, 1986.

Linne, Karsten. "Hunger und Kannibalismus bei Sowjetischen Kriegsgefangenen im Zweiten Weltkrieg." *Zeitschrift Für Geschichtswissenschaft* 58, no. 3 (March 1, 2010): 243–262.

Loader, Michael. "Beria and Khrushchev: The Power Struggle over Nationality Policy and the Case of Latvia." *Europe-Asia Studies* 68, no. 10 (2016): 1759–1792.

Lockenour, Jay. *Soldiers as Citizens: Former Wehrmacht Officers in the Federal Republic of Germany, 1945–1955*. Lincoln: University of Nebraska Press, 2001.

Lukes, Igor. *On the Edge of the Cold War: American Diplomats and Spies in Postwar Prague*. New York: Oxford University Press, 2012.

Lüthi, Lorenz M. *Cold Wars: Asia, The Middle East, Europe*. Cambridge: Cambridge University Press, 2020.

MacGregor, Iain. *The Lighthouse of Stalingrad: The Hidden Truth at the Heart of the Greatest Battle of World War II*. New York: Scribner, 2022.

Maddox, Steven. "Gulag Football: Competitive and Recreational Sport in Stalin's System of Forced Labor." *Kritika: Explorations in Russian and Eurasian History* 19, no. 3 (2018): 509–536. https://doi.org/10.1353/kri.2018.0028.

Maddox, Steven. *Saving Stalin's Imperial City: Historic Preservation in Leningrad, 1930–1950*. Bloomington: Indiana University Press, 2014.

Maier-Lutz, Edeltraud. *Flußkreuzfahrten in Rußland. Unterwegs auf Wolga, Don, Jenissej und Lena*. Berlin: Trescher Verlag, 2005.

Malkki, Liisa H. *Purity and Exile: Violence, Memory, and National Cosmology among Hutu Refugees in Tanzania*. Chicago: University of Chicago Press, 2012.

Margalit, Gilad. *Guilt, Suffering, and Memory: Germany Remembers Its Dead of World War II*. Bloomington: Indiana University Press, 2010.

Maurach, Reinhart. *Die Kriegsverbrecherprozesse gegen deutsche Gefangene in der Sowjetunion*. Hamburg: Arbeitsgemeinschaft vom Roten Kreuz, 1950.

Mazuzan, George T., and Nancy Walker. "Restricted Areas: German Prisoner-of-War Camps in Western New York, 1944–1946." *New York History* 59, no. 1 (January 1978): 54–72.

McDermott, Kevin, and Jeremy Agnew. *The Comintern: A History of International Communism from Lenin to Stalin*. London: Macmillan, 1996.

Merridale, Catherine. *Ivan's War: Life and Death in the Red Army, 1939–1945*. New York: Henry Holt, 2007.

Meyer, Heinz Heinrich, and Hein Mayer. *Kriegsgefangene im Kalten Krieg: Die Kriegsgefangenpolitik der Bundesrepublik Deutschland im amerikanisch-sowjetischen Machtkampf von 1950 bis 1955*. Osnabrück: Biblio, 1998.

Miner, Steven Merritt. *Stalin's Holy War: Religion, Nationalism, and Alliance Politics, 1941–1945*. Chapel Hill: University of North Carolina Press, 2003.

Moeller, Robert G. "'The Last Soldiers of the Great War' and Tales of Family Reunions in the Federal Republic of Germany." *Journal of Women in Culture and Society* 24, no. 1 (1998): 129–145.

Moeller, Robert G. *War Stories: The Search for a Usable Past in the Federal Republic of Germany*. Berkeley: University of California Press, 2001.

Moore, Gary W. *Playing with the Enemy: A Baseball Prodigy, a World at War, and a Field of Broken Dreams*. Philadelphia: Casemate, 2006.

Morina, Christina. "An Experiment in Political Education': Henry W. Ehrmann, Germans POWs in US Reeducation Programs, and the Democratisation of Germany after the Second World War." *War & Society* 27, no. 1 (May 2008): 79–103.

Morré, Jörg. "Umerziehung in der sowjetischen Kriegsgefangenschaft Deutsche und Österricher in der 'Antifa.'" In *Kriegsgefangene des Zweiten Weltkrieges: Gefangennahme, Lagerleben, Rückkehr*, edited by Günter Bischof, Stefan Karner, and Barbara Stelzl-Marx, 152–166. Vienna: Oldenbourg, 2005.

Morrow, James D. *Order within Anarchy: The Laws of War as an International Institution*. Cambridge: Cambridge University Press, 2014.

Müller, Ingo. *Furchtbare Juristen: Die unbewältigte Vergangenheit unserer Justiz*. Munich: Kindler Verlag, 1987.

Muminov, Sehrzod. *Eleven Winters of Discontent: The Siberian Internment and the Making of a New Japan.* Cambridge, MA: Harvard University Press, 2022.

Muzei-Zapovednik Stalingradskaya Bitva. "Iz Istorii Muzeya-Zapovedknika." *Stalingrad-battle.ru.* Accessed March 14, 2019. http://www.stalingrad-battle.ru/index.php?option=com_content&view=article&id=14&Itemid=8.

Muzei-Zapovednik Stalingradskaya Bitva. "Muzei 'Pamyat.'" Accessed March 14, 2019. http://www.stalingrad-battle.ru/index.php?Itemid=38&id=1278&option=com_content&view=article.

Nagornaia, Oksana S. *"Drugoi Voennyi Opyt": Rossiiskie Voennoplennye Pervoi Mirovoi Voiny v Germanii, 1914–1922.* Moscow: Novyi Khronograf, 2010.

Nakonechnyi, Mikhail. "'They Won't Survive for Long': Soviet Officials on Medical Release Procedure." In *Rethinking the Gulag: Identities, Sources, Legacies,* edited by Alan Barenberg and Emily D. Johnson, 103–128. Bloomington: Indiana University Press, 2022.

Naimark, Norman M. *The Russians in Germany: A History of the Soviet Zone of Occupation, 1945–1949.* Cambridge, MA: Belknap Press, 1995.

Nekrasov, Victor. *Front-Line Stalingrad.* South Yorkshire, UK: Pen and Sword, 2012.

Niemetz, Daniel. *Das feldgraue Erbe: Die Wehrmachtseinflüsse im Militär der SBZ/DDR (1948/49–1989).* Berlin: Ch. Links Verlag, 2012.

Novick, Peter. *The Holocaust and Collective Memory: The American Experience.* London: Bloomsbury, 2001.

Overmans, Rüdiger. *Deutsche militärische Verluste im Zweiten Weltkrieg.* Munich: Oldenbourg, 2000.

Overmans, Rüdiger, and Ulrike Goeken-Haidl. *Soldaten hinter Stacheldraht: Deutsche Kriegsgefangene des Zweiten Weltkriegs.* Munich: Ullstein, 2000.

Overy, Richard. *Russia's War: A History of the Soviet War Effort: 1941–1945.* New York: Penguin, 1998.

Ostermann, Christian F., ed. *Uprising in East Germany 1953: The Cold War, the German Question, and the First Major Upheaval behind the Iron Curtain.* Budapest: Central European University Press, 2001.

Pallot, Judith, Laura Piacentini, and Dominique Moran. *Gender, Geography, and Punishment: The Experience of Women in Carceral Russia.* Oxford: Oxford University Press, 2012.

Palmer, Scott W. "How Memory Was Made: The Construction of the Memorial to the Heroes of the Battle of Stalingrad." *Russian Review* 68, no. 3 (2009): 373–407. https://doi.org/10.1111/j.1467-9434.2009.00530.x.

"PDF Software with Text Recognition—ABBYY FineReader 14 OCR." *Abbyy.* Accessed March 14, 2019. https://www.abbyy.com/en-us/finereader/.

Peter, Erwin. *Von Workuta bis Astrachan: Kriegsgefangene aus sowjetischen Lagern berichten.* Graz: Stocker, 1998.

Peter, Erwin, and Aleksandr Egorovich Epifanov. *Stalins Kriegsgefangene: ihr Schicksal in Erinnerungen und nach russischen Archiven.* Graz: Stocker, 1998.

Peterson, Edward Norman. *The Many Faces of Defeat: The German People's Experience in 1945.* Bern: Peter Lang, 1990.

Ploskikh, V. M., and K. Karasaev atyndagy Bishkek gumanitardyk universiteti. *Materialy nauchno-prakticheskoi konferentsii "Sokhranenie istoricheskoi pamiati o*

Velikoi Otechestvennoi voine: problemy i resheniia": (Bishkekskii gumanitarnyi universitet im. K. Karasaeva, 20–21 aprelia 2015 g.), edited by I. A. Masaliev. Bishkek: Turar, 2016.

Pobezhimov, S. I. *Memorial'nyi Muzei Nemetskikh Antifashistov: Filial Tsentral'nogo Muzeya Velikoi Otechestvennoi Voiny. g. Krasnogorsk.* Krasnogorsk: Filial Fonda Rozy Lyuksemburg v Rossiiskoi Federatsii, 2015.

Pohl, J. Otto. *The Stalinist Penal System: A Statistical History of Soviet Repression and Terror, 1930–1953.* Jefferson, NC: McFarland, 1997.

Polisenska, Milada. *Czechoslovak Diplomacy and the Gulag: Deportation of Czechoslovak Citizens to the USSR and the Negotiation for Their Repatriation, 1945–1953.* Translated by Barbara Day. Budapest: Central European University Press, 2015.

Popp, Dianna M., and Gottfried P. Dulias. *Another Bowl of Kapusta: The True Life Story of a World War II Luftwaffe Fighter Pilot and P. O. W. in Russia.* Bloomington, IN: AuthorHouse, 2004.

Preuss, Hans. *Im wilden Sumpfwald am Ladogasee: Leben, Sterben oder Überleben in einem sowjetischen Arbeitslager.* Hanau: Haag und Herchen, 1996.

Rachamimov, Alon. *POWs and the Great War: Captivity on the Eastern Front.* New York: Bloomsbury, 2014.

Ratza, Werner, and Erich Maschke. *Die deutschen Kriegsgefangenen in der Sowjet-union: Der Faktor Arbeit.* Bielefeld: Gieseking, 1973.

Reinisch, Jessica. *The Perils of Peace: The Public Health Crisis in Occupied Germany.* New York: Oxford University Press, 2013.

"Research Starters: Worldwide Deaths in World War II." *National WWII Museum,* New Orleans. Accessed March 14, 2019. https://www.nationalww2museum .org/students-teachers/student-resources/research-starters/research-starters -worldwide-deaths-world-war.

Reuss, Ernst. *Kriegsgefangen im 2. Weltkrieg: wie Deutsche und Russen mit ihren Gegnern umgingen.* Berlin: Edition Ost, 2010.

Rodden, John. *Textbook Reds: Schoolbooks, Ideology, and Eastern German Identity.* University Park: Penn State Press, 2010.

Rosenzweig, Roy, and Steven A. Barnes. *Gulag History.* "Gulag: Many Days Many Lives," n.d. http://gulaghistory.org/.

Rühle, Otto. *Die Ärzte von Stalingrad: Genesung in Jelabuga: Kessel Stalingrad— Antifaschule für ein neues Deutschland—autobiographischer Bericht.* Berlin: Wünsche, 2007.

Sanborn, Joshua A. *Imperial Apocalypse: The Great War and the Destruction of the Russian Empire.* Oxford: Oxford University Press, 2014.

Schenck, Ernst Günther. *Woina Plenni: 10 Jahre Gefangenschaft in sowjetischen Lagern.* Stockach: Bavarian Connection, 1985.

Schuetz, A. D. Hans. *Davai, Davai! Memoir of a German Prisoner of World War II in the Soviet Union.* Jefferson, NC: McFarland, 1997.

Schwarz, Wolfgang, and Erich Maschke. *Zur Geschichte der deutschen Kriegsgefangenen des Zweiten Weltkrieges Bd. 6 Bd. 6.* Bielefeld: Gieseking, 1969.

Schwelling, Birgit. *Heimkehr-Erinnerung-Integration: Der Verband der Heimkehrer, die ehemaligen Kriegsgefangenen und die westdeutsche Nachkriegsgesellschaft.* Leiden: Schöningh, 2010.

Sidorov, S. G. *Trud voennoplennykh v SSSR, 1939–1956 gg.* Volgograd: Izd-vo Volgo-gradskogo gos. universiteta, 2001.

Smith, Arthur L. *Heimkehr aus dem Zweiten Weltkrieg: Die Entlassung der deutschen Kriegsgefangenen.* Berlin: Walter de Gruyter, 1985.

Snyder, Timothy. *Bloodlands: Europe between Hitler and Stalin.* New York: Basic Books, 2010.

Solomon, Peter H. *Soviet Criminal Justice under Stalin.* Cambridge: Cambridge University Press, 1996.

Solzhenitsyn, Aleksandr Isaevich. *The Gulag Archipelago, 1918–1956: An Experiment in Literary Investigation.* New York: Harper & Row, 1975.

Soviet Union Posol'stvo (U.S.). *Soviet War Documents: June, 1941—November, 1943: Addresses, Notes, Orders of the Day, Statements.* Honolulu: University Press of the Pacific, 2003.

Stahel, David. *The Battle for Moscow.* Cambridge: Cambridge University Press, 2017.

Steil, Benn. *The Marshall Plan: Dawn of the Cold War.* New York: Oxford University Press, 2018.

Stites, Richard. *Culture and Entertainment in Wartime Russia.* Bloomington: Indiana University Press, 1995.

Streit, Christian. *Keine Kameraden: Die Wehrmacht und die sowjetischen Kriegsgefangenen 1941–1945.* Bonn: J.H.W. Dietz, 1997.

"Tabula: Extract Tables from PDFs." *Tabula.* June 16, 2013. http://tabula.technology/.

Taubman, William. *Khrushchev: The Man and His Era.* New York: W. W. Norton, 2004.

Thompson, Andy. *Cars of the Soviet Union: The Definitive History.* Yeovil, Somerset: Haynes Publishing, 2008.

Thompson, Antonio. *Men in German Uniform: POWs in America during World War II.* Knoxville: University of Tennessee Press, 2010.

Thurston, Robert W., and Bernd Bonwetsch. *The People's War: Responses to World War II in the Soviet Union.* Champaign: University of Illinois Press, 2000.

Toker, Leona. *Return from the Archipelago: Narratives of Gulag Survivors.* Bloomington: Indiana University Press, 2000.

"Treaties, States Parties, and Commentaries—Hague Convention (IV) on War on Land and Its Annexed Regulations, 1907." *International Committee of the Red Cross.* Accessed March 14, 2019. https://ihl-databases.icrc.org/ihl/INTRO/195.

"Treaties, States Parties, and Commentaries—Russian Federation." *International Committee of the Red Cross.* Accessed March 14, 2019. https://ihl-databases.icrc .org/applic/ihl/ihl.nsf/vwTreatiesByCountrySelected.xsp?xp _countrySelected=RU.

"Treaties, States Parties, and Commentaries—States Parties—Convention Relative to the Treatment of Prisoners of War. Geneva, 27 July 1929." *International Committee of the Red Cross.* Accessed March 14, 2019. https://ihl-databases.icrc .org/applic/ihl/ihl.nsf/States.xsp?xp_viewStates=XPages_NORMStates Parties&xp_treatySelected=305.

"Treaties, States Parties, and Commentaries—States Parties—Convention Relative to the Treatment of Prisoners of War. Geneva, 27 July 1929." *International Committee of the Red Cross.* Accessed March 14, 2019. https://ihl-databases.icrc

.org/applic/ihl/ihl.nsf/States.xsp?xp_viewStates=XPages_NORMStatesPart
ies&xp_treatySelected=305.

Trezise, Thomas. *Witnessing Witnessing: On the Reception of Holocaust Survivor Testimony*. New York: Fordham University Press, 2014.

Trueblood, Benjamin Franklin. *The Two Hague Conferences and Their Results*. Washington, DC: American Peace Society, 1914.

Tumarkin, Nina. "The Great Patriotic War as Myth and Memory." *European Review* 11, no. 4 (2003): 595–611.

Tumarkin, Nina. *The Living & The Dead: The Rise and Fall of the Cult of World War II in Russia*. New York: Basic Books, 1994.

Uhlig, Christa. *Rückkehr aus der Sowjetunion: Politische Erfahrungen und pädagogische Wirkungen: Emigranten und ehemalige Kriegsgefangene in der SBZ und frühen DDR*. Weinheim: Deutscher Studien Verlag, 1998.

U.S.S.R. Council of Ministers, Central Statistical Administration. *The U.S.S.R. Economy: A Statistical Abstract*. London: Lawrence & Wishart, 1957.

Viola, Lynne. *The Unknown Gulag: The Lost World of Stalin's Special Settlements*. New York: Oxford University Press, 2007.

"Voiaki." Slovar' Mul'titran. *Multitran.ru*. Accessed March 14, 2019. https://www
.multitran.ru/c/m.exe?l1=1&l2=2&s=вояки.

Vuchetich, E. V., et al. *Geroiam Stalingradskoi Bitvy: Pamiatnik-Ansambl' Mamaev Kurgan*.Leningrad Khudozhnik RSFSR, 1969.

Weber, Bernhard. *Erlebnisse in und um Stalins geheimen Atombereich: Dokumentation einer ungewöhnlichen Kriegsgefangenschaft 1945—November 1953*. 2nd ed. Aachen: Verlag Mainz, 2002.

Weber, Hermann. *Die DDR 1945–1990*. Oldenbourg Verlag, 2006.

Wegner, Bernd. *From Peace to War: Germany, Soviet Russia, and the World, 1939–1941*. Providence, RI: Berghahn, 1997.

Weiner, Amir. *Making Sense of War: The Second World War and the Fate of the Bolshevik Revolution*. Princeton, NJ: Princeton University Press, 2012.

Weitz, Eric D. *Creating German Communism, 1890–1990: From Popular Protests to Socialist State*. Princeton, NJ: Princeton University Press, 1997.

Werth, Alexander. *Russia at War: 1941–1945*. New York: E. P. Dutton, 1964.

Wertsch, James V. *Voices of Collective Remembering*. Cambridge: Cambridge University Press, 2002.

Wette, Wolfram. *The Wehrmacht: History, Myth, Reality*. Cambridge, MA: Harvard University Press, 2009.

Whitcomb, Roger S. *The Cold War in Retrospect: The Formative Years*. Westport, CT: Greenwood, 1998.

Wienand, Christiane. *Returning Memories: Former Prisoners of War in Divided and Reunited Germany*. Rochester, NY: Camden House, 2015.

Wilkin, Bernard. *Aerial Propaganda and the Wartime Occupation of France, 1914–18*. Boca Raton, FL: Taylor & Francis, 2016.

Winter, J. M. *Remembering War: The Great War between Memory and History in the Twentieth Century*. New Haven: Yale University Press, 2006.

Winter, Jay. *Sites of Memory, Sites of Mourning: The Great War in European Cultural History*. Cambridge: Cambridge University Press, 2014.

Wise, James E. *U-505: The Final Journey*. Annapolis, MD: Naval Institute Press, 2005.

"World Cities." *ArcGIS Online*. Accessed March 14, 2019. http://www.arcgis.com /home/item.html?id=6996f03a1b364dbab4008d99380370ed.

Yezhov, A. *Soviet Statistics*. Moscow: Foreign Language, 1957.

Young, Charles Steuart. *Name, Rank, and Serial Number: Exploiting Korean War POWs at Home and Abroad*. New York: Oxford University Press, 2014.

Young, James Edward. *The Texture of Memory: Holocaust Memorials and Meaning*. New Haven: Yale University Press, 1993.

Zagorul'ko, Maksim Matveevich. *Regional'nye Struktury GUPVI NKVD-MVD SSSR, 1941–1951: Otchetno-Informatsionnye Dokumenty*, Vol. 1. Volgograd: Izdatel', 2005.

Zagorul'ko, Maksim Matveevich. *Regional'nye Struktury GUPVI NKVD-MVD SSSR, 1941–1951: Otchetno-Informatsionnye Dokumenty*, Vol. 2. Volgograd: Izdatel', 2005.

Zagorul'ko, Maksim Matveevich. *Voennoplennye v SSSR 1939–1956: Dokumenty i materialy*. Moscow: Logos, 2000.

Zajda, Joseph I. *Education in the USSR: International Studies in Education and Social Change*. Cham, Switzerland: Elsevier, 2014.

Zaleski, Eugene. *Stalinist Planning for Economic Growth, 1933–1952*. Chapel Hill: University of North Carolina Press, 2012.

Zank, Horst. *Stalingrad: Kessel und Gefangenschaft*. Herford: E. S. Mittler, 1993.

Zerubavel, Yael. *Recovered Roots: Collective Memory and the Making of Israeli National Tradition*. Chicago: University of Chicago Press, 1997.

Zubkova, Elena IUr'evna. *Russia after the War: Hopes, Illusions, and Disappointments, 1945–1957*. Armonk, NY: M. E. Sharpe, 1998.

Zubok, Vladislav M. *A Failed Empire: The Soviet Union in the Cold War from Stalin to Gorbachev*. Chapel Hill: University of North Carolina Press, 2009.

Zubovich, Katherine. *Moscow Monumental: Soviet Skyscrapers and Urban Life in Stalin's Capital*. Princeton, NJ: Princeton University Press, 2021.

Zylmann, Detert. *Daruber Wurde Nicht Gesprochen: Die Geschichte Meines Vaters (Kriegs- und Nachkriegszeit)*. Munich: Grin Verlag Gmbh, 2014.

INDEX

Note: f and t following locators indicate figures and tables, respectively.

rations for German POWs, 30–47; during
and after famine, 41–46; calculation of
daily calories and full calorie tables,
207–208; distributed according to labor
category, 28–29; for enlisted German
POWs from 1943 to 1947, 37, 38t; for
German officer POWs, 31, 32–33t, 34–35;
German POWs on quality and quantity
of, 38–41, 43; increase in, 37–38, 38t, 41;
labor output and size of, 30, 31, 35;
misappropriation of, 45; nutritional
content of, 32–33t, 34–35; ration norms,
31, 32–33t; repatriation of German POWs
in 1946 and, 42, 45–47; Soviet planners
and, 46; for Stalingrad German POWs, 25
Reagan, Ronald, trip to Bitburg, 188–189
reconstruction of Soviet Union. *See* postwar
reconstruction of Soviet Union, German
POWs and
Red Army: capture of German soldiers in
last months of the war, 82; capture of
German supplies, weapons and vehicles,
50; food rations for, 36
Red Cross: camp inspections by, 18, 20;
continued incarceration of German
POWs in the Soviet Union and, 9;
forbidden from entering POW camps,
108; Ulyanovsk State Committee, 192
Red Cross postcards, 60
"Rehabilitation of Nazism" (Russian
Criminal Code), 1
relaxation camps for POWs, 62
religious symbols, in commemoration of
German POWs, 197–198, 198n62
repatriation of German POWs, 203–204.
See also politics of repatriation; in 1946,
42; during 1947, 45–47; 1949–1953, 138–156;
1953–1956, 156–173; after German capitulation, 136; agitprop work during Cold
War and, 122–131; of amnestied war
criminal POWs to East Germany, 161–163;
antifascist reeducation program and early,
103, 135; death of POWs on journey
back to Germany, 46, 52, 71–72; death
of Stalin and, 132, 137, 156–158, 172; of
final German POWs, 137; following
Adenauer's trip to Moscow, 164–167;
German criticism of slow, 114; of ill/
injured POWs, 52, 53–54, 63, 71; political
motivations for, 204–205; reintegration
of former POWs labeled as war criminals
into East and West German societies,
168–169; route for, 139; Soviet statistics
on, 150–151; at war's end, 71–72

repatriation of prisoners of war, Geneva
Convention on, 19, 21
Research Institute of History and Culture of
the Ulyanovsk Region, 10
Revenge of the Domestic (Harsch), 114n44
Rodina Mat' Zovët (The Motherland Calls)
statue, 178, 179, 179f
Romanian POWs, 24
Roosevelt, Theodore, 15
Russia. *See also* Soviet Union: care of war
graves in Germany and in, 190–192; cult
of Great Patriotic War in, 3; German
POWs and war memory, 11–12; invasion
of Ukraine, 201; legacy of World War II
German POWs and politics in, 1–2;
number of German POW camps in,
89–90, 89t; topic of World War II war
dead in, 9, 200–201; use of World War I
POWs as forced labor, 16–17
Russian archives, opening of after collapse
of Soviet Union, 10, 190
Russian Civil War, Mamaev Kurgan and, 181
Russian Federation, commemoration of
German POWs in, 175, 176
Russian Military Prosecutor's Office, 147
Russian nationalism, cult of Great Patriotic
War and, 199
Russians, reconciliation with Germans, 198
Russian Soviet Federative Socialist Republic
(RSFSR), 195: German POWs sent to,
71; Ministry of Culture, 180–181; Penal
Code, "Counterrevolutionary Crimes,"
147
Russian State Archive of Economics
(RGAE), 97n93
Russian State Archive of Literature and Art
(RGALI), 10
Russian State Archive of Socio-Political
History (RGASPI), 10
Russian State Economic Archive (RGAE), 10
Russian State Military Archive (RGVA), 10,
49, 97, 97n93

sanitation: in Gulag, 47–48; shortages of
supplies for POW camps, 49–50
Schenck, Ernst Günther, 99
Schmidt, Elli, 143
Schmidt, Helmut, 185–186
scholarly literature on German POWs in the
Soviet Union, 5–6
Schtrauch, Max, 118
Schuetz, Hans: on antifascist reeducation,
112; on antifascist work among POWs,
104; on medical care in camps, 53; on